Principles
of Appellate
Advocacy

ASPEN COURSEBOOK SERIES

Principles of Appellate Advocacy

SECOND EDITION

DANIEL P. SELMI

Fritz B. Burns Professor of Law
Loyola Law School, Los Angeles

REBECCA A. DELFINO

Clinical Professor of Law
Director of Appellate Advocacy and Moot Court Programs
Director of Field Placement Department
Loyola Law School, Los Angeles

Cover image: Photograph by fivepointsix/Shutterstock.com

To contact Customer Service, e-mail customer.service@aspenpublishing.com, call 1-800-950-5259, or mail correspondence to:

Aspen Publishing
Attn: Order Department
PO Box 990
Frederick, MD 21705

Printed in the United States of America.

1 2 3 4 5 6 7 8 9 0

ISBN 978-1-5438-0889-6

Library of Congress Cataloging-in-Publication Data

Names: Selmi, Daniel P., author. | Delfino, Rebecca A., author.
Title: Principles of appellate advocacy / Daniel P. Selmi (Fritz B. Burns
    Professor of Law, Loyola Law School, Los Angeles), Rebecca A. Delfino
    (Clinical Professor of Law, Director of Appellate Advocacy and Moot
    Court Programs, Director of Field Placement Department, Loyola Law
    School, Los Angeles).
Description: Second edition. | Frederick, MD: Aspen Publishing, [2021] |
    Series: Aspen coursebook series | Includes index. | Summary: "A textbook
    for law school courses on Advanced Legal Writing or Writing an Appellate
    Brief"—Provided by publisher.
Identifiers: LCCN 2020054680 (print) | LCCN 2020054681 (ebook) |
    ISBN 9781543808896 (paperback) | ISBN 9781543831214 (ebook)
Subjects: LCSH: Appellate procedure—United States.
Classification: LCC KF9050 .S45 2021 (print) | LCC KF9050 (ebook) |
    DDC 347.73/8—dc23
LC record available at https://lccn.loc.gov/2020054680
LC ebook record available at https://lccn.loc.gov/2020054681

About Aspen Publishing

Aspen Publishing is a leading provider of educational content and digital learning solutions to law schools in the U.S. and around the world. Aspen provides best-in-class solutions for legal education through authoritative textbooks, written by renowned authors, and breakthrough products such as Connected eBooks, Connected Quizzing, and PracticePerfect.

The Aspen Casebook Series (famously known among law faculty and students as the "red and black" casebooks) encompasses hundreds of highly regarded textbooks in more than eighty disciplines, from large enrollment courses, such as Torts and Contracts to emerging electives such as Sustainability and the Law of Policing. Study aids such as the *Examples & Explanations* and the *Emanuel Law Outlines* series, both highly popular collections, help law students master complex subject matter.

Major products, programs, and initiatives include:

- **Connected eBooks** are enhanced digital textbooks and study aids that come with a suite of online content and learning tools designed to maximize student success. Designed in collaboration with hundreds of faculty and students, the Connected eBook is a significant leap forward in the legal education learning tools available to students.

- **Connected Quizzing** is an easy-to-use formative assessment tool that tests law students' understanding and provides timely feedback to improve learning outcomes. Delivered through CasebookConnect.com, the learning platform already used by students to access their Aspen casebooks, Connected Quizzing is simple to implement and integrates seamlessly with law school course curricula.

- **PracticePerfect** is a visually engaging, interactive study aid to explain commonly encountered legal doctrines through easy-to-understand animated videos, illustrative examples, and numerous practice questions. Developed by a team of experts, PracticePerfect is the ideal study companion for today's law students.

- The **Aspen Learning Library** enables law schools to provide their students with access to the most popular study aids on the market across all of their courses. Available through an annual subscription, the online library consists of study aids in e-book, audio, and video formats with full text search, note-taking, and highlighting capabilities.

- Aspen's **Digital Bookshelf** is an institutional-level online education bookshelf, consolidating everything students and professors need to ensure success. This program ensures that every student has access to affordable course materials from day one.

- **Leading Edge** is a community centered on thinking differently about legal education and putting those thoughts into actionable strategies. At the core of the program is the Leading Edge Conference, an annual gathering of legal education thought leaders looking to pool ideas and identify promising directions of exploration.

For Greg, with thanks for all the hypotheticals.
DPS

For my children, Miranda, Matthew, and Michael, who inspire all of my work.
RAD

CONTENTS

CHAPTER 9

THE INTRODUCTION OR SUMMARY OF ARGUMENT   107

CHAPTER 10

BASIC WRITING AND OTHER MECHANICS   121

Mastering appellate practice is undeniably difficult. For example, it requires a thorough understanding of a wide variety of procedural issues (e.g., whether a party may take an appeal, when to file a notice of appeal, when a cross-appeal is allowed, when the use of a writ is possible, how to compile a record on appeal, how to obtain interlocutory relief pending appeal, etc.). This list just scratches the surface. Moreover, the central part of appellate work—writing professional appellate briefs and making effective oral arguments—requires considerable skill. And the existing evidence, often proclaimed by judges, is that many lawyers are *not* good writers.

Teaching all the needed skills to students is daunting in a 13-week class on appellate advocacy. Given the breadth and nature of the subject, the risk is high that a book will inundate the student with too much information. The student will then "lose the forest for the trees" and conclude the class with only a vague understanding of what is important and what is not. Adding to the conundrum is the fact that both improving students' writing abilities and improving their oral advocacy are highly personal and pedagogically difficult undertakings. This book is designed with these difficulties in mind.

The goal in the first edition was to give students a precise understanding of a bounded set of fundamental principles that apply to writing appellate briefs and engaging in oral arguments before appellate courts. The second edition reinforces that goal with updated references to the law, expanded discussion of complex topics, and new examples from appellate briefs. While the book's structure remains largely the same, the changes in the second edition reflect the feedback we received from users of the first edition.

- Chapter One has been reorganized and expanded to offer new insights into appellate jurisdiction and the distinctions between trial and appellate practice.
- Chapter Three, on the standard of review, has been greatly expanded to more fully illustrate the differences in standards applied by appellate courts.
- Chapter Six, on the statement of the facts and the procedural history, adds new discussion on making effective use of themes and emotion in appellate writing, as well as how to make the most of the recitation of the procedural history.
- Chapter Eight, on building the argument, includes new recommendations on presenting arguments that interpret statutory language.
- Chapter Nine's coverage of how to draft an effective summary of the argument includes new examples that illustrate the principles in the text.

- Chapter 10 delves deeper into the principles of effective appellate writing by emphasizing topic sentences and the use of the "stress position" in sentences.
- Appendix A, the sample appellate brief, has been updated to reflect changes in the law since the publication of the first edition.
- Appendix B has been expanded to include exercises on the standard of review, additional examples of fact statements, and new exercises for students to practice editing and revising. This feature allows students to implement the substantive material from the chapters, an essential step in internalizing their knowledge of appellate advocacy.

The second edition also has a new co-author, Loyola Law School Professor Rebecca A. Delfino, who brings more than twenty years of experience teaching appellate advocacy and directing Loyola's nationally recognized competitive moot court program. Professor Delfino's expertise and insights into the best practices of appellate law are further informed by nearly two decades as an appellate court lawyer on the staff the California Court of Appeal. Professor Delfino joins Professor Daniel P. Selmi, whose extensive appellate experience includes orally arguing over 35 appeals in state and federal courts.

The Second edition continues to reflect three central premises in its approach to the subject of appellate advocacy:

First, it focuses on the core skills of appellate advocacy: brief writing and oral argument. Appellate procedure is undeniably important in practice, but, in the end, appellate writing and oral argument are fundamental—and difficult to learn. So, while the book alerts students to basic points of appellate procedure, it emphasizes the essential skills of brief writing and oral argument.

Second, it has a central theme. To practice appellate law properly, students must learn and then implement a method of thinking: They must be able to put themselves in the place of the judges deciding the appeal. Thinking like an appellate lawyer means thinking like a judge. If students can learn to do so, they will be able to answer for themselves many of the questions that arise during the writing of a brief, and even many of those questions that come up in preparing for an oral argument. Thus, in Chapter Two the book explains this idea, which it denotes as the "perspective principle," and then repeatedly returns to the principle throughout the ensuing chapters. Moreover, wherever possible, the book uses advice from judges—the target audience of lawyers—to illustrate points made.

Third, it sets out precise principles on how to write and argue, because students need specific yet manageable direction for writing a brief and making an oral argument. (General instruction is unhelpful, and excessively detailed instruction overwhelms students.) The principles set forth are limited in number, so as not to inundate, but they are essential. The authors have drawn them from important works on legal writing, from statements that judges have made about written appellate advocacy, and from their own experience as appellate advocates and as a former lawyer for an appellate court.

These principles provide students with a sound basis upon which to enter the practice of law. The principles are not the only ways to write an appellate brief or argue an appeal. They are, however, time-tested and effective ways of doing so. If students adhere to these principles, they *will* write a professional appellate brief, and they *will* know how to make a professional appellate argument.

Lastly, a word of caution: Appellate brief writing is a time-intensive exercise. The course in appellate advocacy undoubtedly will take more of students' time than they estimate. As a Texas appellate judge recognized:

> [B]riefs almost always take more time than originally estimated. That's because the brief writing process is circular, not linear. During drafting, additional potential arguments will surface, requiring more research and a new assessment of what facts are relevant. A good brief requires enough time to go through this cycle several times.

Jim Moseley, *An Appellate Judge's Tips for Writing Persuasive Briefs,* TEXAS LAWYER (April 12, 2012).

So, be forewarned: This class is both hard and time-consuming. In the end, though, the skills that students will acquire are essential for their future careers.

Principles of Appellate Advocacy

The Decision to Appeal

A. **Appeals and the Appellate Process**
   1. Appeals Defined
   2. Appellate Courts and Their Jurisdiction
   3. Appellate Lawyers and Appellate Briefs

B. **Appealable Error**
   1. Identifying Trial Court Errors and Appealable Decisions
   2. The Time for Appeal
   3. The Trial Court Record
   4. Preservation of Issues for Appeal

A. APPEALS AND THE APPELLATE PROCESS

1. Appeals Defined

In legal trials, parties resolve their disputes through the formal and orderly presentation of factual evidence to a fact finder — a jury or trial judge — and legal arguments to a judge. An appeal is a request for "review" of the trier of fact's resolution of the dispute. To win an appeal, the party who lost in the trial court must demonstrate that an error warranting reversal occurred in the lower court. An appeal therefore follows a trial, and the matters raised on appeal are generally confined to the matters presented and argued in the trial court.

The understanding of appeals and the appellate process begins with an examination of the appellate court system and the limited jurisdiction of reviewing courts.

2. Appellate Courts and Their Jurisdiction

Jurisdiction in this context refers to the legal authority that has been conferred on the reviewing court to act on the decisions of the courts subordinate to it. Appellate courts — both the intermediate appeal courts and the courts of last resort, usually state supreme courts — are judicial bodies of limited jurisdiction.

a. Intermediate Appellate Courts. At the federal level, the circuit courts of appeals are the first level of appeal from the district courts, which are the federal trial courts for most matters. At the state level, the court of appeals serves as the first stop on appeal of decisions by trial courts. A few states use different terminology; for example, New York calls its highest court the Court of Appeals. In most states, however, the term *court of appeals* or *court of appeal* refers to the intermediate appellate court. These appellate courts almost always hear appeals in panels of three judges.

Parties, known as "appellants," have received adverse trial court decisions and may take initial appeals from those decisions as a "matter of right." In other words, the intermediate appellate court cannot refuse to hear that appeal. Thus, in many instances, a party appealing to an intermediate appellate court does not have to convince the court to hear the case in the way that it would have to convince a court of last resort, such as the United States Supreme Court. Of course, the court of appeals must have jurisdiction over the particular matter appealed.

The intermediate appellate courts decide most appeals. Here is how one author described the functions performed by the federal circuit courts of appeals:

> Fewer than 15% of circuit court decisions are even appealed to the Supreme Court and fewer than 2% of those appeals are taken by the high court.
>
> Thus, in large measure, it is the circuit courts that create U.S. law. . . . The circuit courts play by far the greatest legal policymaking role in the United States judicial system. . . . [C]ircuit court decisions are almost always about defining the law, and they set binding precedents for the multistate area that the circuit covers.

Frank B. Cross, DECISION MAKING IN THE U.S. COURTS OF APPEAL 4 (2007). Many state courts of appeal perform the same function.

b. The Courts of Last Resort. The courts of last resort are the highest courts in any jurisdiction; they are last and final place to obtain appellate review of a case. The United States Supreme Court and the other courts of last resort in the states, usually denominated state supreme courts, generally have complete discretion over which appeals they wish to hear. To obtain review at these courts, a party that lost in the intermediate appellate court files a petition seeking review — a brief to convince the court that it should hear the case. Although decisions of the United States Supreme Court and the state supreme courts confront important questions of law and set wide-ranging precedents, these courts exercise their discretion to consider only a fraction of the petitions for review each year.

The chances of the Supreme Court granting a petition submitted to it, known as a petition for certiorari, are small, although some factors increase the chances. These factors include the federal government acting as the petitioner; a matter of significant controversy or public importance, such as the constitutionality of the State of Florida's process of re-counting of votes in the 2000 presidential election at issue in *Bush v. Gore*, 531 U.S. 98 (2000) (holding that the use of standardless manual recounts of votes in the State of Florida in that election violated the Equal Protection Clause of the Fourteenth Amendment); or a "split" in the decisions of the circuit courts of appeals in deciding an issue. *See, e.g., Burgess v. United States*, 553 U.S. 124, 128 (2008) ("We granted the writ [of certiorari] . . . to resolve a split among the Circuits on the question Burgess presents: Does a drug crime classified as a misdemeanor by state law, but punishable by more than a year's imprisonment, rank as a 'felony drug offense' under 21 U.S.C. §841(b)(1)(A)?"). When the Supreme Court grants a petition for certiorari, it will identify the issues that it has agreed to hear.

Most state supreme courts likewise have discretion whether to hear almost all the cases on their docket. Counsel files a "petition for review," a "petition for certiorari," or a similar document that tries to convince a state supreme court to review an appeal. Once again, inconsistencies in holdings by the lower courts of appeals in that state can influence whether the court will agree to hear the matter. As with the United States Supreme Court, the chances are not high that a state supreme court will grant the petition.

In both the United States Supreme Court and the state supreme courts, a so-called friend of the court (an individual or entity that is not a party to the litigation) may file a brief supporting a petition that the court take a case. A single "friend of the court" is known by the Latin term *amicus curiae*. An *amicus curiae* brief will often try to inform the court of a case's importance to a general area of law and persuade the court that the case is sufficiently significant for the court to hear it.

3. Appellate Lawyers and Appellate Briefs

The practice of litigation requires that lawyers command and deploy a diverse set of skills on behalf of their clients. The type of skills required depends not only on the factual and legal matters at issue in a case but also on whether the matter will be decided in the trial or appellate court. Appreciating the distinctions in these skill sets is critical to effectively presenting a case on appeal.

Trial lawyers operate within a framework of existing legal precepts, and they gather and develop the facts. Given the conflicting evidence presented, they have a singular goal: to persuade the fact finder to accept a version of the dispute favoring their client. Trial lawyers are also required to rely regularly on their skills as oral advocates; they conduct oral depositions of witnesses, make oral objections and motions to the trial court, and present evidence and argument to a jury. Although trial lawyers prepare written arguments, briefs are not the primary means of persuasion in the trial court.

In addition, the primary audience for the trial lawyer is the jury. In presenting a case to a jury, the trial advocate is not limited to reasoned argument. The trial lawyer can argue irrational or emotional matters to a jury. However, certain rhetorical skills that properly shape the argument before a lay jury may be totally unacceptable when arguing points of law to a judge.

In contrast, appellate lawyers are a different breed. Appellate practice calls upon talents and skills that differ from those utilized in other facets of practicing law. Once a matter is on appeal, the focus shifts from fact development, presentation, and determination to assessment of whether, given the evidence and law presented in the trial court, reversible error occurred. Thus, appellate lawyers focus on the law, specifically whether the fact finder's determination was erroneous under the law or whether the trial court misapplied or misinterpreted the law. When the matter is before the court of last resort, the appellate advocate may be asking the court to resolve a conflict in law or urging reinterpretation of the law.

The means of articulating a point is also different in the appellate courts. The primary means of persuasion in the world of appeals is written advocacy in the form of an appellate brief. One of the classic works on appellate practice has defined an "appellate brief" as "a written argument in support of or in opposition to the order, decree, or judgment below." Frederick Bernays Wiener, Effective Appellate Advocacy 31 (rev. ed. 2003). Although many appellate courts still allow parties to present oral argument, some do not allow it unless the court decides the oral argument will significantly assist the court in reaching a decision. *See, e.g.,* Federal Rules of Appellate Procedure (FRAP) 34, subd. (a)(2) ("Oral argument must be allowed in every case unless a panel of three judges who have examined the briefs and record unanimously agrees that oral argument is unnecessary for any of the following reasons . . . (C) the facts and legal arguments are adequately presented in the briefs and record, and the decisional process would not be significantly aided by oral argument.").

Well before oral arguments are scheduled in all cases, the appellate court has already reviewed the record and the appellate briefs, conducted legal research, and analyzed the issues and arguments in a bench memorandum or draft opinion. In some cases, the court has already reached at least a tentative conclusion as to the outcome of the appeal. Aware of this process, the appellate advocates must devote their substantial efforts to the preparation of the written briefs and rely less on oral advocacy to prevail.

Finally, a significant distinction between the work of trial lawyers and appellate practitioners is that each has a different audience for their work. The audience for appellate briefs is relatively small and is limited to judges, who are educated in the law and usually bring many years of legal experience to each case.[1] The background of this highly skilled and legally sophisticated audience informs the presentation of appellate arguments. Unlike juries, appellate court judges are not persuaded by hyperbolic arguments, or easily swayed by appeal to emotion and irrelevant matters. Thus, appellate lawyers know that their arguments on appeal must be succinct and clear, grounded in reason, and based on legal precedent.

Being a good trial lawyer does not mean that you are also a qualified appellate advocate. Therefore, making sure that your client is represented by a lawyer who has the requisite skill set to prosecute the appeal is critical to success on appeal.

---

[1] Most state supreme courts have *justices* sitting on them, while a few have *judges*. Lower appellate courts are mixed in their terminology. For convenience, this book will use the term *judge* to refer to both.

B. APPEALABLE ERROR

1. Identifying Trial Court Errors and Appealable Decisions

The appellate process begins when a client decides to appeal a decision that is final in the trial court or an order that is appealable. An appellate advocate's work with their client usually commences with the decision of whether to appeal.

a. The Decision to Appeal. The appellate lawyer should be intimately involved with the decision to file an appeal. First, the client may be emotionally upset with the trial court's ruling or the jury's verdict, and thus unable to clearly evaluate whether an appeal is worthwhile. The appellate lawyer must provide an evenhanded viewpoint to help with this decision. This viewpoint should be informed not only by the perspective of the client but also, where the appellate lawyer did not try the case, by the trial counsel's assessment of the errors that occurred in the trial. Because both the client and the trial lawyer were so invested in the outcome of the trial, the appellate lawyer should view the trial lawyer and the client's account of the trial with a degree of skepticism.

Second, nonlawyers — and some trial lawyers — fail to understand that an appeal is not the equivalent of a "second bite at the apple." Instead, an appellate review of findings of fact is narrow. The appellate court's review is often limited by the applicable standard of review, which refers to the amount of deference that the appellate court will apply to the legal determinations of the trial court and the factual determinations of the trier of fact. Keeping the standard of review in mind, the lawyer must be prepared to fairly estimate the chances of succeeding on an appeal of a particular issue.

Most importantly, however, the trial court must have committed actual error. The task of the appellate lawyer is to locate such errors, evaluate the likelihood of an appellate court reversing the trial court's judgment or decision because of those errors, and recommend to the client whether an appeal is warranted.

Given these constraints, a client should not take an appeal without giving that decision considerable thought. Here is advice from the late Supreme Court Justice Ruth Bader Ginsburg on the subject:

> Turning to the starting line, my first words of caution to lawyers contemplating an appeal: perhaps you shouldn't. In the federal courts, of all appeals decided on the merits, over eighty percent are affirmed; the administrative agencies whose actions federal courts review fare almost as well. District court judgments generally survive appeal unmodified, not just because courts of appeals review many issues under a deferential standard, but too often because the appellant's case is exceedingly weak. Appellate review is more than occasionally sought simply because it is available and inexpensive. This is disturbing to appellate judges who face mounting caseloads....

Ruth Bader Ginsburg, *Remarks on Appellate Advocacy*, 50 S.C. L. REV. 567 (1999).

b. Final Judgments and Other Orders. Appellate courts must have jurisdiction over an appeal to decide it. Jurisdictional issues in the courts of appeal largely arise from an appellant's attempts to circumvent what is known as the "final judgment" rule. Under this rule, the trial judge must resolve all issues in a case and enter a final judgment before an appeal may be taken. Orders that trial courts enter while a case is still ongoing are considered "interlocutory"; such orders are not generally intended to be final.

When the case is concluded, any aspect of an interlocutory order that has not become moot may be challenged in an appeal from the final judgment. An interlocutory order is only subject to appellate review if a statute gives the appellate court jurisdiction over the specific ruling being appealed. For example, in many states, statutes allow appellate courts to review decisions such as granting preliminary injunctions or relating to the certification of class actions.

Appellate courts also may have jurisdiction over petitions for "extraordinary writs." A writ is an order from a higher court commanding specific action from a lower court. The best known of these is the writ of mandamus. These writs, however, are discretionary, and appellate courts usually deny such petitions.

Because appellate courts have limited jurisdiction, a lawyer for an appealing party must confirm that a statute gives jurisdiction to the court of appeals. Consider the following short opinion in *King v. Director of Revenue*, 283 S.W. 3d 817, 818 (Mo. Ct. App. 2009):

> The Director of Revenue, State of Missouri (Appellant) appeals from an order granting Jerry King (Respondent) a limited driving privilege.
>
> As an initial matter, this Court must determine whether it has jurisdiction to entertain this appeal. If we lack jurisdiction, we should dismiss the appeal. *Bryant v. City of University City,* 105 S.W.3d 855, 856 (Mo. App. E.D. 2003). "To invoke this Court's jurisdiction, parties must appeal a written decree or order which has been signed by the trial judge and denominated a 'judgment.'" *Jon E. Fuhrer Co. v. Gerhardt,* 955 S.W.2d 212, 213 (Mo. App. E.D. 1997); Rule 74.01(a) . . . .
>
> Here, the order granting Respondent a limited driving privilege is not denominated a "judgment" as required by Rule 74.01(a) . . . .
>
> We dismiss the appeal without prejudice for lack of a final, appealable judgment.

A court can raise lack of jurisdiction on its own. For example, in *City of Alameda v. Federal Aviation Administration*, 285 F.3d 1143 (9th Cir. 2002), the petitioner sought review of an order issued by the Federal Aviation Administration by filing the case directly in the court of appeals. All the parties agreed that the court of appeals had jurisdiction over the case. However, that court — without urging by any party to the case — issued an order concluding otherwise and dismissing the case, which by this point had been fully briefed.

Most disputes over appellate jurisdiction arise from appeals from orders entered *during* litigation at the trial level, rather than from appeals from final trial court judgments. For example, a party may try to appeal from an order granting a preliminary injunction against it, or from an order granting a new trial. In these instances, because the trial court has likely not yet entered a final judgment, the appellant must point to a particular statute that empowers the court of appeals to hear the appeal. Thus, if a party is appealing from the grant of a preliminary injunction, its brief would cite the court of appeals' authority to hear such appeals. *See, e.g.,* 28 U.S.C. §1292(a)(1) (giving jurisdiction to federal courts of appeals to hear appeals of orders "granting, continuing, modifying, refusing or dissolving injunctions"). The brief should also disclose sufficient information from the record for the appellate court to determine that the appeal has been timely filed under the applicable rules of court.

Here is the decision of the court of appeals in *Aventine Renewable Energy v. JP Morgan Securities, Inc.,* 940 N.E.2d 257, 259 (Ill. App. Ct. 2010), in which a related issue arose, the appealability of an order staying an action in the trial court:

> JP Morgan argues that we lack jurisdiction over this appeal. We disagree. Illinois Supreme Court Rule 307(a)(1) provides: "An appeal may be taken to the Appellate Court from an interlocutory order of the court: (1) granting, modifying, refusing, dissolving, or refusing to dissolve or modify an injunction." . . . "A stay is considered injunctive in nature, and thus an order granting or denying a stay fits squarely within Rule 307(a)." [citation omitted]

The lesson is obvious. At the outset of any appeal, the lawyer must ensure that the appellate court has jurisdiction to consider the appeal being filed. Otherwise, counsel may spend a lot of time — and a lot of the client's money — pursuing an appeal, only to find that the court refuses to hear it. Needless to say, the client will not be happy.

2. The Time for Appeal

Counsel initiates an appeal by filing a "notice of appeal." This notice triggers the reviewing court's jurisdiction and officially begins the appeal process. The timing of the notice is critical, and if the lawyer waits too long, the appeal period will pass. If the appellate lawyer fails to timely file a notice of appeal and the time to appeal expires, the reviewing court will not consider the appeal even if it has merit. In this way, the time to appeal operates like a statute of limitations on appellate review.

The Florida statute governing appeals is illustrative:

> (1) The time within which and the method by which the jurisdiction of any court in this state possessed of power to review the action of any other court . . . may be invoked by appeal, certiorari, petition for review or other process by whatever name designated, and the manner of computing such time shall be prescribed by rule of the Supreme Court.

> (2) Failure to invoke the jurisdiction of any such court within the time prescribed by such rules shall divest such court of jurisdiction to review such cause.

Fla. Stat. Ann. §59.081.

A lawyer practicing in this jurisdiction would then consult the Florida Rules of Court and find Florida Rule of Appellate Procedure 9.110, which reads in pertinent part:

> **(b) Commencement.** Jurisdiction of the court under this rule shall be invoked by filing a notice, accompanied by any filing fees prescribed by law, with the clerk of the lower tribunal within 30 days of rendition of the order to be reviewed. . . .

In federal court, Federal Rule of Appellate Procedure (FRAP) 4(a)(1)(A) specifies that an appeal must be filed "within 30 days after entry of the judgment or order appealed from" unless the party is the United States, which is given 60 days.

The filing of other motions in the trial court, such as a motion for judgment notwithstanding the verdict or a motion for a new trial, can affect the time allowed for filing a notice of appeal. The practitioner must carefully research the law in a particular jurisdiction to determine the effect of such other motions on the timing of an appeal.

Additionally, many courts of appeals require appellants to file certain information in a "docketing statement." This information may include the basis for the appellate court's jurisdiction, any related cases, and the procedural status of the case on appeal.

3. The Trial Court Record

In general, an appellate court will hear the appeal based only upon the record of proceedings before the trial court. That record will include the transcript of any oral proceedings before the trial court, sometimes referred to as a "reporter's transcript," and the "clerk's record," which consists of all documents filed in the trial court. Federal Rule of Appellate Procedure 10(a) defines the record on appeal to include: (1) the original papers and exhibits filed in the district court; (2) the transcript of proceedings, if any; and (3) a certified copy of the docket entries prepared by the district clerk. Alternatively, the parties may agree to an "agreed statement" that will become the record on appeal. Fed. R. App. P. 10(d). Because the appellate court will confine its review on appeal to the record in the trial court, if a party wants to refer to evidence or other materials that were not included in the record, the party will have to supplement the record. Most jurisdictions' rules of court specify the procedure to do so by filing a motion for judicial notice or filing a motion to augment the record on appeal.

Counsel for the appealing party bears the burden of designating the record and ensuring its completeness. Statutes and court rules prescribe how this task is to be done, and there are costs involved. The appellant, for example, will likely have to pay a court reporter for the preparation of the transcript of the oral proceedings. In some states, the rules of court allow the appellant to put together the record and certify its completeness, a method that can save money.

Knowledge of the record is essential to the proper prosecution of any appeal. The lawyer must spend the time needed to go through the record carefully. That examination will yield both the facts and the issues upon which the appeal will be decided. For example, if a party is appealing from a judgment after a jury trial, the lawyer for the appellant must know exactly what happened during that trial. Thus, counsel will have to read the entire trial transcript, all the exhibits, and all pleadings made before and during the trial.

When writing an appellate brief, counsel will have to include citations to the record that support references to facts or rulings by the trial court. Furthermore, many appellate courts then require this knowledge to be put to use in another way. They often require the appellant and appellee to file "excerpts of record." These are the most important parts of the record upon which the briefs on appeal rely and that are necessary for the court to resolve the issues.

So there is no way around it. You must immerse yourself in the record and exercise care in doing so. And because the record informs both the decision of which issues to assert on appeal and the legal arguments you will make on appeal, you should make a thorough review of the record before you begin significant legal research. As you review the record, take notes or annotate the record to make locating information in the record easier to find during the subsequent research and writing phases. Careful review of the record at the outset pays large dividends as you undertake the briefing process. In particular, it not only prevents overlooking issues, it avoids starting to brief issues that turn out to be "blind alleys."

Finally, one last tip: If you enter a student moot court competition, you will generally find that the records are quite short. But do not be deceived — read the record *carefully*. You will be surprised at what you learn on the fourth and fifth readings of the record that somehow escaped your attention the first time through.

4. Preservation of Issues for Appeal

Finally, as you review the record, it is important to keep in mind that as a general rule, appellate courts will not consider errors that the parties failed to bring to the attention of the trial court. To assert a claim of error on appeal, trial counsel for an appellant must have "preserved" the claim by properly objecting in the trial court, thereby seeking to have the error corrected at that level. The following excerpt from *Jean v. State*, 2013 WL 3282956, at *5 (Tex. Crim. App. 2013), illustrates the consequences of failing to preserve an error:

> Keller, P.J.:
>
> Appellant, [a defendant in a murder case] maintains that the trial court erred in admitting evidence of an extraneous offense — specifically, testimony from two witnesses that he threatened to kill [his romantic partner] several hours before the fire [at her residence.] We initially address whether appellant preserved this issue for our review. To preserve error for appellate review, a party must make a timely and specific objection or motion at trial, and there must be an adverse ruling by the trial court. Failure to preserve error at trial forfeits the later assertion of that

error on appeal. Almost all error — even constitutional error — may be forfeited if the appellant failed to object. We have consistently held that the failure to object in a timely and specific manner during trial forfeits complaints about the admissibility of evidence. . . .

Appellant made no objections at trial to the testimony concerning the threats. Therefore, appellant has forfeited appellate review of this issue.

Ensuring that an objection was preserved requires the appellate lawyer to comprehensively analyze the trial court record. A failure to put in the time needed for this analysis can result in a waste of attorney and appellate resources, as the *Jean* case illustrates.

Waiver is the general rule applied to those situations in which objections are not properly and timely made in the trial court. Courts apply waiver because it incentivizes parties to put their best case forward in the trial court and allows parties to correct any trial court errors at that time, perhaps obviating the need for appellate review. Some jurisdictions, however, recognize narrow exceptions to this general rule on a case-by-case basis. A waived issue may nonetheless be raised if the issue is a matter of great public interest or relates to the administration of justice (i.e., affecting the fairness, integrity, or public reputation of the judicial proceeding); would result in a "miscarriage of justice"; or involves a situation where the trial court lacked subject matter jurisdiction in the first instance. Invoking these exceptions to the general rule will prove challenging because a court's decision to apply an exception to waiver is generally discretionary.

Summary

- An appeal is a request for "review" by an appellate court of a legal decision or factual determination in a trial court. It is not a re-trial.

- Appellate courts have limited jurisdiction; an appellate court must have jurisdiction over the appeal or it will dismiss it.

- Appeals to intermediate appellate courts generally may be taken as a matter of right. By contrast, appeals to state supreme courts and the United States Supreme Court are discretionary.

- Appellate lawyers have specialized skills that allow them to effectively represent clients at the appellate level.

- Appellate courts usually have jurisdiction over appeals from "final judgments" entered by the trial court, although other means exist for placing issues before appellate courts.

- A party has a limited time to appeal the trial court's judgment, sometimes as few as 30 days after the trial court entered the judgment.

- The appeal will be decided based on the record of proceedings before the trial court, which will include all written documents filed with that court and the reporter's transcript.

- Appellate courts will not consider errors that were not brought to the attention of the trial court and thus were not preserved for appeal.

CHAPTER 2

The Three Overarching Principles of Appellate Brief Writing

A.   **Thinking Like an Appellate Lawyer**

B.   **The Perspective Principle: Seeing the Appeal from the Appellate Court's Viewpoint**
   1.   Putting Yourself in the Shoes of the Appellate Judge
   2.   Blazing a Seamless Trail Through the Briefing Thicket

C.   **The Structural Principle: Build the Brief Around Analyses of Issues and Standards of Review**
   1.   The Core Function of Appellate Judging
   2.   The Relationship Between the Issues and the Function of Appellate Review

D.   **The Organizational Principle: Separate the Analytic Process from the Writing Process**
   1.   Think (Long and Hard) Before You Write
   2.   Reaping the Benefits of Organizing First

A. THINKING LIKE AN APPELLATE LAWYER

After a party has properly appealed a decision by a trial court, the core of the appellate lawyer's work on appeal is producing a quality written brief. An examination of the appellate lawyer's role must focus on the task of writing a brief for an appellate court.

As you are exposed to the work of the appellate lawyer, you must learn and keep in mind three basic principles, what this book terms the *perspective principle*, the *structural principle*, and the *organizational principle*. These principles allow you to answer many questions that will arise during the appellate process.

B. THE PERSPECTIVE PRINCIPLE: SEEING THE APPEAL FROM THE APPELLATE COURT'S VIEWPOINT

1. Putting Yourself in the Shoes of the Appellate Judge

Assume that a new client has hired you to handle the appeal of an important case, and you have thrown yourself into the matter. You have carefully examined the record before the trial court, identified issues to be raised on appeal, and researched the law. You believe that an appellate court can rectify the legal errors that you are certain the trial court committed. Your mind teems with various aspects of the case — the facts, the issues that should be raised on appeal, and the various strands of the law. *You* are now an expert on the entire case.

With such a wealth of knowledge, however, come consequences that you must recognize. One consequence involves how you will use your knowledge. When an individual becomes particularly knowledgeable about a given subject and starts to convey information about it, a tendency arises to assume that the audience shares some of this knowledge or can easily follow reasoning about it. For example, you may assume that the connection between Fact A and Legal Conclusion B is so obvious as to merit little attention in your presentation, comfortable in the belief that the listener will understand the link between the two.

Another consequence of your knowledge stems from the fact that you have come to see the appeal from one perspective: that of your client. After all, the client is paying your bill, and your efforts are aimed at making the best case possible for that client. Accordingly, you can easily become invested in the client's position and begin to view the case narrowly from that client's perspective.

In contrast, consider the viewpoint of the appellate judge. This person is extremely busy, with a pile of briefs to consider. When the judge picks up your brief for the first time, the judge knows absolutely nothing about the case. Additionally, the judge is likely less knowledgeable about the specific law at issue than you are; after all, you have just exhaustively researched the law on the issues raised in the brief. By necessity appellate judges are generalists in their knowledge of law.

Consider, for example, the following list of laws that form the subject matter of some appeals heard by federal appellate judges, taken mostly from William Domnarski, THE OPINION OF THE COURT 91-92 (1996):

- The Social Security Act
- The Hobbs Act

- The Sherman Antitrust Act
- The Age Discrimination in Employment Act
- The Securities Exchange Act of 1934
- The Longshore and Harbor Workers' Compensation Act
- The Federal Deposit Insurance Act
- The Federal Trade Commission Act
- The Administrative Procedure Act
- The Commodity Exchange Act
- The Labor Management Relations Act
- The Interstate Commerce Commission Termination Act
- The Civil Rights Attorney Fees Award Act
- The United States Arbitration Act
- The Bankruptcy Reform Act
- The Racketeer Influenced and Corrupt Organizations Act
- The Affordable Care Act
- The Coronavirus Aid, Relief, and Economic Security Act
- Formerly Incarcerated Reenter Society Transformed Safely Transitioning Every Person Act
- The Employee Retirement Income Security Act
- The Civil Rights Act
- The National Environmental Policy Act
- The Lanham Trademark Act
- The National Labor Relations Act.

No judge is or can be an "expert" on all of these laws. Consequently, the judge necessarily must depend on the lawyers representing the parties for help in gaining an understanding of the law at issue in a particular appeal. The appellate lawyer's task, therefore, is to both educate and explain the law to the court. As one federal appellate judge put it, the first "constraint" on an appellate justice is "reliance to quite a considerable degree on the performance of adversaries." Frank N. Coffin, ON APPEAL: COURTS, LAWYERING, AND JUDGING 258 (1994). Addressing appellate lawyers, another declared, "Your job is to educate and teach us. If you cannot do either, you are not prepared to discharge your appellate function." Leonard I. Garth, *How to Appeal to an Appellate Judge*, 21 LITIGATION 20, 67 (1994).

Unless you take the judge's level of knowledge into account, you cannot write a persuasive brief. For example, suppose that the lawyer, steeped in expertise on a legal issue presented in the case, writes a brief arguing that an exception to a general rule should apply. The brief presumes that the court knows and understands the general rule. Instead of explaining it, the brief jumps into discussing the exception, which forms the basis for the specific issue before the court. In this situation, however, the court might be unable to follow the argument. If so, the lawyer has failed as an appellate advocate.

Therefore, after having mastered the record on appeal and the law involved, the appellate lawyer must step back and look at the case from an entirely different perspective. The lawyer must follow the first principle of appellate writing, denominated here the *perspective principle*: Put yourself in the shoes of the reader, the appellate judge.

It helps to actually envision yourself in the appellate judge's shoes as the judge opens up your brief. Here is how former Judge Richard Posner, an extremely experienced and respected federal appellate judge, put it:

> [T]he key to effective appellate advocacy is to imagine yourself an appellate judge. If you do that you will see immediately that the judge of such a court labors under an immense disadvantage: he has very little time to spend on each case and, in addition, he lacks specialized knowledge of most of the cases that come before him, provided that he is a judge of a generalist court, as most appellate judges in this country are.
>
> The judge so circumstanced is very badly in need of the advocates' help, which is something that for some reason very few advocates seem to understand. The implicit working assumption of most of the lawyers who argue before my court seems to be that the judges have the same knowledge and outlook as the lawyers. That is wrong.

Richard A. Posner, *Convincing a Federal Court of Appeals*, 25 LITIGATION 3 (1999). Former Supreme Court Justice Anthony Kennedy echoes the thought: "I've learned that the judges really want your help." *Bryan Garner Interviews Associate Justice Anthony Kennedy on Legal Writing*, http://www.thelaw.net/bryan-garner-interviews-assoc-justice-anthony-kennedy-on-legal-writing-2/.

Following the perspective principle will lead you to giving that help. You will constantly ask yourself questions like these:

- Have I provided sufficient factual background and legal context for the judges to understand the issues on appeal?
- Can the judges follow my reasoning in applying this case precedent?
- What impression will they get from the opening paragraph of the brief?
- Can the judges see the overall logic of my argument by examining the table of contents in the brief?
- Is my explanation of this complex case precedent sufficiently clear?

This principle — putting yourself in the shoes of the judge — may seem obvious. Do not, however, let its simplicity deceive you. Although the principle is extremely important and useful, it is much harder to employ than it seems. Like all human beings, lawyers naturally tend to look at situations from their own perspective. Compounding the problem is the fact that lawyers are advocates who, by definition, take sides in legal disputes. They deliberately assume a particular perspective, that of their client. Thus, switching viewpoints from the client's perspective to consider an issue from a neutral and quite different perspective — that of a judge — can be difficult.

Applying the principle yields great dividends. For example, consider the following simple question: How will misspellings and typographic errors affect how a judge perceives a brief? If you give it some thought from the judge's perspective, the answer will be obvious. The judge may well conclude that if you are sloppy with spelling and in proofreading the brief, you are probably also sloppy in your use of precedents in the brief. Consequently, the judge may conclude that the assertions in your brief about those precedents are not trustworthy. So the principle teaches you how to answer the question posed in the second sentence of this paragraph.

Here is another example. Consider the insertion of footnotes into an argument. Many lawyers routinely fill briefs with numerous footnotes, reasoning that it is better to get as many points before the court as is possible. But now look at footnotes from the judge's perspective. As one state supreme court justice summarized, "Every time judges read a footnote our attention is distracted. We lose our place on the page, then we go back to find the place we had." Mark Rust, *Mistakes to Avoid on Appeal*, 74 A.B.A. J. 78, 79 (1988).

So, by placing yourselves in the shoes of the reader, you will see that the judge will react in this manner. Then you will ask *whether* you want to run the risk of distracting the judge in this fashion. The perspective principle leads you to the obvious answer: not unless you have a very good reason. As you go through this book, you will see numerous other examples of the perspective principle in action.

The perspective principle is so engrained in good lawyers that they use it unconsciously. They quickly understand how other individuals will view issues in a dispute, and they plan their strategy with their readers' viewpoint in mind. By doing so, they maximize their chances of achieving their clients' goals.

2. Blazing a Seamless Trail Through the Briefing Thicket

The perspective principle requires you to keep firmly in mind that your readers (appellate judges) are not likely to be experts in the area of law at issue. They may have some general knowledge of the applicable law, but their knowledge is almost certainly far below *your* understanding of that law. Here is another quote from Judge Posner:

> Unless the case arises in one of the staple areas of the docket — such as, for my court, sentencing — or involves a purely procedural issue, the lawyer must not assume that the judge knows much about either the field or the case itself, and has to make both of these terrains familiar and comfortable to him. In fact, you have to spoon-feed the judge.

Richard A. Posner, *Convincing a Federal Court of Appeals*, 25 Litigation 3 (1999). An Ohio appellate judge is equally direct in addressing this same point:

> Start by analyzing your audience — for whom are you writing? . . . First, ask yourself how much your audience already knows — about the facts and the law of your case. The answer to the former is *nothing* — the judge knows nothing about your case until that judge picks up the brief. Your problem is that you know so much about your case. . . . But you must explain it to someone who knows nothing about it.

Mark P. Painter, *Appellate Practice — Including Legal Writing From a Judge's Perspective*, https://docuri.com/download/appellate_59b8e66af581717b5b8779b9_pdf.

You must recognize the consequences of the judge's limited knowledge. If you are not careful, the presentation in your brief can easily confuse or lose the reader. It may be clear to *you,* but not to the judge. And that outcome, of course, is disastrous for an advocate. You cannot begin to persuade a court unless it understands what you are saying and follows all the strands of your reasoning.

Thus, your goal is to take your reader seamlessly through your brief. In the words of a Texas appellate judge, "[t]he secret ingredient of a [good] legal argument is 'flow' — that is, an argument which proceeds like the current of a stream, naturally uninterrupted, and logically from beginning to end." Sarah B. Duncan, *Pursuing Quality: Writing a Helpful Brief,* 30 St. Mary's L.J. 1092, 1104 (1999). She continues: "It is important that the appellate court be swept along by the current; that it understand every logical step along the way and arrive with the litigant at the same ultimate point of conclusion in the same frame of mind." *Id.* Only then will the court be in a position to agree with your argument.

The reader can lose the thread of an argument in numerous ways, but the easiest way is through bad writing. The judge might read a sentence and simply not understand it. As the late Justice Scalia and his coauthor, writing expert Bryan Garner, put it, "Literary elegance, erudition, sophistication of expression — these and all other qualities must be sacrificed if they detract from clarity." Antonin Scalia & Bryan A. Garner, *Making Your Case: The Art of Persuading Judges,* as reprinted in 94 A.B.A. J. 41, 42-43 (2008). To ensure clarity, succeeding chapters of this book will lay out certain specific principles that, if diligently followed, will minimize the likelihood that you will "lose" the reader.

Even if your writing is clear, you can also lose the reader if you leave out essential steps in your logic. Because of your familiarity with the material, you may readily assume that the reader will be able to follow all the parts of your reasoning. However, you might inadvertently skip one or two essential steps in your logic, perhaps without even knowing that you did so. This situation happens quite easily.

To avoid making this mistake, keep in mind that good legal writing does not have to be complex. Simplicity is a highly desirable goal. No judge ever became upset with a lawyer because the argument was clearly and deliberately laid out in detail — i.e., was too "simple." You avoid losing the reader by keeping in mind how the brief will read *from that reader's perspective* rather than from your own.

C. THE STRUCTURAL PRINCIPLE: BUILD THE BRIEF AROUND ANALYSES OF ISSUES AND STANDARDS OF REVIEW

1. The Core Function of Appellate Judging

We now move on to another fundamental question: how to structure the appellate brief. You might think that the rules of the appellate court where the case will be heard will tell you how to organize the brief. To a certain degree, you would be correct. For example, the rules will inform you that a brief must contain certain parts, such as a statement of the facts and an argument.

However, the rules will not tell you how to structure the heart of the brief: the argument section. Fortunately (and unsurprisingly), you can answer this question by considering the brief from the perspective of the judges that will hear and decide the case. The appellate judge's function is, of course, to decide the appeal, but the judge goes about that task by deciding *specific issues*. The judge decides the appeal as a whole by aggregating decisions on individual issues.

This core judicial function — deciding issues — drives the organization of any brief. If the purpose of a brief is to persuade a judge to decide issues in your favor, then the brief's organization must center on those issues. Indeed, *any* legal brief, appellate or otherwise, must follow this organizing principle.

From this general principle follow three other conclusions regarding the presentation of issues in the brief. First, the brief must set out the issues clearly and address them separately. The headings in the argument section of your brief (often known as "point headings") will set forth, in summary fashion, your arguments about how the judge should decide the specific issues. In a good brief, the table of contents allows the judge to determine what the issues are in an appeal by reading the argument headings. If the judge cannot do so, then the writer of the brief has failed this part of the lawyer's persuasive task.

Second, the issues must be set out in a logical order. For example, if issues are related — such as when they are part of a three-part test — that relationship dictates the order.

Finally, when the brief changes from a discussion of one issue to another, the reader must always know that this change is taking place. The reader should never have to guess about where the argument stands at any given point in the brief.

2. The Relationship Between the Issues and the Function of Appellate Review

Once you understand the principle that an appellate writer must structure the brief around the analyses of issues, you must take your thinking an important step further. To begin with, *all* courts decide issues, but appellate courts are courts of review. Their function is to determine whether a trial court has made an error of law in deciding the case.

The writer Ambrose Bierce wittily defined an "appeal" as "[i]n law, to put the dice into the box for another throw." Ambrose Bierce, THE DEVIL'S DICTIONARY (1911 Neale: New York), found at http://www.alcyone.com/max/lit/devils/a.html. However, Mr. Bierce's definition inaccurately implies that the appellant gets a completely new opportunity for victory. In actuality, an appellate court functions quite differently from a trial court:

> A successful appellate strategy must start with an understanding of the nature of the appellate process. The most basic, and most often ignored, point of departure

is this: Appellate courts and trial courts do different things. A court of appeals corrects the trial court's legal errors; it does not decide questions of fact.

Jordan B. Cherrick, *Issues, Facts, and Appellate Strategy*, in APPELLATE PRACTICE MANUAL 73, 74 (1992).

In carrying out this function, the court of appeals adjusts its level of review depending on the specific issue that it is considering. When an appellant argues that a finding of fact made in the trial court was erroneous, the appellate court's review is at its most deferential. It will uphold the finding of fact unless it is clearly erroneous. If the trial court exercised its discretion under law in making a decision, the appellate court will merely determine whether the trial court "abused its discretion." By contrast, if the appellate court is reviewing the trial court's interpretation of a statute, the appellate court's review is far less deferential. It will likely undertake an independent review of the trial court's interpretation of the statute to determine the correctness of the trial court's ruling.

Thus, an appellate court applies a *standard of review* to each issue that is before it on an appeal. The standards of review are discussed in detail in the next chapter.

Finally, you should note the relationship between the perspective principle and the standard of review, which is a central part of the structural principle. The standard of review is embedded in the perspective of appellate judges. If you think from their perspective, you will automatically take the standard of review into account.

D. THE ORGANIZATIONAL PRINCIPLE: SEPARATE THE ANALYTIC PROCESS FROM THE WRITING PROCESS

1. Think (Long and Hard) Before You Write

The central role played by issues in an appeal will necessarily lead you to think about the best way to implement the *structural principle* when you write an appellate brief. The easiest way to implement it is to separate the analyses of the issues — in which you decide what the issues are and how you will present them — from the actual writing of the brief. This book terms this separation the *organizational principle*, for it organizes your work in an efficient manner.

Legal writing involves a lengthy and often difficult analytic process. You must examine the record to determine which issues might be raised, research those issues, and weigh the chances of success under the standard of review. The complexity of the law alone ensures that carrying out this process is not easy. However, the difficulty compounds if, at the same time that you are actually writing the brief, you are also still trying to decide what the issues are, the order in which to present them, what cases to use, etc.

You can avoid this unnecessary difficulty. If you separate the analytic process from the physical process of writing, both will benefit. It is not a new idea:

[S]ome aspects of brief-writing advice have been remarkably consistent. Certain aspects of what is deemed bad lawyering when writing an appellate brief emerged early and have persisted over the years. . . . And the advice to this hapless practitioner has remained the same: Think, organize, and edit! . . .

Helen A. Anderson, *Changing Fashions in Advocacy: 100 Years of Brief-Writing Advice*, 11 J. App. Prac. & Process 1, 15 (2010). We will deal with editing later; for now, focus on the "think" and "organize" part.

To some degree, how you accomplish this separation is a matter of personal preference. Traditionalists prepare a formal outline from scratch: "[I]t is generally a good idea to prepare and then refine a detailed outline." *Effective Brief Writing*, in Federal Appellate Practice 296 (2008). Outlining is important because it allows one to test the logic of the argument prior to committing to the writing. Some, however, prefer using organizing tools like CaseMap. Whatever method you choose, however, you *must* perform this organizing task. The conclusion of one of the leading treatises is blunt: "If [the brief] doesn't outline properly, it hasn't been properly analyzed. . . . And, even with an apparently satisfactory outline, a brief that hasn't been properly thought through or researched just doesn't turn out well." Frederick Bernays Wiener, Effective Appellate Advocacy 97 (rev. ed. 2003).

An important part of this organizing process is crafting your argument point headings — i.e., the "table of contents" that sets forth the arguments in the brief. The argument headings will correspond to the specific issues that the court must decide. You will then write subheadings that break down the overall argument on each issue. When you are done, you will have gone a long way toward structuring your brief.

2. Reaping the Benefits of Organizing First

Organizing in this way requires mental discipline. After spending so much time researching and analyzing the issues, your natural tendency will be to jump immediately into writing the brief. Moreover, as you are organizing, at some point you will probably squirm in your chair trying to get the arguments in the correct order or writing a point heading that accurately reflects your intended argument. No matter how difficult the task is, however, keep one important fact in mind: Trying to organize *and* write at the same time is much harder than undertaking these tasks separately. That is why you must organize before you write.

If you follow the organizational principle, three large benefits will flow from your efforts. First, completing the structuring process at the outset means that you will write the first draft of your brief much more quickly. At this point you will not be worrying about *what* to write; instead, you can concentrate on *how* to write the points set forth in the outline. Thus, the actual writing is easier and will flow more smoothly.

Second, and concomitantly, as a result of following the organizational principle, the first draft of your brief will be much more polished than it would have been had you jumped directly into writing. And if the first draft of the brief is good, then it certainly follows that your *final* brief will be improved.

Third, thinking at this point allows you to decide an important question: What is the *theme* that your brief will follow? Simply put, the theme is your overarching reason why the court should rule in your favor. One article described it as "a message that shines through detailed facts and case law for a busy judge." Sarah E. Ricks & Jane L. Istvan, *Effective Brief Writing Despite High Volume Practice: Ten Misconceptions That Result in Bad Briefs*, 38 U. Tol. L. Rev. 1113, 1114 (2007). Your technical legal arguments allow the court to rule in your favor, but your theme convinces the court that it *should* do so. A theme is "the opportunity to go beyond the technical, legal points of your case and give the court a common sense, simple reason why all the technical stuff in your brief makes sense." Henry D. Gabriel, *Preparation and Delivery of Oral Argument in Appellate Courts*, 22 Am. J. Trial Advoc. 571, 584 (1999).

The theme should be part of your organizational effort. The time to develop your theme is now, when you can incorporate it into various parts of your outline. If you put off identifying the theme until later, when you are in the "thicket" of writing, the theme is likely to get short shrift.

Summary

- The first principle of writing an appellate brief, here denominated as the perspective principle, is to put yourself in the shoes of the reader, an appellate judge. You must see the appeal as the judge sees it, from the neutral viewpoint of a person new to the dispute and with limited knowledge, and not as you know it from your base of knowledge.

- If applied correctly, this perspective principle will help you answer many questions that will arise during the briefing of the appeal.

- A second important principle, the structural principle, requires you to organize the brief around the issues that the court must decide.

- In deciding what issues to raise and in formulating the argument, you must always take into account the standard of review that the court will apply.

- Third, you will simplify your task in writing a brief if you separate the analysis of the issues from the actual writing of the brief. The best way to do so is to outline in some fashion before you write.

- Thinking beforehand also allows you to identify the theme that your brief will raise. Developing your theme during your deliberative phase permits you to emphasize the reason you should win throughout your brief.

The Standard of Review

A. THE REVIEW FUNCTION OF APPELLATE COURTS

Recognizing that appellate courts are courts of *review* is a vital component of the perspective principle discussed in Chapter Two. The central function of appellate courts is to examine decisions of the trial court to determine whether reversible error occurred. On some occasions, appellate courts hear cases in the first instance, but the discussion below assumes that the court is reviewing a trial court decision.

The tasks performed by the trial court directly affect how the appellate court carries out its review. Different tests on appeal apply to the review of various decisions made by the trier of fact — the judge or the jury — in the trial court. These tests, known as "standards of review," establish a critical parameter for the appeal: the amount of deference that an appellate court will give to a trial court's decision. The standards exist on a continuum: At one end there is great deference to that decision, while at the other end there is none whatsoever.

For example, the trial court may have committed *legal error* in interpreting the law by using the wrong legal standard in deciding a motion, misinterpreting a statute, or giving an erroneous instruction to the jury. The list of such possible legal errors is long.

In reviewing issues claiming such legal errors, the appellate court essentially sits in the same position as the trial court. The appellate court is just as capable as the trial court of researching and interpreting the law. Accordingly, the court of appeals uses an independent standard of review — a completely new look at the legal issue. It accords no deference to the trial court's decision.

Alternatively, at the other end of the continuum, the appellant may argue that the trial court or the jury erred in making a decision regarding the facts. Perhaps the appellant claims that the overwhelming weight of the evidence contradicts a key factual determination made by the jury. In this situation, different and more deferential considerations apply because the jury was best situated to decide the facts. The trier of fact observed the witnesses firsthand, heard the testimony, and was in a "bird's-eye" position to ascertain the credibility and demeanor of the witnesses. In contrast, the appellate court merely has before it the written record of the testimony. As a result, the appellate court applies a much more deferential standard of review for factual determinations.

The purpose of standards of review, then, is to give the appellate court a lens through which to undertake its review. As one court put it, "Standards of review . . . focus reviewing courts upon their proper role when passing on the conduct of other decision-makers." *Evans v. Eaton Corp. Long Term Disability Plan*, 514 F.3d 315, 320 (4th Cir. 2008).

B. LOCATING THE STANDARD OF REVIEW FOR AN ISSUE

Where does the lawyer find the standard of review that an appellate court will use in deciding a particular issue? Again, the perspective principle supplies the answer. In deciding a case, an appellate judge will have to evaluate a series of issues. For each of those issues, the judge *must* apply a particular standard of review. The court is reviewing what happened in the court below, and it must determine how much deference to accord the trial court on each issue.

Moreover, most issues in appellate litigation recur, so the appellate courts are very likely to have previously considered the same issues in past cases. For example, the appellate judge may be evaluating a criminal case in which the appellant argues insufficient evidence was introduced at trial to support a jury's conclusion of fact. Many past cases will have raised such a claim.

So the answer to the question about where to find the standard of review for a particular issue should be obvious: Past appellate opinions will tell you in almost every instance. If you are deciding whether to raise an issue in an appeal, you will research the law to determine the standard of review that the court will apply to this issue. In rare instances, the issue may be an entirely new one that the court has not considered previously. In that case, you will argue to the court what standard it should apply to this new issue. But you will again start with the existing case law to find the standards of review used in deciding other issues that are closely analogous to the new one raised here.

C. THE PRINCIPAL STANDARDS OF REVIEW

While the various standards of review can vary slightly from state to state, on the whole they are relatively consistent. Below we examine the most common standards of review set forth in excerpts from discussions in recent decisions.

1. *De Novo* Review

The standard of review that gives no deference to the trial court's decision on an issue is known as *de novo* review. In Latin, "de novo" means "from the new"; the court takes an entirely new look at the matter. The most common issues in which *de novo* review applies are pure questions of law, but some others fall into this category as well.

T-Mobile W. LLC v. City & Cty. of San Francisco, 6 Cal. 5th 1107, 1117, 438 P.3d 239, 243-44 (2019):

Section 7901 provides that telephone corporations may construct lines and erect equipment along public roads in ways and locations that do not "incommode the public use of the road." We review the statute's language to determine the scope of the rights it grants to telephone corporations and whether, by granting those rights, the Legislature intended to preempt local regulation based on aesthetic considerations. These questions of law are subject to de novo review. (*Bruns v. E-Commerce Exchange, Inc.* (2011) 51 Cal.4th 717, 724, 122 Cal.Rptr.3d 331, 248 P.3d 1185; *Farm Raised Salmon Cases* (2008) 42 Cal.4th 1077, 1089, fn. 10, 72 Cal.Rptr.3d 112, 175 P.3d 1170.)

Credible Behavioral Health, Inc. v. Johnson, 466 Md. 380, 392-93, 220 A.3d 303, 309-10 (2019):

Next, we must determine whether the district court's interpretation of the promissory note is a legal conclusion. Regarding this issue, we have consistently held that "the interpretation of a contract, including the question of whether the language of a contract is ambiguous, is a question of law subject to *de novo* review." *Myers v. Kayhoe*, 391 Md. 188, 198, 892 A.2d 520, 526 (2006) (citing *Towson v. Conte*, 384 Md. 68, 78, 862 A.2d 941, 946 (2004)).

Ingram v. Brook Chateau, 586 S.W.3d 772, 774 (Mo. 2019):

The overruling of a motion to compel arbitration is reviewed *de novo. Soars v. Easter Seals Midwest*, 563 S.W.3d 111, 113 (Mo. banc 2018). The interpretation of a durable power of attorney is a question of law, also reviewed *de novo. Pearson v. Koster*, 367 S.W.3d 36, 43 (Mo. banc 2012).

2. Abuse of Discretion

A second common standard of review recognizes that the trial court was exercising discretion in making a decision. The court had to weigh certain considerations, and if its judgment fell within the boundaries of its discretion, the court of appeals will find no abuse. As one court explained, an appellate court may find an abuse of discretion when a decision "rest[s] on an impermissible basis" or was "based upon a consideration of irrelevant or inappropriate factors." *Flagg v. Essex Ct. Prosecutor*, 171 N.J. 561, 571, 796 A.2d 182 (2002). This standard of review is thus highly deferential.

In re Accutane Litig., 234 N.J. 340, 391, 191 A.3d 560, 590 (2018):

A reviewing court must apply an abuse of discretion standard to a trial court's determination, after a full Rule 104 hearing, to exclude expert testimony on unreliability grounds. *Hisenaj v. Kuehner*, 194 N.J. 6, 12, 16, 942 A.2d 769 (2008).

Gonzalez-Rivera v. Centro Medico Del Turabo, Inc., 931 F.3d 23, 27 (1st Cir. 2019):

We review for abuse of discretion a district court's order excluding an expert witness as a sanction for noncompliance with a scheduling order. *See Samaan v. St. Joseph Hosp.*, 670 F.3d 21, 35 (1st Cir. 2012). "This standard of review obtains both as to the finding that a discovery violation occurred and as to the appropriateness of the sanction selected." *Santiago-Díaz v. Laboratorio Clínico y de Referencia del Este*, 456 F.3d 272, 275 (1st Cir. 2006).

3. Clearly Erroneous

Another highly deferential standard of review asks whether the decision of the trial court was "clearly erroneous." A finding is clearly erroneous "when although there is evidence to support it, the reviewing court on the entire evidence is left with the definite and firm conviction that a mistake has been committed." *United States v. United States Gypsum Co.*, 333 U.S. 364, 395, 68 S. Ct. 525, 92 L. Ed. 746 (1948). This standard often applies to review of findings of fact made by a trial judge acting as the trier of fact rather than findings of facts made by a jury or administrative entity.

***State v. Smith*, 2016 WI 23, ¶ 26, 367 Wis. 2d 483, 505, 878 N.W.2d 135, 146:**

A competency determination [to stand trial] is functionally a factual finding. *State v. Byrge*, 2000 WI 101, ¶ 33, 237 Wis.2d 197, 614 N.W.2d 477. Therefore, we review the circuit court's competency determination under a clearly erroneous standard of review that is particularized to competency findings. *Garfoot*, 207 Wis.2d at 224, 558 N.W.2d 626; *Byrge*, 237 Wis.2d 197, ¶ 45, 614 N.W.2d 477.

***Credible Behavioral Health, Inc. v. Johnson*, 466 Md. 380, 388, 220 A.3d 303, 307 (2019):**

Under Maryland Rule 8–131(c), an appellate court ". . . will not set aside the judgment of the trial court on the evidence unless clearly erroneous, and will give due regard to the opportunity of the trial court to judge the credibility of the witnesses." Md. Rule 8–131(c); *Nesbit v. Gov't Emps. Ins. Co.*, 382 Md. 65, 72, 854 A.2d 879, 883 (2004).

4. Substantial Evidence

The "substantial evidence" standard is used by many courts to test whether sufficient evidence exists to support a finding of fact. In its application, the substantial evidence standard of review is similar to the clearly erroneous standard. However, unlike the clearly erroneous standard, which is almost exclusively applied to factual findings made by trial judges, the substantial evidence standard of review applies to findings of fact made by a jury. This standard of review is also often used to determine whether findings of fact by administrative agencies were sufficiently supported in the record.

***Exaro Energy III, LLC v. Wyoming Oil & Gas Conservation Comm'n*, 2020 WY 8, ¶¶ 9-11, 455 P.3d 1243, 1248-49 (Wyo. 2020):**

When, as here, both parties submitted evidence at the contested case hearing and an agency's factual findings are involved, we apply the substantial evidence standard of review. *Dale v. S & S Builders, LLC*, 2008 WY 84, ¶ 10, 188 P.3d 554, 558 (Wyo. 2008). . . . Under this standard of review, "we examine the entire record to determine whether there is substantial evidence to support an agency's [factual] findings. If the agency's decision is supported by substantial evidence, we cannot properly substitute our judgment for that of the agency and must uphold the findings on appeal."

***Nero v. S.C. Dep't of Transportation*, 422 S.C. 424, 427, 812 S.E.2d 735, 737 (2018), *reh'g denied* (May 3, 2018):**

"While reasonable minds could have reached a different conclusion based on the record, we must not engage in fact-finding that would disregard the Commission's factual findings on these issues. . . . We find the Commission's findings are supported by substantial evidence." *Hartzell v. Palmetto Collision, LLC*, 415 S.C. 617, 623, 785 S.E.2d 194, 197 (2016).

In litigating appeals, you may find other standards of review not mentioned above. For example, a court may review a decision to determine whether it was "arbitrary or capricious." But the standards just discussed will apply to the vast majority of issues litigated on appeals.

5. Mixed Questions of Law and Fact

Often, of course, a case will present a combination of issues that call for the application of different standards of review. A court may apply *de novo* review for one issue, and then turn to the clearly erroneous standard when addressing the next issue. Sometimes, however, a single issue may seem to implicate more than one standard of review. By far the most common of these is the "mixed question of law and fact." As you will no doubt intuit from the discussion of the standards of review set forth above, such a mixed question would seem to implicate two standards: (1) *de novo* review (since part of it is a question of law), and (2) a deferential standard of review such as "clearly erroneous" (since part of it involves review of a factual determination).

Where they can, courts will separate out the parts of the "mixed question of law and fact" so that these two standards can be separately applied:

> *State v. Hawkins*, **2019-Ohio-4210, 158 Ohio St. 3d 94, 97, 140 N.E.3d 577, 580-81,** *reconsideration denied*, **2019-Ohio-5327, 157 Ohio St. 3d 1524, 137 N.E.3d 109, and** *cert. denied*, **206 L. Ed. 2d 939 (May 18, 2020):**
>
> Appellate review of a ruling on a motion to suppress [evidence] presents a mixed question of law and fact. *State v. Burnside*, 100 Ohio St.3d 152, 2003-Ohio-5372, 797 N.E.2d 71, ¶ 8. An appellate court must accept the trial court's findings of fact if they are supported by competent, credible evidence. *See State v. Fanning*, 1 Ohio St.3d 19, 20, 437 N.E.2d 583 (1982). But the appellate court must decide the legal questions independently, without deference to the trial court's decision. *Burnside* at ¶ 8.

When the law and fact questions seem so intertwined that they cannot be separated, courts may approach each set of questions by determining which ones predominate, or they may use a kind of sliding scale for the standard of review:

> *Intercontinental Hotels Grp. v. Utah Labor Comm'n*, **2019 UT 55, ¶¶ 5-6, 448 P.3d 1270, 1274:**
>
> IHG asks us to reconsider the Labor Commission's order affirming the award of workers' compensation benefits to Ms. Wilson. "Whether the [Labor] [C]ommission correctly or incorrectly denied benefits is 'a traditional mixed question of law and fact.'" And the "standard of review we apply when reviewing a mixed question can be either deferential or non-deferential." "Deference on a mixed question is warranted when the mixed finding is *not* law-like because it does not lend itself to consistent resolution by a uniform body of appellate

precedent or *is* fact-like because the [factfinder] is in a superior position to decide it." In this case, we must review two Labor Commission determinations: one determination that is law-like — whether certain "going and coming" exception factors we identified in a previous case applied to accidents on an employer's premises — and another that is fact-like — whether the accident in this case occurred on the employer's premises. Accordingly, we review the first determination without deference, and the second determination with deference.

As these excerpts illustrate, courts employ a variety of standards of review, and they differ significantly in their effect on the outcome of the appeal. The late Judge Karen Williams of the Fourth Circuit Court of Appeals emphasized the central role that standards of review play in appeals:

> I cannot overstate the importance that the standard of review plays in shaping the appellate judge's outlook on the issue. If we review only for abuse of discretion, the advocate must clearly demonstrate an obvious error, or no relief will be forthcoming. Under the de novo standard of review, however, we are free to reverse a judgment call in a grey area.

Karen J. Williams, *Help Us Help You: A Fourth Circuit Primer on Effective Appellate Oral Arguments*, 50 S.C. L. Rev. 591, 597 (1999). A former chief judge of the District of Columbia Circuit was even more direct: "To the judge, [the standard of review] is everything." Harry T. Edwards & Linda A. Elliott, Federal Courts Standards of Review (2007).

D. WAIVER, PREJUDICE, AND HARMLESS ERROR

Before addressing how lawyers use the standard of review, one essential point needs to be made. The appellant's lawyer may identify an error in the record, research the standard of review, and conclude that the trial court unquestionably erred in its ruling. The lawyer may be absolutely correct in that analysis. Nonetheless, the appeal can still be lost for one of two reasons.

First, at trial, the lawyer who was representing the appealing party must have raised the issue before the court. For example, if the issue concerns the admissibility of certain evidence, the lawyer must have objected to the admission of that evidence. Similarly, if the error concerns prejudice from the venue where the trial was held, the trial lawyer must have filed a motion to change venue. Failure to do so will waive the issue on appeal. *See, e.g., State v. Miranda*, 327 Conn. 451, 461, 174 A.3d 770, 776 (2018) ("'[W]aiver may be effected by action of counsel. . . . When a party consents to or expresses satisfaction with an issue at trial, claims arising from that issue are deemed waived and may not be reviewed on appeal.'").

Second, even if the trial lawyer did not waive the issue, the court's ruling must result in prejudice to the client. "A party seeking reversal for evidentiary error must show that the error was prejudicial, and that the verdict was more probably than not affected as a result." *McCollough v. Johnson, Rodenburg & Lauinger, LLC*, 637 F.3d 939, 953 (9th Cir. 2011). If no prejudice is shown on an issue, the appellate court will not reverse.

Now let's move on to how appellate lawyers use the standards of review.

E. EXPLAINING THE STANDARD OF REVIEW TO THE COURT

When it begins considering an appeal, the appellate court will immediately be concerned with identifying the standard of review that it must apply in reviewing an issue. The court will look to *you*, as counsel for one of the parties, to inform it of the appropriate standard of review in your brief. Federal Rule of Appellate Procedure 28(a) explicitly requires that the appellant's argument must include "for each issue, a concise statement of the applicable standard of review . . . ." But even absent such a rule, effective lawyers will always include a discussion of the standard of review in their brief.

In deciding what your discussion of the standard of review should entail, you will want to apply the perspective principle from Chapter Two. If you do, one thought will immediately arise: If *every* issue on *every* appeal has a standard of review, the appellate court will be well aware from past cases of the different standards of review. Thus, your explanation of the standard of review in the brief need not be lengthy. But you must fully support that explanation with a citation to appropriate case authority in which the court previously found that the standard applied in your type of case. Here is the approach that an Ohio appellate judge recommends in discussing an appeal from the grant of summary judgment:

> [T]he standard for granting summary judgment . . . is the same for the trial court or the appellate court, whether there is a genuine issue of material fact. Just state that in two lines with a citation, and move on. We really do not need a four or five page treatise on the law of summary judgment — but we get one in about 20% of the briefs. . . .

Mark P. Painter, *Appellate Practice — Including Legal Writing from a Judge's Perspective*, 14.

Here are short excerpts from four appellate briefs. Notice how they succinctly set forth the standard of review:

1. Review of an Interpretation of a Statute

This appeal involves interpretation of statutes. In interpreting statutes, this Court applies de novo review. Nickell v. Matlock, 206 Cal.App.4th 934, 940 (2012); *People ex rel. Lockyer v. Shamrock Foods Co.*, 24 Cal.4th 415, 432 (2000). All issues in this appeal are subject to de novo review.

2. Review of Evidentiary Rulings

The District Court's evidentiary rulings, including the admission of expert testimony and potential hearsay evidence, are reviewed for abuses of discretion. *U.S. v. Stinson*, 647 F.3d 1196, 1210 (9th Cir. 2011); *U.S. v. (Kevin) Freeman*, 498 F.3d 893, 900-01 (9th Cir. 2007). The Court reviews "*de novo* the construction or interpretation of the Federal Rules of Evidence, including whether particular evidence falls within the scope of a given rule." *U.S. v. Wells*, 879 F.3d 900, 914 (9th Cir. 2018) (citation omitted).

3. Review of the Grant of a Motion to Dismiss

This is an appeal from an order granting a motion to dismiss for failure to state a claim upon which relief may be granted, pursuant to Rule 12(b)(6), F.R. CIV. P. The standard of review of such an order is de novo, with no deference to the trial judge's ruling. *U.S. v. Lewis*, 411 F.3d 838, 841-842 (7th Cir. 2005); *Autry v. Northwest Premium Services*, 144 F.3d 1037, 1039 (7th Cir. 1998); *Johnson v. Rivera*, 272 F.3d 519, 521 (7th Cir. 2001).

4. Review of a Jury Verdict

"In reviewing the sufficiency of the evidence, we view the evidence in the light most favorable to the jury verdict and will reverse only if no reasonable jury could have found the defendant guilty." *United States v. Landers*, 417 F.3d 958, 963 (8th Cir. 2005).

Many appeals will raise several issues, and each may have a different standard of review. You must inform the court of the appropriate standard for each of those issues. In doing so, however, you must decide how to incorporate this information into your brief.

One possibility is to write one separate section that discusses the standards of review before the argument part of the brief. In some jurisdictions, the rules require such a separate section of the brief, and in these courts you have no choice. Alternatively, if a court rule does not govern this subject, you may choose not to have a single "standard of review" section at the outset of the argument. Instead, you can tell the court what standard to apply as you discuss each individual issue.

Even if a court rule mandates a separate "standard of review" section, you will still need to apply the perspective principle. Applying that principle may tell you that it will be hard for a judge to keep the various standards in mind in reading through the brief. As a result, you will have to remind the court at various points in the brief about the standard it should use for the issues that you are about to discuss.

A final thought: You may initially decide to address the standard of review in the individual parts of the brief rather than in a single section at the beginning. However, as you write the individual parts of the brief, you could find yourself repeatedly restating the same standard. Accordingly, at that point you may need to reconsider your initial decision on this question, and you may decide that dealing with the standard once at the outset of your argument is the better choice. In other words, your initial decision on how to treat the standard of review is subject to change.

F. THE RELATIONSHIP BETWEEN THE STANDARD OF REVIEW AND THE ISSUES RAISED

Take a second and again examine the case excerpts set forth above discussing the standards of review. The difference in the standards should be very apparent. For example, a "de novo" review by the appellate court is a far cry from application of the "clearly erroneous" standard. An appellant obviously stands a better chance of overturning a trial court's decision under the "de novo" review standard than under the "clearly erroneous" standard. As one litigator put it, "The standard of review acts as a sort of gatekeeper, informing potential appellants as to the prudence of appealing a given issue." Jared K. Carter, *Appellate Practice: Tips for Effectively Defining and Using Standards of Review in Appellate Practice*, 44 VT. B.J. at 28 (2018).

These differences are important for two reasons. First, if possible, you should frame a particular issue so that the court will use a standard of review that favors your client. As a federal appeals judge put it, "The task is to frame the issue as one that calls for a standard of review that favors your side. If you can get us to see the issues your way, you may gain a great advantage over your opponent." Paul R. Michel, *Effective Appellate Advocacy*, 24 LITIGATION 19, 21 (1998).

Second, if the standard of review on an issue is clear, the lawyer still has a great deal of control over whether to *raise* that issue on appeal in the first instance. Because the standards of review differ for separate issues, the appellant will want to consider those differences in choosing which issues to raise on appeal.

Of course, the standard of review is not the only consideration in choosing issues. If an issue is weak for your client, you may not win your case even if the standard of review is favorable. Nonetheless, the standard of review can make a considerable difference in the receptiveness of the appellate court to your argument. As one federal appellate judge summarized: "The brief needs to identify what the alleged reversible error is, taking into consideration the standards of review we have to apply, because that standard in many instances determines the outcome." Robert R. Baldock et al., *What Appellate Advocates Seek from Appellate Judges and What Appellate Judges Seek from Appellate Advocates,* 31 N.M. L. REV. 265, 266 (2001).

G. USING THE STANDARD OF REVIEW

After identifying the standard of review and choosing what issues to raise, an appellant must frame the arguments in the brief to meet those standards. To prevail, you must show the court *why* the standard is met on the particular issue that you are raising. In the words of one appellate judge, you must "weave it throughout your brief." Robert H. Thomas, *Preparing an Effective Appellate Brief— The Expert View*, J. APPELLATE ISSUES 26, 27 (Spring 2012) (citing comments of Judge N. Randy Smith). Here are three examples from briefs showing how the argument incorporates the standard of review. Note how the argument under a *de novo* standard differs from the arguments under the other two standards of review.

1. Using the *"De Novo"* Standard

This Court reviews the district court's interpretation of a statute *de novo. City of L.A. v. United States Doc*, 307 F.3d 859, 868 (9th Cir. 2002). This Court also reviews legal rulings by the district court *de novo*. See *United States v. Middleton*, 231 F.3d 1207, 1209-10 (9th Cir. 2000); *City of L.A. v. United States Doc*, 307 F.3d 859, 868 (9th Cir. 2002) . . . .

In construing the "plain meaning" of a statute, "the court must look to the particular statutory language at issue, as well as the language and design of the statute as a whole." *U.S. v. Lewis*, 67 F.3d 225, 228-29 (9th Cir. 1995) ("Particular phrases must be construed in light of the overall purpose and structure of the whole statutory scheme.")

[T]he language of the Employee Retirement Income Security Act ("ERISA"), 29 USC Section 1133, itself states that an insurer must specifically state the "specific reasons" it is denying a claim in order to "afford" the insured a "full and fair review." Construing the plain language of ERISA, there is no reason to believe that Congress mistakenly substituted "specific reasons" for "specific policy provision" or meant anything other than what the statute expressly states.

ERISA's implementing regulation, 29 C.F.R. § 2560.503-1(g), makes it even more clear that ERISA's requirement that an insurer notify the insured of the specific reasons for its denial is not synonymous with notifying the insured of the plan provision at issue. Section 2560.503-1(g) clearly and separately requires that the insurer do both. As Section 2560.503-1(g) states in pertinent part, the insurer must notify the claimant of any "adverse benefit determination . . . in a manner calculated to be understood by the claimant." The notification shall include the following information:

(i) *The specific reason or reasons for the adverse determination*; [and]
(ii) *Reference to the specific plan provisions on which the determination is based*;

If the "specific reason" and the "plan provision" were synonymous, there would have been no need for ERISA's implementing regulation to expressly require that an insurer notify an insured of both . . . .

2. Using the "Clear Error" Standard

On the issue of whether it was a breach of the standard of care for Dr. Wolfe to obstruct the left ureter with a stitch, the District Court properly found that Dr. Zaslau's opinions on the issue were contradictory. (J.A. 1265-1266). Dr. Zaslau opined that patients do not expect to have a ureteral injury after an anterior colporrhaphy repair but at the same time admitted that Dr. Wolfe's surgery was properly performed. (J.A. 785, 852). Dr. Zaslau also admitted that in his practice he had placed a stitch through a ureter, but did not believe that he was negligent because he had identified it intraoperatively by use of cystoscopy. (J.A. 857). Based upon this inconsistent testimony from Dr. Zaslau, the District Court properly found that Appellants had not established that placing a stitch through the ureter was a breach of the standard care. (J.A. 1270-1272, 1275-6 1276). This finding is not clearly erroneous and should be affirmed.

3. Using the "Abuse of Discretion" Standard

The trial court imposed a substantively unreasonable sentence. The standard sentencing range for an individual convicted of a depredation offense without any significant criminal history is 0 to 6 months. In this case, the range more than tripled to 15 to 21 months due to the possession of a firearm. The trial court increased the sentence even further to 36 months.

The record shows that Wisecarver is an exceptional individual and has led a very clean life. He has served in the military and received an honorable discharge for medical reasons. He has served his community in firefighting and law enforcement, raised a child as a single parent, and does not use alcohol or drugs. He is a highly respected neighbor who frequently helps others without asking for anything in return. He has a reputation of veracity and peacefulness; his criminal history consists of three minor traffic tickets. He was minding his own business on his own property when the depredation offense occurred.

Under these circumstances, the trial court's decision to substantially increase the sentence to over twice the lower end of the guideline range imposes a sentence that is greater than necessary. Such a sentence is substantively unreasonable and an abuse of discretion.

Incorporating the standard of review into your argument is likely to involve a new thinking process for you. In the rush of performing the multiple tasks of brief writing, you can easily overlook it. However, the appellate lawyer does so at great risk. *You* may overlook the standard of review, but the court certainly will not.

Summary

- Appellate courts are courts of review and thus perform a very different function than trial courts. In reviewing various decisions of the trial court, appellate courts apply different "standards of review," which establish the amount of deference that an appellate court will give to the decisions of the trial court.

- The standard of review shapes how a court approaches its review of an issue. Thus, the appellate lawyer must identify the standard of review that applies to an issue and incorporate that standard into the argument.

- You may have a separate "standard of review" section in your brief. Alternatively, you may discuss the applicable standard for different issues in the different parts of the brief that address those issues.

- Your argument will incorporate the standard of review and aim to satisfy that standard. Equally important, you may choose to raise or not raise certain issues depending on how easily you can satisfy the particular standard of review for the issue.

CHAPTER 4

An Overview of the Appellate Brief

A. TYPES OF APPELLATE BRIEFS

The principal task of the appellate lawyer is to prepare and file a convincing brief. Appellate judges unanimously agree that while oral argument can affect the outcome in a few instances, most appellate decisions are reached based on the briefs. So writing the brief is the critical job.

The typical appeal involves an opening brief filed by the appellant (sometimes called the petitioner), and an opposition brief filed later by the appellee (sometimes called the respondent). Finally, the appellant may file a reply brief if it so chooses.

Many lawyers take advantage of this opportunity because it allows them to have the last written word in the appeal.

In general, the appellant's brief sets forth the facts of the case, the issues on appeal, and the arguments about why the appellant believes that the trial court erred and should be reversed. The appellee's brief then responds to the issues that the appellant has raised and includes any additional facts that the appellee deems pertinent. It will generally follow the order in which the appellant's brief has addressed issues, unless a very good reason exists to depart from that order. The reply brief, if any, then responds to any new points raised in the appellee's brief, but it cannot raise new issues.

One other important type of brief used less frequently is an amicus curiae ("friend of the court") brief. This brief is not filed by a party to the litigation; rather, an amicus brief is filed by an outside party that has an interest in the legal issues raised by the appeal. Most important cases in the U.S. Supreme Court attract a large number of amicus curiae briefs. For example, the Chamber of Commerce may file a brief in a case raising an important business-related issue, or a labor union might file in a case raising labor issues.

An amicus curiae brief does not reiterate the briefing by the parties to the appeal. Instead, it tries to illuminate the issues by giving the court legal background or other information beyond the confines of the record that it otherwise might not receive. Thus, while the writing of an amicus curiae brief will use the writing skills taught in this book, its content will look quite different.

The appellate court and the rules of court will set a timetable establishing the dates when the various briefs are due.

B. DETERMINING THE CONTENTS OF AN APPELLATE BRIEF

As a law student, you should have a basic grasp of brief writing from your legal writing class. However, appellate briefs are subject to detailed requirements set by statute and rules of court. For example, Illinois Rule 341 sets forth the following requirements for supreme court briefs filed in that state:

(h) Appellant's Brief. The appellant's brief shall contain the following parts in the order named:

(1) A table of contents, including a summary statement, entitled "Points and Authorities," of the points argued and the authorities cited in the Argument. This shall consist of the headings of the points and subpoints as in the Argument, with the citation under each heading of the authorities relied upon or distinguished, and a reference to the page of the brief on which each heading and each authority appear. Cases shall be cited as near as may be in the order of their importance.

(2) An introductory paragraph stating (i) the nature of the action and of the judgment appealed from and whether the judgment is based upon the verdict of a jury, and (ii) whether any question is raised on the pleadings and, if so, the nature of the question.

(3) A statement of the issue or issues presented for review, without detail or citation of authorities. . . . The appellant must include a concise statement of the applicable standard of review for each issue, with citation to authority, either in the discussion of the issue in the argument or under a separate heading placed before the discussion in the argument.

(4) A statement of jurisdiction:

(i) In a case appealed to the Supreme Court directly from the trial court or as a matter of right from the Appellate Court, a brief statement under the heading "Jurisdiction" of the jurisdictional grounds for the appeal to the Supreme Court.

(ii) In a case appealed to the Appellate Court, a brief, but precise statement or explanation under the heading "Jurisdiction" of the basis for appeal including the supreme court rule or other law which confers jurisdiction upon the reviewing court; the facts of the case which bring it within this rule or other law; and the date that the order being appealed was entered and any other facts which are necessary to demonstrate that the appeal is timely. In appeals from a judgment as to all the claims and all the parties, the statement shall demonstrate the disposition of all claims and all parties. All facts recited in this statement shall be supported by page references to the record on appeal.

(5) In a case involving the construction or validity of a statute, constitutional provision, treaty, ordinance, or regulation, the pertinent parts of the provision verbatim, with a citation of the place where it may be found, all under an appropriate heading, such as "Statutes Involved." If the provision involved is lengthy, its citation alone will suffice at this point, and its pertinent text shall be set forth in an appendix.

(6) Statement of Facts, which shall contain the facts necessary to an understanding of the case, stated accurately and fairly without argument or comment, and with appropriate reference to the pages of the record on appeal . . . .

(7) Argument, which shall contain the contentions of the appellant and the reasons therefor . . . .

(i) Briefs of Appellee and Other Parties. The brief for the appellee and other parties shall conform to the foregoing requirements, except that items (2), (3), (4), (5), [and] (6) . . . of paragraph (h) of this rule need not be included except to the extent that the presentation by the appellant is deemed unsatisfactory.

(j) Reply Brief. The reply brief, if any, shall be confined strictly to replying to arguments presented in the brief of the appellee and need contain only Argument.

In the federal courts of appeals, Federal Rule of Appellate Procedure 28(a) sets out a list of analogous requirements. Furthermore, each federal appellate circuit has individual requirements that you must identify and follow.

The requirements for an appellate brief thus can vary somewhat from jurisdiction to jurisdiction. For example, the part of the Illinois Rule requiring a "Points and Authorities" is not found in most other states. However, you will find that the basic requirements for appellate briefs are relatively consistent in appellate courts throughout the country.

C. THE BASIC PARTS OF AN APPELLATE BRIEF

Here are the basic parts of an appellate brief. Later chapters of this book will discuss these parts in detail.

1. Jurisdictional Statement

Federal court rules require you to include a jurisdictional statement setting forth the basis of the appellate court's jurisdiction. Many state courts have a similar requirement.

2. Statement of Issues

Most court rules ask you to include a statement of the issues presented for appellate review. However, even if the rules do not include this requirement, you should put yourself in the shoes of the judge. Wouldn't you want to know precisely what the issues in the case are? Furthermore, from the advocate's viewpoint, the statement of issues is an important opportunity to shape the entire presentation of the brief. Good lawyers include a statement of the issues even if the rules do not specifically require one.

3. Statement of Facts

This part of the brief lays out the facts of the case for the appellate judges. The facts are taken solely from the record on appeal; the lawyer cannot take facts from outside the record, even if true, and insert them in the statement of facts unless the lawyer has sought permission to augment the record. A citation to the record on appeal must accompany each fact.

The lawyer has three goals in mind when writing the statement of facts. First, it must include all of the principal and dispositive facts necessary to argue the issues addressed in the brief. Second, it must tell a story that is favorable to the lawyer's client. That story will be consistent with the "theme" of the brief, a subject discussed above in Chapter Two. Third, the statement of facts must be scrupulously accurate.

4. Statement of the Case

Many rules of court speak of a "statement of the case." For example, Rule 28 of the Federal Rules of Appellate Procedure declares that an appellant's brief must contain "a statement of the case briefly indicating the nature of the case, the course of proceedings, and the disposition below." Massachusetts Rule of Appellate Procedure 16 likewise dictates that the statement of the case should discuss the same three topics.

The appellate court needs to know the procedural background of the case—the court from which the appeal is taken and the decision that is being appealed. These facts are crucial for the appellate court to determine whether it has jurisdiction over the appeal.

The terminology of court rules varies with respect to the statement of the case. Some rules require the brief to include both the statement of facts and the procedural background of the case. Others just say a statement of the case is needed but do not define it. Whatever the specific content required by the rule, the court of appeals will need to know about the facts and the procedural background of the appeal. Both sets of information are essential to the appellate court's review function.

5. Standard of Review

As discussed in Chapter Three, the brief must inform the appellate court about the standards of review that it should apply to the various issues. Does the court apply "de novo" review, i.e., give no deference to the trial court's conclusions? Or does some other standard apply, such as the "clearly erroneous" standard, or the "substantial evidence" standard?

Some briefs will contain a separate section on the standards of review to be applied, while others will deal with this subject within each specific argument. But make no mistake about it: Your brief must address the standard of review, whether in a separate section or not. If it does not, the first question you may face at oral argument could likely be: "Counsel, what standard of review do we apply, and why wasn't that standard set forth in your brief?"

6. Summary of Argument/Introduction

Although some jurisdictions do not specifically require a summary of argument, good practice dictates including one even if no rule requires it. The summary gives the court a quick overview of the entire argument, affording the judges an opportunity to see the entire picture of the appeal. This part of the brief, very likely the first or second section that the appellate judge will read, sets the tone for the brief. It succinctly summarizes the substance of the appeal. A summary of the argument is usually placed in the brief immediately before the argument section.

To succeed, the summary of argument must do more than just state the arguments in shortened form. It must also paint your client's position in the best light and thus hopefully begin to move the court toward viewing your client's position favorably. The summary can accomplish this goal by touching on important equities in your client's favor or setting forth the policy justifications supporting your client's position.

Sometimes a brief will contain an "introduction" rather than a "summary of argument." A significant difference between them is that an introduction section will be placed in the brief before the statement of the facts, while a summary of the argument section immediately follows the statement of the case. In addition, introductions sometimes include a brief description of the procedural history of the case, telling the reader how the matter arrived at the appellate court. The function of the introduction, however, is largely the same as the summary of the argument. Both allow counsel to preview the major issues and arguments in the case and to present a party's theory and theme.

7. Argument

This part of the brief contains the heart of the case on appeal, the legal argument why that party should prevail. The appellate brief structures the argument around "point headings." In one sentence or phrase, each point heading informs the reader about the argument that is set forth immediately below the heading.

8. Conclusion

You will need a conclusion to wrap up your brief. The conclusion is very short, often just a couple of sentences in a single paragraph. Its most important function is telling the court precisely what relief you seek from the appellate process, whether you are an appellant or an appellee.

The relief may be a request that the appellate court reverse the judgment of the court below and direct the trial court to enter judgment for your client. Alternatively, it may be more involved, such as a request for reversal with specific direction to the trial court. Whatever the case, the chief function of the conclusion in the brief is to give the appellate judge a place to turn to and find the precise relief that a party wants from the court.

In summary, the table of contents in an appellate brief will look something like this:

Table of Authorities
[Introduction]
Statement of Issues
Jurisdictional Statement
Statement of Facts
Procedural History [or Statement of the Case]
[Summary of the Argument]
Standard of Review
Argument
Conclusion

D. THE MECHANICS OF PRODUCING THE BRIEF

As you have seen, statutes and court rules dictate a large part of an appellate brief's content. These sources give you information about the substance of the brief as well as about the technical requirements. The latter include page limits (or, more likely in today's era of word processors, word limits) on the brief, allowed typeface, required line spacing, content of the cover page, content of the table of contents and table of authorities, and the color of the brief's cover. The jurisdiction may also require the party to attach an appendix of the leading authorities cited. Finally, you will be told how to file and serve the brief.

These requirements must be checked carefully, for some of them can be quite idiosyncratic. For example, if you file a brief in the District of Columbia Circuit Court of Appeals, you will discover Circuit Rule 28(a)(2), which declares:

> (2) In the left-hand margin of the table of authorities in all briefs, an asterisk may be placed next to those authorities on which the brief principally relies, together with a notation at the bottom of the first page of the table stating: "Authorities upon which we chiefly rely are marked with asterisks." . . . The table of authorities must identify each page of the brief on which the authority is cited; *passim* or similar terms may not be used.

In pondering this requirement, you might conclude that this definitional "notation" would work better at the *top* of the table of authorities. The court, however, has decreed otherwise, and you therefore must both remember it and place it at the bottom of the first page.

Some of these rules may seem to be a nuisance, but they have very important consequences. When you attempt to file your brief, the clerk of the court often stamps "received" on the brief instead of "filed." Then, out of your sight, the clerk will examine the "received" brief to see if it conforms to the court's rules. If you have filed your brief on the last day allowed under the court's timetable, you may find out on the following day that the clerk has decided your brief does not comply with the rules. Now you may have a big problem. When you fix the error and try to refile, your brief is *late*, and you may need a court order allowing the late filing.

Furthermore, even if the violation makes it past the Clerk's Office and the brief is filed, violations of rules concerning page, word, and type restrictions have other consequences. As a former chief judge of the Ninth Circuit Court of Appeals pithily warned, a violation of a requirement concerning typeface or maximum length "tells the judges that the lawyer is the type of sleazeball who is willing to cheat on a small procedural rule and therefore probably will lie about the record or forget to cite controlling authority." Alex Kozinski, *The Wrong Stuff,* BYU L. REV. 325, 327 (1992).

Of course, it could be even more embarrassing. A story has it that when John Marshall Harlan—later a Supreme Court Justice—briefed an appeal in the Second

Circuit Court of Appeals, the brief was overly long. The clerk did not reject it. However, when Harlan's senior partner stood up to argue at the oral argument, the famous Justice Learned Hand inquired as to who wrote the brief. The senior partner—thinking that Justice Hand was about to bestow a compliment—graciously identified Harlan as the principal author. Justice Hand then said that the brief was too long and that he wouldn't read it—and then threw the brief over the bench toward the counsel table where Harlan sat. Andrew L. Frey, *How to Write a Good Appellate Brief,* https://www.mayerbrown.com/en/perspectives-events/publications/no-date/how-to-write-a-good-appellate-brief.

So find and follow the requirements carefully. You won't have to duck at oral argument. End of story.

Summary

- The three briefs usually filed in an appeal are the appellant's opening brief, the appellee's brief, and the appellant's reply brief. There are also other types of briefs, such as the brief of an amicus curiae, or "friend of the court."

- The court's rules, and perhaps the statutes in a state, establish the content required for the brief.

- The basic parts of an appellate brief are the jurisdictional statement, the statement of issues, the statement of facts, the statement of the case (or procedural history), the standard of review, the summary of argument (or introduction), the argument, and the conclusion.

- Court rules also establish specific rules regarding the length of the brief, the typeface required, the contents of the cover page, and numerous other details. A court clerk can reject your brief if you do not follow these rules.

The Statement of Issues

A. THE PURPOSE OF SEPARATELY STATING THE ISSUES

Assume that you are an appellate judge picking up a brief for the first time. You are part of a three-judge panel, but you have been assigned to carry out the internal analysis of one appeal before oral argument. Your chambers will produce a draft opinion or a detailed bench memo that will circulate to the other two appellate judges who will hear the case.

You would like to quickly identify the issues in the appeal for two reasons. First, you want to estimate how complex the appeal will be. Second, you are interested in identifying the area of law that the appeal concerns. So, for enlightenment, you immediately turn to the statement of issues or, as it is termed in some appellate courts, the *questions presented*. *See* Bryan A. Garner, *The Future of Appellate Advocacy*, 54 Duq. L. Rev. 311, 314 (2016) ("Any reasonable judge wants to know immediately upon picking up a brief what the question to be decided is.").

From the standpoint of the appellate lawyer, the statement of issues thus presents an important opportunity to persuade court that you should win. You can clarify for the court exactly what the appeal is about from your client's viewpoint. At the same time, you can frame the issues in a way that will favor the outcome you desire. So, while the statement of issues is on a single page in the brief, it can play an important role in beginning to persuade the court in your client's favor. As Karl Llewelyn said in a speech on appellate lawyering:

> [T]he first thing that comes up is the issue and the first art is the framing of the issue so that if your framing is accepted the case comes out your way. . . . Second, you have to capture the issue, because your opponent will be framing an issue very differently. You have got to so frame yours that it "sells the Court," to use the term of the market place . . . so that it "captures the field." . . . And third, you have to build a technique of phrasing of your issue which . . . will stick your capture into the Court's head so that it can't forget it.

Karl N. Llewellyn, *A Lecture on Appellate Advocacy*, 29 U. CHI. L. REV. 627, 630 (1962), reproduced in 7 J. APP. PRAC. & PROCESS 173, 177 (2005).

In short, you have much to accomplish in the small number of words that comprise the statement of issues.

B. DRAFTING THE STATEMENT OF ISSUES

1. Selecting the Issues

The appellant's lawyer begins work on the statement of issues by considering the number of issues to be raised. Lawyers are trained to find issues, and the potential issues tend to multiply as the lawyer becomes familiar with the record (always making sure, of course, that the issue was preserved for appeal in the court below and that the error was prejudicial). So you must choose the issues that you will argue in your brief. How do you decide how many issues to raise?

Certainly the number of issues in an appeal depends on the nature of the case and the particular decision that is appealed. An extremely complex antitrust case or a capital murder trial can raise a multitude of issues for appeal, while a basic appeal could conceivably raise only one issue. Similarly, an appeal from the denial of a preliminary injunction may raise fewer issues than an appeal from a judgment entered after a lengthy trial. So the nature of the appeal, to a significant extent, dictates how many issues should be addressed in your brief.

But this principle only takes you so far, for a limiting factor is at work. Judges expect you to raise only *substantial* issues on appeal, and they assume — rightly so in most cases — that only a few issues in any given appeal will truly be substantial. If the underlying case appears to be simple, a brief that raises numerous issues gives the appearance of the lawyer "throwing" everything possible at the court, hoping that one of those issues will "stick."

Judges decry this practice. In one study of Texas appellate judges, 43 percent of the judges said that appeals should raise two to four issues, while 52 percent set the range at three to five issues. No judge said it was wise to raise seven or more issues. JoAnn Storey & Kent Rutter, *Inside the Mind of an Appellate Judge: 25 Lessons from the Appellate Judicial Survey*, 73 TEX. B.J. 116 (2010).

Raising numerous issues is sometimes referred to as filing a "shotgun" brief, because the lawyer shoots a bunch of issues at the court and hopes for the best. Courts do not like this type of brief, for it makes more work for a court than the case really merits. Moreover, from the appellant's viewpoint, if there are one or two truly meritorious issues, they may get lost in the "forest" of multiple issues. A Delaware appellate judge referred to this kind of situation as the "clutter effect," because "[w]eaker issues tend to obscure the focus of the argument and diminish the entire presentation." Joseph A. Del Sole, *What Makes a Successful Appellate Advocate?*, 10 LAWYERS J. 5 (2008). In the worst scenario, the appellate judge may see the multitude of issues and then ignore some of them. *See* S. Jay Plager, J., *Remarks, Sixteenth Annual Judicial Conference of the United States Court of Appeals for the Federal Circuit*, 193 F.R.D. 263, 277 (1999) (Judge Plager's statement that "I can't remember ever sitting on a case that was decided by the ninth or tenth 'Question Presented,' and in part that may be because I can't ever remember having read that far into the 'Question Presented' . . ."); Hon. Joel F. Dubina, *How to Litigate Successfully in the United States Court of Appeals for the Eleventh Circuit*, 49 CUMB. L. REV. 297, 300 (2018-2019) ("More often than not, [lawyers] try to convey too much information and cover too many issues.").

Inevitably, choosing which issues to include is a question of finding an appropriate balance. "Part of the craft of counseling is the ability to balance the *possible* contribution of the issue . . . against the undiluted loss of impact and persuasion of a brief that wastes the court's time on side trails that lead nowhere." Albert Tate, Jr., *The Art of Brief Writing: What a Judge Wants to Read*, in APPELLATE PRACTICE MANUAL 197, 201 (Priscilla Anne Schwab ed., 1992).

Above all, keep in mind that a tighter brief with a limited number of issues is more likely to prevail. So as a very rough rule of thumb, the statement of issues should normally set forth *no more* than four issues. As the website of a Washington appellate court cautions, as the arguments raised exceed four, "with each succeeding argument, you have a higher psychological threshold to mount." Washington State Court of Appeals, Division I, *Brief Writing—Best Practices*, https://www.courts.wa.gov/ appellate_trial_courts/?fa=atc.display_divs&folderID=div1&fileID=briefWriting.

Of course, if the brief is written for a state supreme court where the court granted review on certain specific issues, you will be limited to those issues. Moreover, in criminal cases where a defendant has a constitutional right to an effective counsel, the lawyer can be ethically obligated to raise a much larger number of issues. As a general rule, however, four or fewer main issues will almost always suffice in the "typical" appeal. If you find yourself with more than four, think again. As one judge said, "The key to effective written advocacy . . . is selectivity, not fertility." Stephen J. Dwyer et al., *How to Write, Edit, and Review Persuasive Briefs: Seven Guidelines from One Judge and Two Lawyers*, 31 SEATTLE U. L. REV. 417, 422 (2008).

2. Formulating the Issue

The rules of the appeal court will likely dictate the form of the issue statement. In some jurisdictions, especially in the intermediate appellate courts, the parties are permitted to state the issues in the form of a declarative statement. Here is an example:

> Substantial evidence in the record supported the juvenile dependency court's order declaring the children dependents of where the parents exposed the children to domestic abuse in the home. *See* Cal. App. Rules of Ct. 8.204(a)(1)(B).

Alternatively, a common practice in the federal circuit courts and the state and federal supreme courts is to state the issue in the form of a question. Lawyers often begin the statement of issues with the phrase "Did the court." For example, an issue may be stated as:

> Did the trial court err in refusing to admit into evidence the second will signed by Respondent?

Another common practice is to begin the issue statement with the word "Whether":

> Whether the one year statute of limitations bars respondent's tort action where the injury occurred three years before the lawsuit was filed.

The rules of the jurisdiction often require that the issue statement be brief, thus assuming that the writer will state the issue in one sentence. Use of one sentence for an issue statement is by far the most common method. It has the advantage of quickly encapsulating the issue for the court.

However, some legal writing professionals have proposed that for complex issues, the court may need background information to understand the issue presented. In those cases, they recommend that the brief writer use one or two sentences to set up the statement of an issue, and then follow with the actual issue in the form of a question. Writing expert Bryan Garner has termed this type of framing as "deep issues." Bryan A. Garner, *The Deep Issue: A New Approach to Framing Legal Questions,* 5 SCRIBES J. LEGAL WRITING 1 (1994/1995).

For example, the preliminary sentences might tell the court about the content of a specific statute. Armed with that knowledge, the court can understand the issue then presented. Here are two examples:

1. Statute of Limitations Issue

An importer may file a protest with United States Customs and Border Protection challenging the imposition or collection of duties. The controlling statute, 19 U.S.C. §1515(a), provides that Customs "within two years from the date a protest was filed . . . , shall review the protest and shall allow or deny such protest in whole or in part" and specifically prohibits Customs from exceeding the statute's "two-year limitation."

The question presented is:

Whether Customs may withhold disposition of a protest indefinitely despite the plain mandate in 19 U.S.C. §1515(a) that Customs "shall review the protest and shall allow or deny such protest in whole or in part" within two years.

2. Constitutional Equal Protection Issue

Section 3 of the Defense of Marriage Act (DOMA) defines the term *marriage* for all purposes under federal law, including the provision of federal benefits, as "only a legal union between one man and one woman as husband and wife." 1 U.S.C. 7. It similarly defines the term *spouse* as "a person of the opposite sex who is a husband or a wife." *Ibid.* The question presented is:

Whether Section 3 of DOMA violates the Fifth Amendment's guarantee of equal protection of the laws as applied to persons of the same sex who are legally married under the laws of their State.

If the issue statement is a single sentence, it should not be overly long — otherwise, the court may be unable to understand it. So apply a 40-word limit for a sentence setting forth the statement. (Sentence length is discussed later in Chapter Ten.) In some cases, however, you may wish to extend the question's length so as to frame the issue more favorably for your client. You can do so and exceed 40 words by using a numbering system to break the question down to ensure that it is readable:

> Did the district court correctly dismiss Tessler's constitutional claims where he (1) spoke as an employee, and not as a citizen addressing matters of public concern; (2) has no fundamental constitutional right to government employment; and (3) has an adequate post-deprivation remedy in a state court article 78 proceeding to challenge his termination?

3. Questions, Law, and Facts

As an advocate, you seek to present the court with the *precise* issues that it must decide. Usually, you will use both law and facts to achieve this goal. The reason is that the court is not deciding a legal issue in the abstract. Rather, it is deciding the issue within the factual context in which the issue has arisen — that is, within the facts of the present case.

Another reason for using facts in the issues presented is that you want to state the issues as narrowly as possible. Courts seek to decide only the specific issue before them; they do not promulgate broad "declaratory rulings" on a statute's meaning when the case before them presents only one particular set of facts. A technique for narrowing the issue to its leanest form is to frame it in terms of the specific facts before the court.

To summarize, the best statements of issues use both facts and law. They incorporate key facts of the present case. The lawyer will not state the issue as:

Did the statute of limitations bar Mr. Smith's malpractice action?

Instead, the statement will incorporate facts:

Did the two-year statute of limitations bar Mr. Smith's malpractice action where his operation occurred more than three years before the filing of the suit, but he felt no ill effects until more than two years after the operation?

The second statement obviously gives the court more information. Crucially, however, it also allows the advocate to employ facts favorable to the client's side and to frame the issue in a way that begins to generate some sympathy for the client's position. How can it be fair to bar Mr. Smith in a situation where the statute of limitations had run out before he even knew that he was injured?

Remember the admonition, set forth above, to keep issue statements at a maximum of 40 words. Does the statement of the issue in Mr. Smith's appeal above comply? Yes — barely. This situation is typical. You will often find that the word length of your issue statements starts to creep up when you insert facts. You must, however, fight the tendency to state the issue in an overly lengthy manner. It is always of central importance that the court understands what you are writing, for without that understanding, you have conveyed nothing to the court. If the sentence is too long, it will lose the reader.

So you use key facts without making the sentence overly lengthy. It's a tough job. You should expect to revise issue statements several times in the writing process, keeping in mind that they create the first and often lasting impression on the reader.

4. Choosing What to Emphasize

In deciding what to include in a statement of issues, you must carefully evaluate the persuasiveness of the options available to you. If the wording of a statute seems particularly favorable, then your statement should emphasize that wording. If, in contrast, some factual development casts your position in a good light, you may want to put those facts in the statement.

Consider the following two opposing statements of the question presented filed in a case before the U.S. Supreme Court:

Does the National Labor Relations Board have authority to decide cases with only two sitting members, where 29 U.S.C. §153(b) provides that "three members of the Board shall, at all times, constitute a quorum of the Board"?

Whether Section 3(b) of the National Labor Relations Act, 29 U.S.C. 153(b), authorizes the National Labor Relations Board to act when only two of its five positions are filled, if the Board has previously delegated its full powers to a three-member group of the Board that includes the two current members.

Notice the difference in approach. The first statement emphasizes the law by quoting the statutory provision stating that three members of the Board constitute a quorum. The second statement, by contrast, emphasizes that the Board had previously delegated its powers to a three-member group.

Here are two more contrasting examples:

Whether the Fourth Amendment prohibits public school officials from conducting a search of a student suspected of possessing and distributing a prescription drug on campus in violation of school policy.

Whether it is reasonable to subject a thirteen-year-old girl to the indignity of a strip search based on an unreliable accusation that she previously possessed ibuprofen and no information that she possessed ibuprofen in her undergarments at the time of the search.

The first issue statement emphasizes the basis for the search (suspicion of possessing a drug) and the fact that such possession violated school policy. The respondent's issue statement, by contrast, centers on the personal violation of the student's body and attacks the information on which the suspicion was founded. It also names the drug, ibuprofen, presumably because the court will be familiar with it and may see it as less dangerous.

Here is one final set of statements:

Whether petitioner "use[d] [a] communication facility in causing or facilitating a felony" drug distribution, in violation of 21 U.S.C. 843(b), by using his cell phone to arrange with a drug dealer several purchases of cocaine for his own personal consumption.

Whether the use of a telephone to buy drugs for personal use "facilitates" the commission of a drug "felony," in violation of 21 U.S.C. §843(b), on the theory that the crime facilitated by the buyer (1) is not his purchase of drugs for personal use (a misdemeanor), but (2) is the seller's distribution of the drugs to him (a felony).

Can you see the difference in emphasis? The first one emphasizes use of a cell phone, tying it to the language "use[d] a communication facility." The latter is not concerned with the cell phone; rather, it points out that, while the defendant was buying drugs for personal use, the government is charging him with facilitating the *seller's* crime. In each case the lawyer focused on incorporating the law or facts most helpful to the client.

5. Ordering the Issues

Next, the brief writer must decide the order in which to present the issues. Of course, your statement of issues will present them in the same order that you argue them in the brief's argument section, which comes after the statement of issues. But what *is* that order?

The perspective principle can answer this question. If you were a judge, your attention would be at its peak when you first start reading — that is, at the beginning of the brief. Even the best written brief can become a bit tedious on the forty-second page. So use this insight to your advantage: As a general rule, always put your strongest argument or arguments first.

There is, however, an exception to this rule. In certain appeals, logic dictates that some issues precede others. For example, one of the issues before the appellate court may be whether a trial court had jurisdiction to hear the case at the trial level. Jurisdiction is an issue that logically comes first in a brief, for if the trial court lacked jurisdiction, the issues raised on the merits of the appeal become irrelevant. Alternatively, consider a case involving a state tort claims act that requires a plaintiff to file a claim with a public agency before bringing suit against that agency. In writing the appellate brief for this case, it may make sense to discuss the issue of whether the claim was properly filed before other issues of substantive tort law.

To summarize: Start with the idea that you want to put your strongest issues first. Then ask yourself whether this arrangement of the order of the issues would be logical. Your good judgment will allow you to answer this question and properly order your statement of issues.

Finally, we have been discussing the appellant's brief. Must the appellee accept the order of issues presented by the appellant? The answer is no, but in this situation applying the perspective principle counsels some caution. If you were an appellate judge reading an appellant's brief, it would be much easier for you if the appellee's brief responded to the issues in the same order as the appellant presented them. If it did, you could more easily "match" the arguments in the two briefs when considering those issues. Furthermore, from the appellee's perspective, addressing the issues in the same order as the appellant gives an appearance of strength. You are confronting the issues directly, not obfuscating them.

Still, there is always a concern about the overall persuasiveness of the appellee's brief. Perhaps the appellant has underplayed a significant jurisdictional issue, "burying" it in the body of its brief. Because this issue could determine the outcome of the appeal, the appellee could highlight that issue by placing it before the court at a much earlier part of its brief.

However, think hard about whether to depart from the order in the appellant's brief. If you change the order, explain to the court why you have done so.

6. Referring to Parties

Assume that you represent the appellant John Jones and are beginning to write the statement of issues. How should you refer to him? Should you just call him "Appellant," "Jones," or "Mr. Jones"?

By now, you know what this next sentence will say: Put yourself in the shoes of the judge. Ask yourself which of these choices will make it easier for the judge — who has no knowledge of the parties before picking up the brief — to keep track of that party as she reads the brief. A little thought will provide the answer: Personalizing the case works best. A reader will more easily remember a specific name or specific description than a generic designation like "appellant." Thus, using the party's name usually works better, and adding a title (Mr. or Ms.) lends the party dignity.

The Federal Rules of Appellate Procedure mandate this practice. Rule 28(d) states:

> (d) References to Parties. In briefs and at oral argument, counsel should minimize use of the terms "appellant" and "appellee." To make briefs clear, counsel should use the parties' actual names or the designations used in the lower court or agency proceeding, or such descriptive terms as "the employee," "the injured person," "the taxpayer," "the ship," "the stevedore."

C. RECOGNIZING A GOOD STATEMENT OF AN ISSUE

How do you know when you have written a good statement of an issue? Once again, ask yourself why the statement of an issue is important to the court. The answer: because the court must *decide* that issue. As an appellate advocate, your goal is to make it as easy as possible for the court to carry out that task.

You will succeed in achieving this goal if the court can easily turn your statement of an issue into its holding on that issue. In other words, if you have stated the issue properly in terms of both fact and law, the court can quickly turn that question into an answer. Consider again this statement of the issue:

> Did the three-year statute of limitations bar Mr. Smith's malpractice action where the operation occurred more than three years before the filing of the suit, but he felt no ill effects until more than two years after the operation?

A court could easily and efficiently answer that question in an opinion:

> We hold that where the nature of the operation hid its adverse effects from the plaintiff for more than two years, the three-year statute of limitations did not bar the plaintiff's malpractice action.

If you can easily turn your statement of the issue into a holding on that issue, you have written a good statement.

Summary

- While quite short, the statement of issues both clarifies for the court the legal questions at issue on the appeal and affords an opportunity to frame those issues favorably to your client.

- The number of issues that you raise depends upon the complexity of the appeal. Courts dislike briefs that raise too many issues, so you must carefully consider which issues are most likely to result in a favorable outcome for your client.

- The issue is often framed in terms of a declaratory sentence, but it can also be a question or a statement beginning with the word "whether." The issue incorporates both facts and law. The issue should not be overly long; a 40-word limit is prudent.

- You may choose to emphasize facts or law in your issue statement, depending on which makes your case more persuasive.

- In ordering your issues, use your strongest issue first unless there is some logical reason why another — perhaps weaker — issue should come first. Appellees do not have to accept the order of issues presented by the appellant. However, they may wish to do so for the convenience of the court.

- Use proper names or designations (for example, "landlord") in your statement of issues, not "appellant" or "respondent."

- A good statement of issues allows the court to easily turn the statement into a holding on that issue.

Appendix B contains exercises that ask you to evaluate statements of issues in light of the principles discussed in this chapter.

CHAPTER 6

The Prelude: The Statement of Facts and the Procedural History

A. THE STATEMENT OF FACTS

1. Supplying Dispositive Facts

Assume that a case is on appeal after a lengthy trial. Unquestionably, the appellate court needs to learn about the facts of the case. But which facts does the court need to hear about? Certainly it does not need to learn all of them; the statement of facts in an appellate brief is *not* a summary of all the evidence presented in the court below. Rather, facts culled from the trial court record are included in this statement to serve two purposes, one functional and one persuasive.

To recognize the first purpose, think back to the structural principle presented in Chapter Two. Because appellate courts decide specific legal issues made up of both facts and law, you must organize the brief around the issues. The function of the statement of facts is to give the court all the facts it needs to decide the issues raised. In deciding them, courts use precedent decisions in situations where the facts of the precedent and the facts of the present case are analogous. The facts can also form the basis of a policy argument.

Accordingly, the court must know certain facts about the present case so it can compare them to the facts in a precedent. Such facts are known as "dispositive" facts because they directly affect the outcome on appeal. Your first task in preparing the statement of facts is to identify those dispositive facts that you will use.

2. Context Facts: Telling a Story

The dispositive facts do not arise in a vacuum. They exist in a broader context of time, place, people, and events that you supply to orient the reader. Conveying these context facts allows the statement of facts to serve a second purpose: to begin the persuasive process. Consider the following statement by the former chief judge of the Second Circuit Court of Appeals:

> Let the narrative of facts tell a compelling story. The facts are, almost without exception, the heart of the case on appeal. . . . The facts generate the force that impels the judge's will in your direction.

Irving R. Kaufman, *Appellate Advocacy in the Federal Courts, Address Before Association of the Bar of the City of New York* (April 21, 1977). Chief Justice John Roberts is even more emphatic on this point:

> It's got to be a good story. Every lawsuit is a story . . . . I don't care if it's about a dry contract interpretation; you've got two people who want to accomplish some-thing, and they're coming together—that's a story. And you've got to tell a good story . . . you want it to be a little bit of a page-turner, to have some sense of drama, some building up to the legal argument.

Bryan A. Garner, *Interview with Supreme Court Justice John Roberts,* 13 SCRIBES 5, 16 (2010). That story is told in the statement of facts.

Judges are also concerned about the justice of the situation presented by the appeal. Like other human beings, judges react when presented with good behavior or bad behavior. "An appellate writer will ask what 'bottom line' point she is trying to prove? Why is her client's cause *just*, or why is the other side's cause *unjust*?" Kenneth D. Chestek, *The Plot Thickens: The Appellate Brief as Story,* 14 J. LEGAL WRITING INST.

127, 146 (2008). The statement of facts allows the advocate to portray his client's behavior in a positive light, an important initial step in the persuasive process.

So you need to tell a story, and like all stories, you need a plot. You set forth the plot in the statement of facts. And remember that the statement of facts is not an argument; instead, it is a story about what happened. Save the argument for its proper place in the brief. You do not want to make legal arguments in your statement of facts.

Finally, do not get "carried away" with your story. You still bear an ethical obligation of informing the court fairly of the facts.

3. Identifying the Relevant and Dispositive Facts from the Record

The dispositive facts used in the argument section of a brief should appear in the statement of facts. In writing the statement of facts, the appellate lawyer's goal is to give the court the basic facts that it must know to decide the case. Hopefully, if you carry out that task correctly, the judges will retain those basic facts as they begin reading your argument. You can elaborate on facts in the argument, but you should not present important new ones there.

If the brief is to set forth the relevant and dispositive facts, then you must know what those facts are *before* you write the statement of facts. To begin this process, you must read the full record on appeal and familiarize yourself with the factual universe available to you. However, to know which facts are relevant, you must first analyze the legal issues on appeal and decide which ones you will raise in the brief. You must also know what story or theme underlies your appeal.

In other words, writing the statement of facts is an iterative process. You will go back and forth between doing research and consulting the record. You need an initial familiarity with the facts to do the research, but as you do the research, you may spot a new issue. If you do, facts that seemed irrelevant to you before now become important, so you return to the record to check them.

4. Lining Up the Facts in Order

Theoretically, you can present the facts in several ways. You could start with the dispositive facts, the ones at the heart of the case, and after presenting them fill in with other, less significant facts. Alternatively, you could organize your statement of facts around specific individuals or entities, and the roles that they played leading up to the lawsuit. Or you could start with the damages first and then fill in the events leading to those damages.

Although each of these approaches is plausible, in most cases you will not use them. Remember that the appellate court has *no* previous knowledge of the facts of your appeal; you are writing, so to speak, on a "clean slate." Your goal is to make it as easy as possible for the appellate judges to learn the facts of the case and to retain them for their use when reading the argument section of the brief.

The easiest way to help someone retain new facts is to present them in *chronological order*. Fortunately, this method is also the easiest way to tell a story.

Do not, however, jump right into chronology. Instead, begin the story by introducing your client to the reader. Provide some brief information—a couple of sentences to a short paragraph—about your client's background and history to humanize and personalize them. Giving the reader some backstory on your client will provide helpful context for your client's actions at issue in the appeal and may also generate empathy for the client's position.

After you have introduced your client, you should work your way chronologically through the various relevant and dispositive facts. Do not get ahead of yourself and then backtrack. Instead, seamlessly lead the reader through the passage of time, setting forth how the tale progressed. End at the point before the case is filed; events occurring later belong in the procedural history of the case.

Consider the following short statement of facts in a retaliatory firing case. Notice how the statement of facts begins with humanizing background information followed by use of chronological order to tell the story of the case:

> Alvin Adams and Betty Bickel, life-long residents of Williamstown, were both 25 years-old, and engaged to be married. They were also both employees of Parks Corporation, and their relationship "was common knowledge at Parks Corporation. . . ." App. 55.
>
> In September 2006, Bickel filed a charge with the Equal Employment Opportunity Commission, asserting that her supervisors had discriminated against her based on her gender. Bickel alleged that the company had demoted her twice because of her gender and that, for the same reason, she was paid less than a male employee.
>
> On February 15, 2007, the Commission notified Parks Corporation of Bickel's charge. Soon thereafter, an executive of Parks Corporation directed Bickel's supervisor, Charlie Cook, to prepare a memorandum indicating that Adams would be dismissed. On March 7, 2007, barely three weeks after receiving notice of Bickel's charge, Parks Corporation dismissed Adams.

Chronological order is an important and sometimes unappreciated tool. If a reader (here, a judge) is not familiar with a story, the judge will have a hard time mentally moving back and forth in time if the story is told out of chronological order. In all likelihood, that reader will not be able easily to follow the thread of events.

The principle is not absolute. As a matter of strategy, consider that in some cases there are two competing and opposite versions of the underlying events—one from your client's perspective and another from the opposing party. In that instance, tell your client's version first to get the reader to see the facts from your client's viewpoint before they read the other side's version.

There may also be some instances in which telling the entire story chronologically is not the best way to present the facts. For example, perhaps the appeal concerns two parallel sets of events. You may want to relate one set of events first and then move to the other, even though this method requires you to backtrack. In that instance it may be easier to keep track of the facts by presenting them separately.

But depart from chronological order *only* after giving it serious thought and concluding that the benefits of departing from that order outweigh the loss in the reader's ability to follow your factual presentation.

One final point: Setting forth facts chronologically does not mean inundating the reader with dates. A series of sentences beginning "On ___, 2020," stultifies your story. By including unnecessary dates, "you create the false impression that the case includes a time-sensitive issue, which the reader will then search for in vain." Brian L. Porto, *Improving Your Appellate Briefs: The Best Advice from Bench, Bar, and Academy*, 37 Vt. B.J. 1, 63 (2011). Of course, dates *are* critical in certain appeals such as, for example, those involving statutes of limitation, notice, or deadlines. But most appeals are not date sensitive, and there is no need to over-particularize with details that are not relevant to the outcome.

You can convey chronology through words. Many are available: then, later, after, subsequently, etc. Use them and keep the actual dates to a minimum.

5. Accuracy and the "Favorable Light"

You have an ethical obligation to be scrupulously accurate in presenting the facts. The obligation for accuracy takes two forms. First, all the facts in your statement of facts must be sourced in the record on appeal. You cannot use facts outside of the record.

Equally important, you cannot overstate facts in a way that the record does not support. If you exaggerate, not only do you risk the court's imposition of sanctions against you, you will lose your credibility with the court. The *rest* of your brief, including your legal argument, will immediately become suspect to the court. After all, if the lawyer misrepresented the facts in the statement of facts, won't the writer misrepresent facts from a precedent as well? As a former judge on the Ninth Circuit warned: "A brief writer should summarize facts with scrupulous accuracy. Misstating the record can irretrievably damage your credibility with the court. You don't want to waste precious time at oral argument trying to rehabilitate yourself." Arthur L. Alarcon, *Points on Appeal*, in Appellate Practice Manual 95, 97 (Priscilla Anne Schwab ed., 1992).

Your statement of facts impliedly represents to the court that it is accurate; it stands as an invitation to the judges to test and verify your assertions of fact if they wish. Thus, citations to the record on appeal must accompany the facts that you set forth in your statement of facts. Many lawyers use short forms "App." (for Record on Appeal) or "CT" (Clerk's Transcript) for those citations to the record. Rules of court also can instruct you about the form of the citation. Here is an example:

> Mr. Smith's operation was scheduled for April 23, 2004, and went smoothly. App. 342. Two years later, however, he began suffering from horrible stomach pains that did not go away. App. 456. After numerous visits from Mr. Smith, Dr. Hawthorne recommended exploratory surgery. App. 523. Dr. Hawthorn undertook that surgery on February 8, 2006. App. 620.

When in doubt about whether a citation to the record is necessary, include it. You want to *invite* the court to check your representation of the facts and to make it easy for the court to do so.

At the same time, however, you are an advocate telling a story, and you want to tell that story favorably for your client. You want to persuade the court of your client's cause. How does an advocate persuade in a statement of facts?

The appellate advocate does so through careful choice of words. The appellate lawyer gets to choose the words that describe the facts, and that word choice can make a huge difference. Consider the following two statements of the same underlying facts:

> Herbert shoved Walker backward into a steel beam, splitting Walker's head open. A stream of blood gushed, falling into Walker's eyes and mouth.

> Walker was pushed and fell back into a beam, cutting his head.

Both versions of these facts discuss the same incident. But the first two sentences slant much more favorably toward Walker (the plaintiff). The second version softens the impact by using the passive voice ("was pushed"), so that Herbert's actions are not highlighted. It also minimizes the blood from the injury by using a weaker verb ("cut" rather than "gushed").

Again, though, remember that in choosing words you must be accurate at all times. You are walking a verbal tightrope between colorful, accurate advocacy and unsupportable exaggeration. If you use words that do not accurately describe the facts or that exaggerate them, you will suffer in the long run. But within the range of factual accuracy, you can advocate. As an Illinois appellate justice described the task, "You can tell your side of the case and still state the facts 'accurately and fairly without argument or comment.'" Robert W. Cook, *An Appellate Justice's Quick Guide to Appeals*, 97 ILL. B.J. 132, 136 (2009) (citing Ill. S. Ct. Rule 341(h)(6)).

In particular, choose your verbs carefully and make careful and limited use of descriptive adjectives and adverbs to add effect. Err on the side of subtlety and avoid being bombastic. Consider the following two examples:

> Lying through her teeth, the witness invented a story about her whereabouts on the night of the crime.

> Contradicting the testimony of the previous four witnesses, the witness told the jury that she was not present at the crime scene.

The first sentence is an "over the top" accusation. The second is more professional and more convincing.

You do not, however, need to eliminate all emotion from your fact statements. Although persuasion is effectively achieved by focusing on the facts in the record that support the logical and rational result, do not forget that appellate judges are also human beings who may have emotional reactions to the cases before them. Therefore, when appropriate, do not neglect to emphasize those facts that, although perhaps not dispositive to the outcome, appeal to the judge's humanity.

Consider, for example, *Adoptive Couple v. Baby Girl,* 570 U.S. 637 (2013), a case addressing the congressional intent of the Indian Child Welfare Act, 25 U.S.C. §1912 and §1915(a), relating to the placement and adoption of Native American Indian children with non-Indian parents. The case concerned whether the provision that bars involuntary termination of an Indian parent's rights applied when the Indian parent never had custody of the child. Although neither dispositive nor directly relevant to the issues on appeal, the Petitioners, the adoptive parents, included the following facts in their opening brief:

> Adoptive Parents supported Mother financially and emotionally during her pregnancy and shortly after Baby Girl's birth. They spoke to Mother weekly, and Adoptive Mother traveled to visit her in Oklahoma in August 2009. They paid for medical expenses associated with the pregnancy. Pet. App. 5a.

> . . . Adoptive Parents were in the delivery room during the delivery, and Adoptive Father cut the umbilical cord. [Biological] Father sought no contact with Baby Girl in the months after her birth, despite knowing her due date. Pet. App. 8a; Trial Tr. 489-90.

> When Baby Girl was placed with Adoptive Parents . . . [Biological] Mother and Father had never lived together, and Father had neither supported Mother with pregnancy-related expenses nor provided support for the child. Pet. App. 4a. . . . Father "took no pro-active steps to protect his parental rights to the child" in the eight months after he became aware of Baby Girl's pending birth. . . .

Petitioners Brief, pp. 9-10.

And those emotional facts resonated with the majority of the Court because they appeared in the opinion:

> Adoptive Couple supported Birth Mother both emotionally and financially throughout her pregnancy. Adoptive Couple was present at Baby Girl's birth in Oklahoma . . . and Adoptive Father even cut the umbilical cord. . . .

> It is undisputed that, for the duration of the pregnancy and the first four months after Baby Girl's birth, Biological Father provided no financial assistance to Birth Mother or Baby Girl, even though he had the ability to do so. Indeed, Biological Father "made no meaningful attempts to assume his responsibility of parenthood" during this period.

Adoptive Couple v. Baby Girl, 570 U.S. at 644.

Other points to consider in highlighting facts favorable for your client: If the record contains a quotation—such as trial testimony—that is particularly good for your client, include it in the fact statement. In addition, when describing favorable facts, use more sentences to describe those circumstances. Doing so forces the reader to spend more time reading and thinking about those facts.

Finally, how do you deal with unfavorable facts? You cannot simply ignore them. Leaving out relevant facts can rise to a level that violates your ethical duties to fairly state the case to the court. Furthermore, as a practical matter, if you do not mention them, your opponent certainly will—and will also point out your failure to include them.

Consider the example of an Illinois child custody case in which the appellant was the child's biological father. He was appealing an order terminating his parental rights. His brief stated that he was in the county jail and that the child's mother had passed away. It failed to point out that the father had been imprisoned for murdering the mother. Needless to say, the opposition jumped in to trumpet the fact. Maria Pellegrino, *Brief-Writing Tips for the Illinois Appellate Court*, 96 ILL. B.J. 412, 415 (2008). As one of the authors of a classic treatise on appellate advocacy put it, it is much better to "[d]raw the sting of the unpleasant facts by presenting them yourself." Frederick Bernays Wiener, EFFECTIVE APPELLATE ADVOCACY 39 (rev. ed. 2004).

You have tactics to consider. One tactic is to mention them in generic language. Paraphrase the record, using words that will blunt the negative impact to describe bad facts, and do not quote from the record when describing them. Also, tuck them within other facts that do not harm your client and use fewer sentences to describe them, hoping that they will not impact the reader as fully. Alternatively, you can take a frank approach in mentioning the facts, to show the court that these facts are not determinative.

6. Setting Up the Subheadings as Guideposts

Depending on the case, the statement of facts can become somewhat lengthy. As it grows longer, the reader encounters more difficulty "keeping up" with the flow. After working through several pages of facts, a judge seeing yet another full page of facts can become discouraged.

An important method for helping the reader through the facts is to break up the statement of facts with subheadings. In a few words the subheading should tell the reader what material will follow immediately in the part of the statement of facts below that subheading. The subheadings should be short, informative, and accurate. They also signal the readers about when they can mentally "take a break" in their reading. All readers need those breaks.

Consider, for example, the following sequential subheadings in a malpractice case:

    A. The Initial Diagnosis of a Tumor by Defendant Dr. Wiese
    B. The Operation by Dr. Wiese and his Failure to Remove the Scalpel
    C. The Second Operation and the Discovery of Dr. Wiese's Scalpel
    D. The Lengthy Recovery by Mr. Jones and his Painful, Permanent Disability

Notice how each of these subheadings allows the reader to anticipate the facts that will be coming up in that subsection. The subheadings cause the reader to break up the story mentally, making it easier to retain the facts. They also convey the information chronologically ("initial diagnosis," "operation," "second operation," "lengthy recovery"). Finally, the language in each subheading enhances the plaintiff's

(Mr. Jones's) case through the choice of language: "failure to remove," "lengthy recovery," and "painful, permanent disability."

7. Applying the Principles

As you can see from reading this chapter, writing a good statement of facts is not a simple process. Here is an example of a statement of facts that incorporates the principles discussed above:

A. The Police Investigation of Appellant Marco Gunther

For the five years prior to his arrest, Maple City Police Department drug enforcement officers had been investigating appellant Marco Gunther. Investigators suspected that appellant, who had no discernable occupation or legal and regular employment, made a living selling drugs throughout the county.

B. The Informant and the Plan About a Drug Transaction

In early September 2020, Maple City police officers interrogated a confidential informant, who informed them of a potential sale of illegal drugs. App. 12. The informant said that he would be buying one kilogram of cocaine from appellant. App. 13. The sale would occur on September 15, 2020, at the Krazy Kup restaurant in Maple City. Id.

The police and the informant then agreed upon a plan in which the police would arrest the seller during the transaction. App. 27. The informant would first go to the restaurant and meet with appellant. App. 28. Once the informant actually saw the kilogram of cocaine on the premises, he would tell the appellant that he was going outside to get the money for the purchase. The informant would then signal the police, who would move in and arrest appellant. Id.

C. The Police Raid and the Detention of Appellant

On September 15, the police concealed themselves outside the restaurant, and the informant went inside. App. 128. The police next saw appellant enter the restaurant. Police testified that appellant was "hunched over" as he walked and, in the view of the police, appeared as if he was trying to conceal something. Id. According to the police, appellant's clothing had a large "bulge" in it. App. 129.

Two minutes after appellant entered the restaurant, the informant exited the building and gave the prearranged signal to the police. App. 226. At about 6 p.m., police officers moved into the restaurant and secured it. App. 247. The police initially found three individuals inside: a waitress, a customer, and Mario Vega, who was the owner of the restaurant and later a codefendant. Id.

The police then saw the head of a fourth individual, appellant, appear out of a small office. App. 255. The police secured appellant, handcuffed him, but did not enter the office. Looking inside the office, they could see that it was very small and that no one else was in it. Id. One police officer, Officer Spain, testified that he saw a small package on a desk in the office. App. 260.

D. The Search Warrant, the Search of the Restaurant Office, and the Subsequent Interviews

Rather than conduct an immediate search, Officer Spain left the restaurant to obtain a warrant permitting the police to search the office for drugs. App. 301. The warrant issued at 7:10 p.m. App. 308. Thereafter, the police served the warrant on Mr. Vega and searched the small office in the restaurant. App. 311. A police dog trained to recognize drugs sniffed at the package on the desk, which was wrapped in duct tape. The police opened the package and found that it contained a large quantity of cocaine. Id.

After the search, the police interviewed Mr. Vega and read appellant his "Miranda" rights. App. 402. Appellant admitted that he had obtained the drugs from a supplier and gone to the restaurant with the drugs "stuffed into his waist line." App. 404. Once inside the restaurant, he went into the small office and was still there when the police entered the building. App. 405.

First, notice how the statement begins with relevant background and then proceeds in chronological order. The reader can readily picture how the sequence of events progressed. The subheadings help by previewing for the reader what is to come. For example, subheading B—"The Police Raid and the Detention of Appellant"—accurately summarizes the three next paragraphs. A citation to the record accompanies each fact.

You probably could tell that the statement was written from the standpoint of the prosecution. The wording was chosen accordingly; it is a conservative presentation suited to the seriousness of a prosecution. It emphasized that the events unfolded just as the informant had said they would. Thus, it then seems unsurprising that the drugs were found on the desk.

B. THE PROCEDURAL HISTORY

1. The Function of the Procedural History

The procedural history starts where the narrative in the statement of facts leaves off. It tells the court how the case arrived at the point where an appeal was taken. The procedural history section of the brief is sometimes called the *statement of the case*, but in some jurisdictions that term also can include the statement of facts. Whatever the specific terminology, however, the brief must include the procedural background of the case.

The procedural history serves the basic function of allowing the appellate court to confirm that it has jurisdiction over the appeal. You will tell the court why it has jurisdiction at the end of this part of the brief (or perhaps, in a separate section of the brief, if the court rules so require). You will do so by citing the statute that gives the court jurisdiction to hear the appeal.

Finally, the trial court entered a judgment or made certain rulings from which you are appealing, and the court of appeals needs to know about them. Now is the time to present that information.

2. Only Essential History Wanted

Unlike the statement of facts, the procedural history is a bit of an interlude. You are transitioning from the statement of facts, which usually comes before the procedural history, to the all-important argument, which comes next. Accordingly, you want to get the procedural history across quickly, especially if your client lost below, so you include only the most essential information.

Although you should not clutter your brief with a lengthy recitation of the procedural history, there may be some aspect of the lower court's decision that is significant, helpful, and perhaps dispositive to your appeal. If so, you should refer to it in your description of the procedural facts. For example, in this excerpt from petitioner's brief, notice how the brief writer describes the procedural history the case:

> Respondent filed suit in the Middle District of Pennsylvania. He claimed his employer, Petitioner St. Michael's, violated Title I of the Americans with Disabilities Act ("ADA"), 42 U.S.C. §12101 et seq (1990) when it fired him from his job as an athletic trainer at the private catholic school after he became disabled. St. Michael's asserted that both the First Amendment's ministerial exception and Respondent's status as an independent contractor barred his ADA claim.
>
> After a bench trial, district court entered judgment for St. Michael's, finding Respondent "failed to meet his burden of proof against" St. Michael's. The district court found that Respondent supplied his own equipment, tracked his hours worked, and hired his own assistants—all of which demonstrated that Respondent worked as an independent contractor. Further, the court found the balance of the relevant legal factors also weighed in favor of St. Michael's characterization of Respondent as a "minister," including that Respondent led prayers before games, and supervised one of the religious clubs on campus. Accordingly, the district court rejected Respondent's ADA claim because both the common law agency test and the First Amendment defenses prohibited it.
>
> Respondent appealed to Third Circuit Court of Appeals, which reversed. Without citing any authority, the Third Circuit applied an "independent" assessment of the mixed question of fact and law, finding St. Michael's hired Respondent as an employee, and not an independent contractor. Circuit Judge Jorden dissented, observing that "applying a de novo standard splits from the majority of the circuit courts." He further elaborated that deciding "whether a person is an employee or an independent contractor is a fact intensive analysis that should be reviewed [for] clear error." The dissent concluded that had the court applied the appropriate standard of review, it would have most certainly affirmed. The Third Circuit also reversed the district court's finding of the ministerial exception, focusing solely on the fact that the Respondent's job related to student physical fitness rather than spirituality. The court of appeals, noting the particular friction created between the two defenses, "refuse[d] to engage in the analysis" that allowed the district court to find St. Michael's burden had been met on its defenses.

Here the petitioner uses the description of the district court's findings in the bench trial to focus the reader's attention on the factual aspects that the petitioner maintains are the most critical to the outcome. Thereafter, the petitioner discloses the procedural history at the circuit court to describe the lower court's ruling and undermine it by pointing out that the court of appeals failed to cite to authority for some points and did not engage in analysis of others. Moreover, by highlighting the dissent, the writer previews the arguments it will assert later in the brief.

Remember, however, that only procedural history is included in this section. As with the statement of facts, this is not the place in the brief to argue the issues.

3. Applying the Principles

Here is an example of a procedural history:

> Longtin filed suit against Tutter under the Columbia Fair Employment Act. App. 213. Tutter filed a motion for summary judgment arguing, among other defenses, that Longtin was not incapacitated because she continued to perform a similar job at Kaiser Drugs. App. 346. Longtin opposed the motion, supported by Dr. Adolf's declaration and her own declaration. App. 399.
>
> After a hearing, the trial court granted Tutter's motion, finding that Longtin was not incapacitated under the Fair Employment Act because she still performed similar duties at Kaiser. App. 615. The trial court entered judgment for Tutter, and Longtin appealed. App. 705. In a two-to-one decision, the District Court of Appeals affirmed the grant of summary judgment. Slip Op. 6.

The example is short and to the point, as a procedural history should be. It quickly summarizes the nature of the suit and proceeds to the trial court's grant of summary judgment. The history contains no extraneous facts or legal argument. It then quickly details who appealed and the outcome of that appeal. From this procedural history, the higher court now considering the case can quickly determine whether it will have jurisdiction.

Summary

- The statement of facts identifies the key facts needed for use in making the legal argument. It also, however, allows the appellate lawyer to tell a story about the client's case.

- The statement of facts should include all important facts used in the argument section of the brief. Accordingly, deciding which facts are relevant depends in large part on the issues that you decide to raise after completing your legal research.

- In most cases the best way to present the facts is in chronological order.

- Your statement of facts must be scrupulously accurate and supported by the record. Leaving out unfavorable facts might violate your ethical obligations to the court. Moreover, in many cases it is better to present an unfavorable fact yourself in the best light possible, rather than leave it to your opponent. Additionally, you can include facts that appeal to the judges' humanity.

- You must support your statement of a fact with a citation to where it can be found in the record of trial court proceedings.

- Subheadings can be very useful in guiding the reader through the statement of facts.

- The procedural history tells the court how the case proceeded through the lower court or courts so that the appellate court can assure itself that it has jurisdiction over the appeal.

- Include the most essential history of the litigation in the procedural history and be strategic in the way in which you describe it.

Appendix B contains exercises that ask you to evaluate statements of facts in light of the principles discussed in this chapter.

CHAPTER 7

The Road Map: Point Headings

A. CREATING A "ROAD MAP" BEFORE WRITING THE ARGUMENT

1. Extending Your Analytical Thinking

We now turn to the heart of the brief: the argument. Let's start by setting the scene. As the lawyer for the appellant, you have become familiar with the record compiled in the trial court. You have completed your legal research and have written solid first drafts of your statement of the issues and statement of facts. Are you ready to begin writing the argument?

Not quite. Remember the organizational principle set forth in Chapter Two of this book: You need to separate your thinking from your writing as much as you can. When you begin to focus on the argument, you want to think about it as much as possible *before* you actually start writing. Creating the argument is analytically difficult, and at this point in the appellate lawyering process, you may be tempted to just start writing and see "how it goes." However, the farther you can carry out your analytical thinking before writing, the better off you will be. The goal is to have a relatively complete framework for the argument before you actually begin writing it.

There is a second point to consider. Remind yourself of the structural principle from Chapter Two: Appellate courts decide issues. You have already completed a great deal of analysis about the issues and have made "semifinal" decisions about those that you intend to raise. Now, you must begin to think about how you will argue the issues that you have chosen. You must identify "sub-issues" that will arise under the broader main issues. And you must bring organization to these thoughts, which is a key ingredient of a good brief according to an experienced federal court of appeals judge: "Good organization will be like a road map to the judges, enabling them to follow from the beginning to the end without getting lost." Joel F. Dubina, *How to Litigate Successful in the United States Court of Appeals for the Eleventh Circuit*, 49 Cumb. L. Rev. 297, 301 (2018-2019).

To carry out these tasks, you will begin by once again undertaking a familiar exercise.

2. A Look at the Table of Contents

Apply the perspective principle and put yourself, yet again, in the shoes of an appellate judge. You have been assigned as the judge who will "work up" the case and send a draft opinion or detailed bench memorandum to your fellow judges. You are sitting in chambers with the briefs in front of you. You know nothing about the appeal, but you want to get an idea about the issues. So you pick up the appellant's brief and — do what?

You could start on page one and read the entire brief. But you are very busy, and there are faster ways to obtain the "snapshot" of issues that you desire. Here is how a famous judge on the First Circuit described the process that he followed in beginning work on an appeal. After first noting the names of the lawyers, the firms on the brief, and the identity of the trial judge, he would then move on as follows: "I next want to see what kind of a case this is. There are three signposts: the table of contents, the statement of issues, and the summary of the argument." Frank M. Coffin, On Appeal: Courts, Lawyering and Judging 111 (1994).

What the reader will see in the table of contents are the headings and sub-headings of the various arguments found in the brief. These are known as "point headings" or "argument headings." They lay out the structure of the appellate brief. The judge can read them and quickly obtain an overview of what the case is about and what your position is on those issues. As the Washington state court of appeals advises appellate lawyers, "The Court should be able to read [the table of contents] to understand what the case is about and to see how you want us to decide each issue that is being raised." Washington State Court of Appeals, Division I, "Briefly Speaking" — Best Writing — Best Practices, https://www.courts.wa.gov/appellate_trial_courts/?fa=atc.display_divs&folderID=div1&fileID=briefWriting.

The point headings serve other purposes as well. The judge can gain a sense of the complexity of the case from them. In addition, you want to "pique the court's interest with a well-developed table of contents." Jon B. Eisenberg, *California Practice Guide: Civil Appeals and Writs* 9:5. You also want to begin convincing the court through the point headings. As one author put it: "You write every word, every sentence, and every paragraph in the argument of a brief for only one reason: to advance the argument. It follows that headings, too, should advance the argument." William Pannill, *Appeals: The Classic Guide*, 45 LITIGATION 38, 43 (2019).

Finally, a judge reading point headings will form an initial impression of your competence as appellate counsel. You want that impression to be favorable.

In short, point headings are a critical part of your brief, so you need to think carefully about what they must accomplish. Moreover, as you will see below, writing good point headings is difficult. That effort, however, pays enormous dividends, both in the actual writing of the brief and in its overall persuasiveness. If you craft excellent point headings, writing the rest of the brief will be a much easier task than would otherwise be the case. Time spent writing good point headings saves even more time later.

3. The Multiple Functions of Point Headings

A "point" is a specific ground for ruling in favor of a party's position on appeal. Point headings are usually complete declarative sentences that argue for a specific conclusion.

Here are two examples taken from briefs (with slight edits and omissions) filed by the parties in the case that resulted in the Supreme Court's 2020 decision *United States Forest Serv. v. Cowpasture River Pres. Ass'n*, 140 S. Ct. 1837, 207 L. Ed. 2d 186 (2020). The case was about a challenge to the Forest Service's approval of a pipeline that would cross the famous Appalachian Trail. Presented first are the point headings from the brief of the federal defendants, who had lost in the court of appeals and thus were petitioners in the Supreme Court:

I. The Forest Service has authority to grant a pipeline right-of-way through federal lands in National Forests

II. The Trails Act does not convert National Forest lands traversed by the Appalachian Trail into "lands in the National Park System"
   A. Congress's designation of a national scenic trail does not transfer administrative authority over National Forest "lands" crossed by that trail
      1. The Trails Act, which distinguishes between a "trail" and the "lands" it traverses, charges the Secretary of the Interior only with administration of "a trail"

    2. The Trails Act's allocation of authority recognizes that federal lands traversed by the Appalachian Trail remain under the administrative jurisdiction of other federal agencies

  B. The broader legal and practical context confirms that National Forest lands traversed by the Trail remain under the Forest Service's administrative jurisdiction

III. The court of appeals misinterpreted the Trails Act and the Mineral Leasing Act

  A. The court of appeals ignored the Trails Act's distinction between a trail and the lands that it traverses

  B. The court of appeals misunderstood the Mineral Leasing Act's definition of "agency head"

By reading point headings I, II, and III, you can see what the case is about and how the federal government has structured its arguments. Point I broadly argues that the Forest Service has authority to grant rights-of-way for pipelines through National Forests. Having set out this authority, Point II then contends that the "Trails Act" doesn't affect that authority here because the land traversed is not "in the National Park system" — and thus is not subject to regulation by a different agency under different standards. Finally, Point III argues that the court of appeals misinterpreted the statutes at issue.

Now let's see how the other side responded, attempting to gain affirmance of the decision of the court of appeals:

  I. THE FOREST SERVICE LACKS AUTHORITY TO GRANT A PIPELINE RIGHT-OF-WAY BECAUSE THE APPALACHIAN TRAIL IS LAND IN THE NATIONAL PARK SYSTEM

    A. Plain Statutory Text Places the Trail in the Park System and Precludes Agency Approval of Oil-and-Gas Pipelines

    B. Statutory History Confirms That the Appalachian Trail Is in the Park System and Carved out of the Leasing Act

    C. A Half-Century of Agency Interpretation Acknowledges That the Appalachian Trail Is "in the National Park System"

  II. THE FOREST SERVICE CANNOT SEPARATE THE "TRAIL" FROM THE FEDERAL "LANDS" DEDICATED TO THE TRAIL

    A. Common Usage, Statutory Text, and Agency Practice Confirm That the Trail Is an Area of Land

      1. The Word "Trail" Ordinarily Refers to an Area of Land

      2. The Trails Act and the Organic Act Confirm That the Park Service Administers the Trail as an Area of Land

    B. Neither the 1983 Trails Act Amendments nor the 1911 Weeks Act Excludes the Trail from the Park System

      1. The 1983 Amendments Do Not Affect the Park Service's Administration of the Trail

      2. The Weeks Act Does Not Affect the Park Service's Administration of the Trail

Here, Point I is quite different from the one made in the government's brief. It contends that the Appalachian Trail is actually in the National Park System, and thus the Forest Service has no authority over it to grant a right-of-way for a pipeline. Point II hones in on what the plaintiffs see as a fatal weakness of the Forest Service position: that the "trail" cannot be separated from the "lands" it occupies.

Point headings are important for several reasons, some of which should now be apparent to you:

A. They require the writer of the brief to organize the argument. To draft the headings, you must decide what your main arguments are, for the principal point headings must reflect those arguments. You have read in Chapter Two that outlining your argument is vital to organizing a logical brief; crafting point headings is central to that outlining process. As one recent article put it, a major benefit of this effort "is that it forces the writer to think about the analysis, to make decisions about the analysis, and to structure the analysis, all before writing." Jacob M. Carpenter, *Identifying Inefficiencies: Exploring Ways to Write Briefs More Quickly Within the Time Demands of Legal Practice*, 18 WYO. L. REV. 409, 428 (2018).

You will also need to decide the order in which you will present the arguments. Next, you will have to decide what subarguments support each overall argument. These will become the subheadings under a broader "umbrella" point.

For example, consider subheadings A through E of the following argument from the briefs in another Supreme Court case:

Congress authorized the National Labor Relations Board to operate with a two-member quorum of a three-member group to which the Board previously delegated its full powers.

A. The plain language of Section 3(b) demonstrates that the Board can operate in these circumstances.

B. The history of the Wagner Act and the legislative history of the Taft-Hartley Act confirm that Section 3(b)'s two-member group quorum requirement operates as an exception to the three-member Board quorum requirement.

C. Congress's decision to permit the Board to delegate its authority to a three-member group that may take action with a two-member quorum is consistent with background principles governing the operation of government agencies.

D. The Board's determination is entitled to deference.

E. The policy arguments petitioner and its amici advance in support of their view are incorrect and irrelevant.

The reader can easily see the logic of the five arguments. The brief first argues that the statute on its face allows a two-member group quorum and then that the legislative history of the law in question confirms this conclusion. Next, the brief argues that the two-member quorum falls within normal operational principles of governing agencies. Finally, the brief concludes with an argument that the court should defer to the agency's interpretation, and that the policy arguments offered by the opposing side are wrong.

Here is another example from part of a brief in a Supreme Court case on the right of presidential "electors" to cast their ballots as they wish:

> I. **The Text and Original Understanding of the Constitution Demonstrate State Authority to Remove or Penalize Electors Who Violate the Conditions of their Appointment**
> A. Article II Places No Limits on State Ability to Impose and Enforce Conditions on Elector Appointment and to Remove Those Who Fail to Comply
> B. The Twelfth Amendment Confirms State Authority to Impose and Enforce Conditions on Elector Appointment
> C. The Electors' Contrary Reading of the Text and Original Understanding Cannot Withstand Scrutiny

Can you see the logic of the three sub-arguments? Why were they placed in that order?

B. Second, point headings act as powerful argumentative devices. A good set of point headings will convey (1) what issues are being addressed, (2) how the court should decide those issues, and (3) why the court should decide them that way. By careful word choice, you can add to the persuasiveness of the point headings, just as you can add persuasiveness to the statement of facts.

Here is a set of point headings challenging the constitutionality of a traffic stop:

> I. **The Traffic Stop of Mr. Snapp's Vehicle Was Unlawful.**
> A. The trooper lacked a reasonable, articulable suspicion that a traffic infraction had occurred.
> B. The record fails to show that the two small air fresheners hanging from the rear view mirror constituted an obstruction of Mr. Snapp's view.
> C. The record fails to demonstrate that Mr. Snapp violated any laws pertaining to the use or condition of seatbelts.

The point headings challenge three possible justifications for the traffic stop. In particular, heading B paints a picture of the car favorable to Mr. Snapp, implying that "two small air fresheners" could hardly obstruct anyone's view.

C. Third, when situated in the brief itself, the point headings act as a transition device — that is, a preview of where the argument is going. An overall heading previews for the reader the precise argument that will unfold under that heading. The judge is aware of this function and, accordingly, is likely to pay special attention to it.

In the following example from an action alleging a violation of the Civil Rights Act, consider how subheading 2 acts as a transition device for the reader:

A. DEPUTY STARK IS ENTITLED TO QUALIFIED IMMUNITY FROM CLAIMS THAT PLAINTIFF WAS ARRESTED WITHOUT PROBABLE CAUSE IN VIOLATION OF PLAINTIFF'S FOURTH AMENDMENT RIGHTS.

    1. No Fourth Amendment Violation Occurred Because Deputy Stark Had Probable Cause To Arrest Plaintiff For Public Intoxication.

    2. Even If Deputy Stark Did Not Have Probable Cause To Arrest Plaintiff, He Was Nonetheless Entitled To Qualified Immunity Because A Reasonable Officer In His Shoes Could Believe Probable Cause Existed.

The "Even if" point heading allows the reader to readily understand the two-part logic of the argument. According to this brief, no Fourth Amendment violation occurred (subheading 1), but if one did, it doesn't matter because the deputy was immune from suit (subheading 2).

These are three very important reasons for paying close attention to drafting the point headings in your brief. A brief without excellent point headings is unlikely to be persuasive.

4. Thinking About the Order of the Issues

At this stage you also need to consider carefully the order of your arguments. Here you must follow two general principles (with one exception) that we have discussed before.

The first general principle is to put your strongest argument first. You will see why if you apply the perspective principle. When is the appellate judge freshest and paying the most attention to the brief? Answer: at the beginning of the brief. Briefs are not like mystery books; they do not build suspense and interest up to the very end. Instead, readers gradually lose momentum as they plow through a brief. So capitalize on the reader's maximum interest at the outset by placing your strongest argument first.

The second general rule is to present your affirmative case before dealing with your opponent's case. You want your brief to appear *positive*. Ask yourself what the court will think if your first point heading reads:

A. The holding in *Smith v. Jones* is Distinguishable from the Present Case Because . . .

The judge will very likely assume that (1) the *Smith v. Jones* case must be very important because you have led off with it, and (2) the case must be troublesome for you — why else would you begin by distinguishing a case? In effect, you have let the opponent dictate the presentation of *your* case. You do not want to put yourself in that position.

The exception to these two principles stems from logic. From a judicial perspective, some arguments necessarily arise before others. For example, take a situation in which a state tort claims act applies to a private citizen who is bringing a negligence action against the state government. The act requires that a plaintiff present a claim for damages to the public entity, which then has a period of time in which to consider that claim. Importantly, the failure to present a proper claim precludes the filing of a suit.

Assume that you represent the defendant public entity and have two issues that you wish to argue: (1) the plaintiff failed to present a proper claim before suing, and (2) your client's actions were not the actual cause of the plaintiff's injury. Logically speaking, the claim issue seems to come first. If the plaintiff did not file a proper claim, the case ends and the court does not need to reach the substantive issue in the case (i.e., the actual causation issue). Thus, if you can convince the court that you are right on the first issue, the court likely will not need to decide the other issue. Similar reasoning would apply to claims like lack of jurisdiction, lack of standing, expiration of the statute of limitations, etc.

Looked at another way, how would you feel if you were an appellate judge who (1) read all of a lengthy argument about the substantive causation issue, and then (2) read the claim issue and concluded that the claim was unquestionably defective? You would not be happy about the extra reading on the substantive issue that you had to do.

Keep in mind, though, that the two overall principles — put your strongest arguments first and present your affirmative case first — are very powerful ones. Think carefully before you lead with a weaker argument. Do so only if the brief will otherwise appear illogical.

B. WRITING A POINT HEADING

1. Complete Sentences That Use Facts and Persuade

Now we will turn to actually writing the point headings. A point heading is almost always a complete sentence. You want a forceful, clear, argumentative sentence. You do not want phrases that are uninformative, such as:

> A. Penal Code Section 1234 Applies to this Case.
>   1. The Language of Section 1234.
>   2. The Legislative History of Section 1234.

Heading A does not tell you why Section 1234 applies. Subheadings 1 and 2 likewise squander an opportunity to persuade; they are phrases, not full sentences. You want to use the headings to advance your argument, not merely to neutrally tell the reader about the general topic being addressed. Consider the following:

> A. Penal Code Section 1234 Applies to the Discharge by Mr. Ames of a Weapon Inside his automobile.
>   1. The Language of Section 1234 expressly applies to weapons fired "at or in vehicles," and Mr. Ames fired his gun out the window of his car while driving it.
>   2. The legislative history of Section 1234 confirms that the statute was broadened to include the use of firearms in vehicles.

These headings advance the argument in persuasive language.

Second, how long should point headings be? Read the following heading:

> I. The Order Approving the Negotiated Settlement Agreement Between American Casualty Insurance Company and the Hellman Company Was in Error and Must Be Reversed Because the Parties Failed to Assign Any Value to the Noncontingent Portions of the Settlement and Because Adams Construction, as a Nonsettling Party, Did Not Receive the Specific Credit to Which It Was Statutorily Entitled With Respect to the Contingent Portions of the Settlement.

The heading is generally understandable (with difficulty) but quite hard to plow through. The reason is obvious: The sentence is long, over 60 words. The reader might well look at the heading and decide to skip over it, knowing that reading it will not be pleasant.

Because a point heading is a sentence, it cannot be too long. You are trying to convey a single idea to the reader, and it is critical that the headings read easily. This book will address sentence length in Chapter Ten; for now, however, you should aim for a sentence that is no longer than 40 words. If the point heading is longer than that, you will need some ordering device — perhaps a (1) and a (2) — to help the reader. For the same reason, you will want to use active voice instead of passive voice (another subject discussed in Chapter Ten) unless you have a good reason to do otherwise.

Third, because they are part of the argument, the best point headings include both law and facts in them. You need facts because the court is deciding the case based on those facts; it is not issuing a general declaration about what the law should be in a given area. So you want to personalize and particularize the point heading by using the facts of the case.

For example, a point heading might read:

> A. The Landlord Owed a Duty of Care to Smith.

The heading gets across the overall conclusion sought by the party filing the brief. But it is not persuasive. It does not tell us *why* the landlord owed a duty of care — it is missing the "because" statement. Adding the "because" statement to this heading "jump starts" the persuasiveness of the argument:

> A. The Landlord Owed a Duty of Care to Mr. Smith Because She had Specifically Invited Him to Visit Her Office and Discuss a Potential Business Venture.

This heading is much better. It tells the reader why the landlord owed a duty based on the facts of the case.

Here is another example of what you do *not* want:

> A. The Trial Court Properly Granted the Motion to Dismiss.

Again, the "because" explanation is missing. Instead, you want this type of point heading:

> A. The Trial Court Properly Granted the Motion to Dismiss Because Mr. Lopez's Injury Occurred in 2015 and the Four-Year Statute of Limitations Expired Before His Complaint Was Filed in 2020.

Note how much more informative *and* persuasive the second heading is. It argues for a conclusion and uses the facts to explain why that conclusion is proper.

Finally, are there any exceptions to the rule that point headings should be a complete sentence? When writing the point heading for the standard of review, many lawyers will simply use the short heading "Standard of Review." The argument for this practice is that the standard of review section is not likely to be long, so a shorter heading is appropriate. We believe, however, that good appellate practice requires the lawyer to use *every* tool available to help persuade the judge. So we recommend following the normal rule for point headings on the standard of review by incorporating facts and using a complete sentence. Which of the two headings immediately below is more persuasive?

STANDARD OF REVIEW

THE COURT EMPLOYS "DE NOVO" REVIEW OF THE TRIAL COURT'S INSTRUCTION TO THE JURY ON HOW TO EVALUATE THE REASONABLENESS OF DEFENDANT'S CONDUCT IN AN EMERGENCY.

2. Subheadings That Break Down the Overall Argument

Your brief will place subheadings under most of the principal point headings. As shown above, subheadings break up an overall argument. Thus, when the subheadings under an argument are considered together, as a whole they must logically support the overall argument.

For example, assume that the court is determining whether the trial court properly applied a four-part test in granting a preliminary injunction, and you are defending that decision. The main heading would argue your overall point: that the court correctly granted the injunction because you met the four-part test. Then, under that main point heading, you might have four subheadings (A, B, C, and D; or 1, 2, 3, and 4) corresponding to the four parts of the test.

Another reason for having subheadings is that the written argument under a main point heading is just too long. As a rule of thumb, if the brief goes longer than four (or at the very most, five) pages under a single heading, you will benefit from adding subheadings to break up the overall point. The readers will be grateful, for doing so helps them get through the material more easily.

Use only "paired" subheadings. In other words, if the overall point heading is a Roman numeral, do not use a subheading "A" without a subheading "B." The reason is simple: By definition, a single subheading under an overall point cannot fully break up that overall point into logical parts. Instead, it will either just restate the overall point (which serves no purpose) or address only part of that overall point (thus leaving a gap in the argument — the missing second part).

Finally, remember once again that the key purpose of subheadings is to break up a larger argument. Thus, the subheadings must split up the overall point for the reader. If a subheading does not fit as part of an overall, larger heading, something is wrong.

3. Conventions to Follow in Drafting Headings

There is room for debate about the style to use in headings. Some lawyers put the main headings in capital letters. Others argue that capital letters make the heading too difficult to read. They claim that a heading should read just like a normal sentence, but it should be put in bold face type. Still others capitalize the first letter of all but the article words (the, an, etc.) in their headings. Older briefs tended to underline the point headings.

Unless the court has a rule covering the subject, decide for yourself which convention that you will follow. The examples above in this chapter use different styles. Take another look at them and apply the perspective principle: What convention would make the headings more readable to a judge? (And, yes, the best appellate lawyers do carefully consider how their brief will look.)

Finally, do not refer to Appellant and Appellee, or Appellant and Respondent, in your point headings. Use individual names or descriptive names (for example, employer, Smith).

C. USING POINT HEADINGS AS AN ORGANIZING TOOL

As you can gather from the discussion above, writing good point headings is difficult. You have important goals and many constraints in writing them. Nonetheless, they are inordinately valuable as an organizing tool.

When you start writing the point headings, allocate sufficient time. You will need it. You will likely agonize over some of the choices: Should this argument go first? Do the subheadings fit under the overall heading, or is this subheading really a different argument? Why is it so hard to shorten this heading? Have I really captured the argument that I am making? Or worse: Do I really *understand* the argument that I am trying to make here?

When you have a good draft of the headings, put them aside for a day and then come back to them. Do they still make sense? Most importantly, if you were a judge reading them for the first time, would you get the overview of the argument that Judge Coffin sought?

Now for some positive news about point headings. When you complete the draft of the point headings, you are well on the way to writing a good brief, for you have already structured your entire argument. You have used the organizational principle from Chapter Two. From an intellectual standpoint, the hardest part of writing the argument is largely behind you.

Finally, an odd point. The discussion above should have convinced you that point headings play a vital role in the appellate brief. In the experience of the authors of this book, however, many lawyers pay insufficient attention to point headings. They write dull, short ones, choosing instead to concentrate on the actual writing of the argument. Avoid that mistake. Take full advantage of the opportunities that point headings present.

Summary

- The court should be able to look at the point headings under the argument section of the brief and understand both what the issues are about and how you want the court to decide the case.

- Point headings help the drafter of the brief organize the argument. They also begin to convince the court how to decide the issues.

- In drafting the point headings, generally place your strongest argument first unless there is a logical reason why a weaker argument should come before it.

- A point heading usually should be a complete sentence, should include facts and law, and should tell the court why it should reach a particular conclusion.

- Use subheadings at least every four or five pages to break down an overall argument.

Appendix B contains exercises that ask you to evaluate sets of point headings in light of the principles discussed in this chapter.

CHAPTER 8

Building the Argument: Cases, Statutes, and Transitions

A. USING CASES AND STATUTES

1. The Mental Process of Using a Case Precedent

The centerpiece of any appellate brief is the use of legal authority. The basic types you should cite in your brief are primary authorities: case precedents, statutes, and constitutional provisions. In this chapter we discuss constructing an argument using legal authority. We will consider cases first and then turn to statutes and constitutions.

The goal in using a precedent case in a brief is to convince the court either that it should follow the precedent in the present case or distinguish the precedent from the present case. For the sake of convenience, assume that we are trying to get the court to follow the precedent rather than distinguish it. What does it take to convince a reader to follow a precedent?

Go back to the perspective principle and put yourself in the shoes of the reader. Ask yourself what the reader must know about the precedent case to apply it. A little thought will lead you to identify three different sets of information:

1.   The precedent has to present the same issue as one of the issues that is pending in the case now before the court on your appeal. So, the appellate judge must know what that issue is and keep it in mind when using the precedent.

2.   The judge will follow the holding of the precedent on the issue only if it presents the same facts as, or at least facts analogous to, the present case. Accordingly, the appellate judge must know the facts of the precedent case. Note that the judge is only interested in the facts relevant to the issue presented; giving the judge other facts will simply clutter up the argument or, at worst, distract the judge.

3.   Finally, the judge must know the precise holding — or rule — established by the precedent on the issue that is presented, because you are asking the judge to reach the same conclusion here.

Now we turn to the present case. Again, the core of any use of a precedent is whether the facts in it are analogous to the present case. Thus, in addition to the relevant facts of the precedent, the appellate judge must know the facts of the present case. To reiterate, only the *relevant* facts are needed; unwanted are those numerous other facts in the case that have nothing to do with the issue.

Next comes the critical stage of the analysis. The court will have to compare the facts of the precedent to those of the present case. Therefore, the lawyer will need to make this comparison for the court in the brief. The purpose of this comparison is to demonstrate how the present case and the precedent case are similar. If they are similar, the principle of *stare decisis* requires the court to conclude that the outcome of the issue in the present case should be the same as the outcome found in the precedent.

From the student's (and, indeed, even the experienced lawyer's) standpoint, this comparison can be difficult to execute. In rare situations, the facts of the precedent and the facts of the present case are virtually the same (a situation referred to as the precedent being "on all fours"). In most instances, however, they will not be exactly the same. Accordingly, you are trying to convince the court that the facts of the two cases are "close enough" that the court should follow the precedent.

It requires hard thinking on the lawyer's part to make that showing. You must first compare the cases mentally to be sure in your mind that the facts in the two cases are analogous. Then this comparison must be put into writing. The tendency that the brief writer must avoid is shirking this comparison by stating the facts of the precedent, going on to state the facts of the present case, and then assuming that the reader can see the comparison. The problem here is that the reader may not see the comparison as easily as you see it. (You are the expert in this area, remember?) And if the reader does not see the analogy, then you have failed as an advocate.

Another possibility is that you are unsure about why the two cases are analogous. However, instead of confronting your uncertainties "head on," you just write up a vague comparison, hoping the judge will do the missing mental work for you. But the judge may refuse to make that effort. Or, even worse, the judge may do the comparison and conclude that the case should *not* be followed — exactly the opposite outcome that you intend.

Finally, the comparison needs to be completed by stating your conclusion about how the issue in the present case must come out in light of the precedent.

If you go back to the beginning of this discussion on the use of cases and start counting, you will see that there were six separate steps required to use a precedent properly. To review, the six steps necessary to use a case precedent are:

1. Defining the issue presented for decision in the present case.
2. Reciting the facts of the precedent case that are relevant to that issue.
3. Explaining the holding (or rule) of the precedent case on that issue, including why the precedent court reached that conclusion.
4. Reciting the facts of the present case that are relevant to the issue presented.
5. Comparing the facts of the precedent case to those of the present case to show that the two are analogous. Here is where you apply the precedent to the present case.
6. Stating a conclusion about how the issue in the present case should come out.

These six steps are the core of the legal analysis when you use a precedent. None of this should come as a surprise to you, as all first-year writing classes cover this type of core legal analysis. Indeed, the analysis has led to an explosion of acronyms that generally stand for the same basic information. Perhaps the most common is "IRAC," short for (1) issue, (2) rule, (3) analysis, and (4) conclusion. Others featured in legal writing texts include:

CRAC: Conclusion, Rule, Application, Conclusion
CRuPAC: Conclusion, Rule, P (Rule proof or explanation), Application of Rule, Conclusion
IREXAC: Issue, Rule, Explanation, Application, Conclusion
TREAC: Topic sentence that states a conclusion, Rule, Explanation, Application, Conclusion

There are others. All, however, exhibit common principles. *See* Tracy Turner, *Finding Consensus in Legal Writing Discourse Regarding Organizational Structure: A Review and Analysis of the Use of IRAC and Its Progenies,* 9 LEGAL COMMN'C & RHETORIC, J. ASS'N LEGAL WRITING DIRECTORS, 351 (2012).

The six steps outlined above are consistent with these approaches. As discussed below, you do not always need to do such a detailed analysis of all six steps when using precedents. However, you need to understand those steps to correctly decide when a shortened version of the six steps is allowable.

A useful test is to go through your draft brief and place a number — one through six — before each separate step of your analysis. Here is an example:

> The issue [#1] is whether the evidence in the record demonstrates that the prosecution qualified Officer Henson under Rule 702 of the Federal Rules of Evidence as an expert witness on drug arrests. The decision in *United States v. Williams,* 212 F.3d 1305 (D.C. Cir. 2000), considered this same issue.
>
> In *Williams,* [#2] Special Agent Stewart testified that he had arrested 11 individuals on drug charges and recovered 11 weapons from them. Id. at 1309. The court held [#3] that this background was an insufficient foundation to qualify Special Agent Stewart as an expert on drug arrests under Rule 702. According to the court, fewer than one dozen arrests involving possession of a firearm was insufficient to qualify him as an expert, particularly without evidence that any of those arrests involved a drug user. Id.
>
> The foundation laid in this case is even weaker than the one in *Williams,* and the same result must obtain. Here, the only testimony [#4] elicited by the prosecution about Officer Henson's background was that he had worked for the police for five years as an investigator and for five years previously with the Metropolitan Transit Authority. The prosecution offered no testimony about Officer Henson's training and experience in the field of drug trafficking. [#5] If one dozen arrests on drug charges was insufficient to qualify Agent Stewart as an expert on drug arrests in *Williams,* then Officer Henson's background, which featured no arrests or even training on drug arrests, also is unquestionably insufficient. [#6] Accordingly, the trial court correctly found that Officer Henson could not testify as an expert under Rule 702.

If one of those numbers is missing, ask yourself whether you have brought your reader fully through the analytic process in applying the precedent. If you inappropriately shorten the steps, you will greatly increase the chance that the reader will not follow your logic, and thus that you will fail in your advocacy.

2. When a Complete Analysis Is Needed

You will not always need to use the full six steps when you employ a case in a brief. Most importantly, you do not need all of them when you cite a case to establish a legal principle that is needed to lay preliminary groundwork for a more specific argument. For example:

- You might be establishing the standard that the court is to apply in deciding a motion for preliminary injunction (that is, the prerequisites that a plaintiff must meet to obtain that relief).
- You might be telling the court of appeals what standard of review applies in the particular case.
- You might be setting forth the test that a trial court is to use in granting a motion for summary judgment.

In these instances, you are not going to use the facts of the precedent cases; instead, you are just laying out broad legal principles that the court will follow. But when you get to the core discussion on the issues in a brief and are asking the court to apply a precedent case, you will need to consider all six steps. When you become an experienced legal writer, using the six-step analysis becomes second nature; you will employ it without really thinking about it. In some instances, you will be able to imply a step, and the reader will be able to follow you. As a beginning writer of appellate briefs, however, you must discipline yourself to make sure that you understand and think about all six steps.

Once you get used to the idea of the six steps as a method, you (as a beginning legal writer) will have two other related questions about its use. One question is whether the six steps must always be used in the same order. The answer is no. Most importantly, it is possible — even desirable — to tell the reader what the outcome is [#6] at the beginning after stating the issue [#1]. Many legal writing texts recommend this approach. You would then repeat your conclusion at the end. Another variation is to state the holding of the precedent [#3] and then discuss its facts [#2].

3. Applying Statutes and Constitutional Provisions

You use much the same technique in applying statutes and constitutional provisions. The starting point is, once again, the issue presented. In this situation, however, instead of using a precedent case to decide that issue, application of the statute's words will decide it. So you need to tell the court what the issue is and that a statute controls in this situation. Then you need to give the court the precise text of the statute that will decide the issue.

To apply the statute, the next step is to lay out the facts that are relevant to the application of the statute. The brief then applies the facts to the statutory language. Finally, you set forth the conclusion on the issue.

In applying statutes, you should be mindful of the courts' approach to interpreting statutes. Language in statutes and constitutions is sometimes clear, but other times it is not. If the meaning is plain and unambiguous, the court will generally apply the ordinary meaning to the facts. But if the language is unclear and ambiguous, then it must be interpreted. The court's objective in interpreting statutes is to determine the intent of the legislature and, in the case of a constitutional provision, to determine the framers' intent.

With this objective in mind, the brief writer should assist the court in constru- ing the law by explaining the law's meaning in the brief, and in so doing, follow- ing the maxims of construction that the court will apply in determining the intent of the law. Specifically, the court first examines the words at issue, looking at how those words are defined in definitional sections of the statute as well as consid- ering non-legal definitions. The court will next consider how the words are used elsewhere in the statute or chapter, or other parts of the law. The court will also look at the statute as a whole, harmonizing the various elements by considering each clause and section in the context of the overall statutory framework. As Chief Justice Taney described the process more than a century ago: "In expounding a statute, we must not be guided by a single sentence or member of a sentence, but look to the provisions of the whole law, and to its object and policy." *United States v. Boisdoré's Heirs,* 49 U.S. (8 How.) 113, 122 (1850).

Finally, the court may review the legislative history of the statute to discern the objectives of the legislators. Examining the language, legal framework, and his- tory of the law will inform the court's effort to ascertain a meaning that meets the apparent intent of the legislature. The court wants to promote the purpose of the statute while avoiding absurd consequences. *People v. Jenkins,* 10 Cal. 4th 234, 246, 893 P.2d 1224, 1231 (1995).

Here is an example. In *Sebelius v. Cloer,* 569 U.S. 369, 376 (2013), the Supreme Court considered when a claimant could recover attorney's fees and costs for fil- ing a petition for compensation under the National Childhood Vaccine Injury Act (NCVIA). The question before the Court required it to interpret the meaning of the phrase "filing a petition," and in so doing the Court applies the maxims of statutory construction:

> As in any statutory construction case, "[w]e start, of course, with the statu- tory text," and proceed from the understanding that "[u]nless otherwise defined, statutory terms are generally interpreted in accordance with their ordinary meaning." [Citation.] The Act's fees provision ties eligibility for attorney's fees broadly to "any proceeding on such petition," referring specifically to "a peti- tion filed under section 300aa-11." [Citation.] Section 300aa-11 provides that "[a] proceeding for compensation" is "initiated" by "service upon the Secretary" and "the filing of a petition containing" certain documentation with the clerk of the Court of Federal Claims who then "immediately forward[s] the filed petition" for assignment to a special master. § 300aa-11(a)(1).

> Nothing in these two provisions suggests that the reason for the subse- quent dismissal of a petition, such as its untimeliness, nullifies the initial fil- ing of that petition. We have explained that "[a]n application is 'filed,' as that term is commonly understood, when it is delivered to, and accepted by, the appropriate court officer for placement into the official record." [Citation.] When this ordinary meaning is applied to the text of the statute, it is clear that an NCVIA petition which is delivered to the clerk of the court, forwarded for processing, and adjudicated in a proceeding before a special master is a

"petition filed under section 300aa-11." 42 U.S.C. § 300aa-15(e)(1). And so long as such a petition was brought in good faith and with a reasonable basis, it is eligible for an award of attorney's fees, even if it is ultimately unsuccessful. Ibid. If Congress had intended to limit fee awards to timely petitions, it could easily have done so.

4. The Basic Building Blocks of Argument

While the use of cases and statutes will form the core of the legal analysis, the argument in the brief will contain other material. For example, you will present preliminary authority that brings the reader to the point where the case or statute can be applied. This material will chiefly involve identifying the specific issues that the court must decide in the case and perhaps breaking down those issues into sub-issues. Thus, if the case involves the appeal of the grant of a preliminary injunction, the brief may set forth the traditional four-part test in determining whether to grant such relief.

The brief might also contain policy arguments in favor of a certain outcome. Those arguments usually will appear at the end of the brief.

But the core of the brief will be the use of cases and statutes, for they constitute the basic "building blocks" of an argument in a brief.

B. CONSTRUCTING AN ARGUMENT ON AN ISSUE

1. A Review of What You Already Know

You already know some of the important principles about how to write the argument section of your brief. For example, you know to put your strongest argument first (unless there is a good reason not to). You know to present your own positive arguments before you rebut your opponent's arguments. You know that policy arguments belong after the arguments that use primary authority. You know that, in using cases, you must be cognizant of the six steps (or a variation of that method if you are applying a statute). And you know that the argument below a point heading must reflect that heading.

Now we need to delve more deeply into the actual argument.

2. Setting Up the Argument: Supplying the Necessary Legal Background

The core of your argument will deal with a very precise issue because your research has honed down the case to that issue, which almost always will be one of a series of issues. So you are now mentally at the epicenter of the appeal. But you traveled a lengthy road to get to this place. You researched, accumulated, and assimilated background information about the area of law that the case involves. In doing so, you may have made certain false turns before you "saw the light" and got back on the main road.

In short, you did not just jump from the state of your knowledge when you began (ignorance of the facts and the law) to where you are now (mastery of both the facts and the law). You *learned* along the way.

You must keep that learning process in mind. The perspective principle teaches you that the judge has to follow the same road that you took (although the judge must skip the wrong turns). So you need to set up the issue by giving readers the necessary background on the law that will lead them to the place where they can consider your specific argument on that issue.

For example, assume that you are writing an appellant's brief for the defendant in a tort case. The case involves a plaintiff who was attacked by a third party in a parking garage that was owned by your client. The specific question at issue is whether the defendant, your client, owed a duty to the plaintiff. What is the background information needed by the reader? Depending on the jurisdiction you are in, you may well need to educate your reader on the following points:

1.   The common law rule was that a landowner owed no duty of care to third parties.
2.   The jurisdiction abolished that rule and held that landowners, in some situations, owe a limited duty.
3.   The test for that limited duty is . . . .

You will need to support these introductory points by citations to authority. But you do not need to use the full six steps. You are simply working your way through what should be the uncontested development of law. In the end, you arrive at the specific issue, and you are ready to use the cases that have the most analogous facts.

The amount of space used in the brief to set out the introductory material varies. But you should assume that the reader is not an expert in the area of law that applies in your case. Therefore, you should first explain and teach the reader about the law, starting with the *broad legal principles* at issue. Then you should proceed from there to explain and teach the reader about the applicable law step by step until you reach the *narrow legal question* at issue on appeal. This organizational approach is illustrated using an inverted triangle. (See Figure 1.)

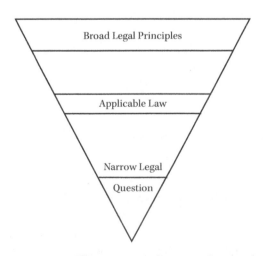

Figure 1.   Illustration of inverted triangle approach to organizing legal principles within a brief.

Consider how this writer uses the inverted triangle approach to organize the legal principles on the following question: When does a voluntary encounter with law enforcement evolve into an unlawful seizure under the Fourth Amendment?

The Fourth Amendment to the United States Constitution guarantees "[t]he right of the people to be secure in their persons, houses, papers, and effects, against unreasonable searches and seizures." U.S. CONST. amend. IV.

"[A] person is seized, thereby triggering a Fourth Amendment analysis of the police action, 'when an officer, by means of physical force or show of authority, has in some way restrained the liberty of a citizen.'" *Terry v. Ohio*, 392 U.S. 1, 19 n. 16, 88 S.Ct. 1868, 20 L.Ed.2d 889 (1968). If no physical force is involved, a seizure by show of authority occurs when the totality of circumstances surrounding the incident would communicate to a reasonable person that he or she is not free to leave and the person submits to the show of authority. Id.

"'[L]aw enforcement officers do not violate the Fourth Amendment by merely approaching an individual on the street or in another public place, by asking him if he is willing to answer some questions, by putting questions to him if he is willing to listen, or by offering in evidence in a criminal prosecution his voluntary answers to such questions.'" *Florida v. Bostick*, 501 U.S. 429, 434, 111 S.Ct. 2382, 115 L.Ed.2d 389 (1991) (quoting *Florida v. Royer*, 460 U.S. 491, 497, 103 S.Ct. 1319, 75 L.Ed.2d 229 (1983)). Thus, a voluntary encounter is not automatically transformed into a seizure when an individual who has been approached and questioned by an officer voluntarily responds to the officer's questions or request for identification. *See INS v. Delgado*, 466 U.S. 210, 216, 104 S.Ct. 1758, 80 L.Ed.2d 247 (1984) ("While most citizens will respond to a police request, the fact that people do so, and do so without being told they are free not to respond, hardly eliminates the consensual nature of the response.")

But, under some circumstances, what begins as a voluntary encounter can evolve into a seizure. "To determine if this evolution has occurred, the United States Supreme Court has devised a 'totality of the circumstances' test. Under the test, law enforcement interaction with a person is voluntary, not a detention, if the officer's conduct conveys to a reasonable person that he or she is free to refuse the officer's requests or otherwise end the encounter. The courts have delineated several nonexclusive factors to consider in applying this test: the presence of more than one officer, the display of a weapon, physical contact by the officer, use of a commanding tone of voice, activation of sirens or flashers, a command to halt or approach, and an attempt to control the ability to flee. *See United States v. Mendenhall*, 446 U.S. 544, 554-55, 100 S.Ct. 1870, 1877-78, 64 L.Ed.2d 497 (1980). No one factor is legally determinative, dispositive, or paramount. The outcome does not turn on the presence or absence of a single controlling or infallible touchstone and requires careful scrutiny of all the surrounding circumstances. *See United States v. Harrison*, 639 F.3d 1273, 1280 (10th Cir. 2011).

By starting the analysis with the broadest relevant point, namely the language of the Fourth Amendment, the writer orients the reader into the law, providing the legal context of the issue. The writer therefore sets the stage for applying the law to a narrow issue on appeal. This method of organizing the law may be no more than a couple of paragraphs or it may be a couple of pages. It could occupy all the space under your first large point heading. Below, we will talk more about what to do at the very bottom of the pyramid — how to frame the specific issue the court must decide.

There is another matter you must consider as you are stating a principle of law and leading a reader through this type of preliminary material: How many cases should you cite? One? Three? Six? Long lists of citations to cases are known as "string citations." They do not help. You only need to cite to one case or statute to support a point of black letter law.

For example, if the brief makes the point that "only relevant evidence is admissible," a citation to the evidence code is sufficient authentication. Likewise, if a case is directly on point from your jurisdiction's highest court, you need to cite only that one case to support your argument. If, however, the case law provides only indirect support for your argument, then you will likely want to cite a few cases and illustrate that support by using introductory signals and parenthetical explanations to demonstrate the relevance of the citations.

Consider the following example from a brief filed by the publisher in a defamation case. The plaintiff was contending that the defendant published books knowing of fraudulent statements in them. The publisher first established the broad legal protection accorded by the First Amendment:

A. Statements Within the Books: The First Amendment and Common Law Bar Plaintiffs' Claims Against Penguin for Publishing Nondefamatory Falsehoods or Inaccuracies in the Books

The First Amendment accords the highest protections to speech about matters of public concern. *Snyder v. Phelps*, 131 S. Ct. 1207, 1211 (2010); *Simon & Schuster v. Members of the New York State Crime Victims Bd.*, 502 U.S. 105 (1991). The Books — bestselling autobiographies about Mortenson's efforts to build schools for children in Pakistan and Afghanistan — are clearly speech about matters of public concern, and hence entitled to maximum First Amendment protection. The question raised by the Fourth Amended Complaint is whether nondefamatory intentional falsehoods embedded within speech about matters of public concern are actionable as fraud. The answer is no.

When First Amendment protection is at its maximum, it bars liability for both the nondefamatory "intentional lie" and for the "careless error" because both are inevitable consequences of free debate and expression. *Gertz v. Robert Welch, Inc.*, 418 U.S. 323, 340 (1974). "The First Amendment requires that we protect some falsehood in order to protect speech that matters." *Gertz*, 418 U.S. at 341; *accord, New York Times v. Sullivan*, 376 U.S. 254, 271-72 (1964) ("[E]rroneous statement is inevitable in free debate," and "it must be protected if the freedoms of expression are to have the 'breathing space' that they 'need . . . to survive.' "), *citing N.A.A.C.P. v. Button*, 371 U.S. 415, 445 (1963) (First Amendment protection does not turn upon "the truth, popularity, or social utility of the ideas and beliefs which are offered"); *see also State v. Woods*, 221 Mont. 17, 23 (1986) ("The defendant's right to speak is not limited to speaking the truth").

The Books express ideas, and the First Amendment guards even inaccuracies or falsehoods in the expression of ideas:

> [Such] expression, be it oral, literary, pictorial, or theatrical, is integrally related to the exposition of thought that may shape our concepts of the whole universe of man. Although such expression may convey factual information relevant to social and individual decisionmaking, it is protected by the Constitution, whether or not it contains factual representations and even if it includes inaccurate assertions of fact. Indeed, disregard of the "truth" may be employed to give force to the underlying idea expressed by the speaker. "Under the First Amendment there is no such thing as a false idea," and the only way that ideas can be suppressed is through "the competition of other ideas."

Virginia State Board of Pharmacy v. Virginia Citizens Consumer Council, 425 U.S. 748, 779-780 (1976) (Stewart, J., concurring) (quoting *Gertz*, 418 U.S. at 339). *Accord, Cantwell v. Connecticut*, 310 U.S. 296, 310 (1940).

. . .

First Amendment protection for false statements applies particularly to publishers when, as here, they are publishing nonfictional works containing (at least hypothetically) verifiable statements of fact, such as autobiographies. If a bookseller were held liable for the content of his books, "he will tend to restrict the books he sells to those he has inspected; and thus the State will have imposed a restriction upon the distribution of constitutionally protected as well as [unprotected] literature." *New York Times Co. v. Sullivan*, 376 U.S. 254, 278 (1964).

Note the purpose served by this part of the argument. The defendant is laying out the general law of defamation within the context of this particular case. It gives the reader the background information needed to understand the *specific* cases that the brief will then go on to use. There, the brief will compare the facts of the cases used to the facts of the present case. Here, though, the brief is painting a broader general picture revolving around a central theme: that the First Amendment broadly protects publishers from many defamation claims.

3. Previewing the Upcoming Argument

Assume that you have laid out the needed legal background and are now about to make a specific argument. Your point heading summarizes the argument. Should you just launch into the argument by identifying the issue and then starting to use authority — whether cases or a statute — to resolve that issue?

You could do so. But do you want to make your reader wade through the entire argument to find out what it is about and how it comes out? Your reader would more easily understand the specific features of your argument on this issue if, at the outset, the reader knew something about where the discussion will go. Hence, you want to tell your reader where the argument will come out at the outset.

You do so with an introductory paragraph. Consider what the judge will know after reading the following paragraph under heading "I" at the beginning of the appellant's argument:

I.   The district court erred in determining that the complaint failed to state a cause of action for the illegal search of her property and seizure of the dogs in violation of the Fourth Amendment.

While the PSPCA did obtain a warrant to search Willard's property, there was no probable cause to support the issuing of the warrant, rendering the warrant constitutionally defective. Furthermore, the warrant did not extend to cover the search and seizure by the PSPCA agents. The PSPCA's search and seizure of her dogs were patently unreasonable and as such infringed on Willard's Fourth Amendment rights.

A.   The PSPCA's warrant did not render the search and seizure constitutional because there was no probable cause to support the issuing of the warrant.

In three short introductory sentences, the brief encapsulates the argument that the appellant will make under point heading I. The short summary allows the reader to anticipate what is to come, and thus helps ensure that the reader at all times understands the flow of the argument.

Here is another example of such an introductory summary:

I.   THE DISTRICT COURT HAS JURISDICTION OVER MS. VELEZ'S ALIEN TORT STATUTE CLAIMS

The district court committed clear legal error in finding that it lacked jurisdiction over Ms. Velez's trafficking and forced labor claims under the Alien Tort Statute ("ATS"), 28 U.S.C. §1350. Contrary to the plain language of the statute, the district court imposed an additional, unwritten requirement that a tort actionable under the ATS must have occurred *outside* the United States. The district court also erroneously held that the passage of 18 U.S.C. §1595, a provision of the Trafficking Victims Protection Reauthorization Act ("TVPRA"), had "implicitly withdrawn" jurisdiction over Ms. Velez's ATS claims.

A.   The District Court Erred in Dismissing Ms. Velez's ATS Claims on the Basis That Defendants' Conduct Occurred within the United States

Again, the short paragraph acts as a preview. The judge now expects a two-part argument: (1) that a tort under the Alien Tort Statute does not require conduct outside of the United States; and (2) that a second act did not "implicitly withdraw" jurisdiction. The brief can then flow smoothly into those arguments.

4. Framing the Specific Issue

The structural principle, explained in Chapter Two, holds that because courts decide issues, you must frame your brief around specific issues. In addition to general background on an issue of the type set forth above, you will need to give the court the necessary law that will identify the specific issue that it must decide. As discussed above, you accomplish this goal by citing authority for the propositions needed to establish the issue.

Consider the initial part of an argument made under the antitrust laws. Note how it quickly and efficiently narrows down the kind of "injury" that antitrust law protects:

A. Plaintiffs Do Not and Cannot Allege Antitrust Injury Because the Alleged Discovery Violations Do Not Injure Interests Protected by the Antitrust Laws.

Section 4 of the Clayton Act permits "any person who shall be injured in his business or property by reason of anything forbidden in the antitrust laws" to sue for treble damages. 15 U.S.C. §15. The Supreme Court has interpreted this language to require a showing of "antitrust injury." *Associated Gen. Contractors of Cal., Inc. v. Cal. State Council of Carpenters*, 459 U.S. 519, 536 (1983); *Brunswick Corp. v. Pueblo Bowl-O-Mat, Inc.*, 429 U.S. 477, 489 (1977). Antitrust injury is:

> injury of the type the antitrust laws were intended to prevent and that flows from that which makes defendants' acts unlawful. The injury should reflect the anticompetitive effect either of the violation or of anticompetitive acts made possible by the violation. It should, in short, be 'the type of loss that the claimed violations . . . would be likely to cause.'

Brunswick Corp., 429 U.S. at 489 (quoting *Zenith Radio Corp. v. Hazeltine Research*, 395 U.S. 100, 125 (1969)).

Accordingly, to establish antitrust standing under Section 4 of the Clayton Act, a plaintiff must demonstrate (1) "that the interests allegedly injured by the defendant fall within the scope of antitrust protection," and (2) "that the defendant's conduct contributed to his injury." *In re Multidistrict Vehicle Air Pollution M.D.L.*, 481 F.2d 122, 130 n.11 (9th Cir. 1973). If a plaintiff cannot plead both of these requirements, the complaint must be dismissed. *See, e.g., Associated Gen. Contractors*, 459 U.S. at 546; *Vehicle Air Pollution*, 481 F.2d at 129-130.

After reading these paragraphs, the reader can easily anticipate where the argument will go next — to claim that the injury alleged by the plaintiffs is not the type of injury that the antitrust law protects. The writer accomplishes this task by setting forth principles and then citing authority (here, cases) to support those principles. Gradually, the argument settles on the specific issues that the court must decide on the appeal.

Here is another example of "drilling down" on the specific issue in a defamation appeal:

A. Audition's Fleeting, First-Name References Do Not Disparage Plaintiff to a "Considerable Segment in the Community"

As the district court correctly held, Plaintiff's defamation claim fails as a matter of law because the "number of people [who] would have been able to recognize the book's oblique references to the plaintiff is "small" and that group, "according to the Complaint," "would also likely have been aware of the circumstances of [plaintiff's] expulsion that were the subject matter of the accused statements." Pl. Add. 21. To be defamatory, a statement must be understood by a "considerable . . . segment in the community" to disparage the plaintiff rather than someone else. *E.g., Amrak Prods.,* 410 F.3d at 72-73. If only a small group would identify the plaintiff as the statement's subject or acquire any negative impression of her because of it, that statement is incapable of sufficiently damaging the plaintiff's reputation and is not actionable. Id. "[W]hether a communication is reasonably susceptible of a defamatory meaning [. . .] is a question of law for the court." Id. at 72 (citing *Phelan v. May Dep't Stores Co.,* 443 Mass. 52, 56, 819 N.E.2d 550, 554 (2004)).

In *Amrak Productions Inc. v. Morton,* for example, . . .

By the time the second paragraph appears, the reader knows that a "considerable" segment of the community must understand that the allegedly defamatory statement refers to the plaintiff and not to someone else. The new paragraph then starts by referring to a specific case. You can anticipate what will come next — at this point the writer is in a position to use the six steps outlined above. The brief will now set out the facts and holding of the precedent, and then compare those facts to the facts of the present case. It will then reach a conclusion on the "considerable segment in the community" issue.

5. Making Factual Comparisons

In using case law, the heart of the analytic process is the comparison — showing the court why the precedent case is analogous to the case before the court, and thus should control its outcome. The easiest (and rarest) situation is where the facts of the precedent are the same, or virtually the same, as the case that the court must decide. Here is an example of a brief citing that type of case. The issue was whether the court-appointed counsel for a minor could be deemed a "state actor" for purposes of liability under the federal Civil Rights Act:

Two cases have directly addressed the issue of whether or not a minor's counsel can be deemed to be a state actor, such that section 1983 liability can attach. *Deluz v. Cohen, supra,* 2011 U.S. Dist. LEXIS 16285; *Berman v. McManus, supra,* 2011 U.S. Dist. LEXIS 57841. In each case, the court concluded that a court-appointed minor's counsel is not a state actor for the purposes of section 1983 claims. *DeLuz, supra,* at *14; *Berman, supra,* at *57-58.

Berman is very similar to the instant case. There, a disgruntled father involved in a custody dispute filed suit against a number of individuals, including the court-appointed minor's counsel. Id. at *5-6. As to the minor's counsel, the plaintiff in *Berman* alleged eleven different "incidents" arising out of the minor's counsel's performance of her duties. Id. at *11-12. The father's allegations also included a claim under section 1983, accusing the minor's counsel of fraudulent actions in order to deprive the father of his visitation rights and familial relationship with his daughters. Id.

The court in *Berman* dismissed the section 1983 claim for lack of subject matter jurisdiction. Id. at *58-59. In so doing, the court found that the minor's counsel was not a state actor — a prerequisite to liability under section 1983. Id. According to the court, while a private actor can theoretically act under the color of state law, the alleged infringement of federal rights must be "fairly attributable" to the state in order for section 1983 liability to attach. Id., citing *Kirtley v. Rainey, supra,* 326 F.3d at 1092. However, as the court persuasively found in *Berman,* actions taken by a court-appointed minor's counsel are not fairly attributable to the state, because a court-appointed minor's counsel is more like a public defender, a state-appointed guardian ad litem, or a court-appointed minor's counsel in a juvenile delinquency proceeding. *Berman* at *58-59. In each of those circumstances, courts have found that the attorney was not acting under the color of state law. Id. at *57-58, citing *Polk County v. Dodson,* 454 U.S. 312, 325 (1981) [public defender]; *Miranda v. Clark County, Nev.,* 319 F.3d 465, 468 (9th Cir. 2003) [same]; *Kirtley v. Rainey, supra,* 326 F.3d at 1092-1096 [guardian ad litem]; *Malachowski v. City of Keene,* 787 F.2d 704, 710 (1st Cir. 1986) [juvenile's counsel in delinquency proceeding].

[A]s the court[] in . . . *Berman* . . . held, and as the district court in this case also held, a minor's counsel is similar in all material respects to a public defender, guardian ad litem, or juvenile's counsel in a delinquency proceeding. [Accordingly, they] should be treated as such for purposes of section 1983 liability.

Notice how the brief includes all six of the steps outlined above in this chapter. It (1) identifies the issue, (2) sets out the facts of the precedent, (3) sets out the holding of the precedent, (4) identifies the facts of the present case, (5) compares them with the facts of the precedent, and (6) reaches a conclusion. As the facts of a precedent become more different from the present case, the difficulty in comparing the cases rises.

Here is another excerpt from a brief addressing the "primary assumption of risk" doctrine in tort law. The brief first cites cases to establish a general principle that naturally occurring hazards are inherent in skiing and a ski operator has no duty to eliminate them. Then, the brief turns to analogizing the facts of two precedents to those of the present case:

Many cases uphold application of assumption of risk to skiers or snowboarders that are injured or killed in falls on steep slopes. In *O'Donoghue*, for example, the plaintiff chose to ski on an advanced run, saw an opening between some trees where he thought he could cross over to another ski run, but realized too late the run bordered an unmarked ravine filled with boulders. Traveling too fast to stop, O'Donoghue fell into the ravine, suffering severe injuries. (*O'Donoghue*, 30 Cal. App. 4th at 191.) In affirming summary judgment for the ski area, the appellate court rejected as "irrelevant" O'Donoghue's claim that he never saw the ravine before he fell into it. (Id. at 193.) As the court observed, "plaintiff was purposely skiing on an advanced run. . . . He could expect to encounter more hazards on the advanced run than on training or beginner slopes. . . . Defendant cannot be expected to change the entire mountain to insure plaintiff's safety." (Ibid.)

Similarly, in *Kane*, 88 Cal. App. 4th 204, judgment was directed for the ski area where plaintiffs claimed they had not seen a dangerous canyon. There, John and Colleen Kane participated in a skills clinic as part of their training as volunteer National Ski Patrollers. The instructor brought the clinic class to the most difficult trail at the ski area and asked the participants to ski a portion of the trail that was icy and spotted with trees, rocks, and stumps. The Kanes were reluctant, but the instructor urged them on. (Id. at 207-208.) John Kane fell when one of his skis lost its edge on the icy snow, and he slid downhill and over the edge of the trail into Bow Canyon. When his wife attempted to ski down to look over the edge of the trail, she also fell and slid into the canyon. John Kane died, and Colleen Kane was severely injured. (Id. at 208.)

In her wrongful death suit, Ms. Kane alleged negligence and recklessness in the way the clinic was conducted. . . . [T]he appellate court . . . directed a verdict entered in favor of defendants, based on the doctrine of primary assumption of risk. While the instructor "[p]lainly . . . did not properly assess the ability and stamina of the Kanes or the fatal hazard posed by Bow Canyon," "[f]alling and thereby being injured or even killed are inherent dangers of skiing." (Id. at 213-14.) The court concluded: "Were operators of ski resorts required to entirely eliminate the danger of falling in difficult terrain, the prospect of liability would effectively terminate the business of ski resort operation." (Id. at 214 [internal citations omitted].)

Jessica — like O'Donoghue and the Kanes — lost control, fell, slid, and struck rocks below. Each of the risks Jessica encountered is an inherent risk of skiing and snowboarding. Alpine Meadows had neither a duty to eliminate those risks nor to reduce them. They are inherent in the sport. The Plaintiffs' claims were properly dismissed.

In using cases, focus carefully on the comparison you are making between the precedent and the present case. In many briefs, particularly those of young lawyers, the tendency is to describe the facts of the precedent case and then start a new paragraph that reads something like this:

> Here, as in the *Smith* case, the plaintiff was aware of facts sufficient to put him on notice of the cause of action . . .

There is no real comparison of the two cases. Instead, the "as in the *Smith* case" phrase leaves the comparison to the reader. Avoid that tendency. Make your comparisons sharp. Here is an example of a convincing comparison from a brief filed by the Solicitor General of the United States. At issue is the applicability of the Court's earlier holding in *Fedorenko v. United States*, 449 U.S. 490 (1981):

> Third, petitioner suggests (Br. 43 n.12) that the *Fedorenko* analysis does not apply because (in his view) his conduct was less egregious than Fedorenko's. There is no textual basis for such a result; if a person assisted in persecution, he is barred under both the DPA and INA. In any event, petitioner's conduct is strikingly similar to Fedorenko's: both were trained to serve as prison guards after a period of incarceration by armed forces; both stood guard as persons were tortured and killed on account of protected grounds; both were armed and charged with keeping prisoners from escaping; both received payment for their services; and both served as guards for several years. Compare *Fedorenko*, 449 U.S. at 494, 498-500 & n.12, with Pet. App. 12a-13a, 15a-16a; J.A. [Joint Appendix]18-20, 26, 40, 42, 58-59; A.R. 328-383. Just as this Court refused to rewrite the statutory text to excuse Fedorenko, it should refuse to rewrite the INA for petitioner.

6. Distinguishing Cases

At times you will find yourself distinguishing cases cited by opposing counsel. A case is obviously distinguishable if it raises a different issue than the one before the court in the appeal you are briefing. More likely, however, you will find yourself trying to distinguish the case by showing that critical facts differ from the facts of the precedent.

Here is an edited sample from a brief in a criminal case where the issue was probable cause to make a warrantless arrest. Notice the clear contrast of the facts of the precedent *Blackmon* case from those of the present case:

> The *Blackmon* decision, *supra*, is instructive. There, the officers' reasonable suspicion ripened into probable cause when their attempts to make verbal contact with Blackmon failed and he remained unresponsive to twenty commands by the officers that Blackmon, suspected of violating a protection order and believed to be high on PCP, get on the ground. Blackmon then "raised his fists as if he was ready to fight." 662 F.3d at 985-86. This Court determined officers at this point had probable cause to arrest Blackmon for resisting arrest. *Id.* at 986.

In contrast to the verbal contact initiated by the officers in *Blackmon*, in the present case Officer Stein made no attempt to make verbal contact or communicate with Winarske. Stein simply approached the car in which Winarske was sitting, ordered him out, handcuffed Winarske, and evidently placed him under arrest. Unlike *Blackmon*, where the suspect would not reply to commands and seemed ready to fight, Winarske was not unresponsive to Stein's commands and did not resist Stein. Different from the circumstances in *Blackmon* where this Court found probable cause existed, the totality of the circumstances in Winarske's case demonstrate that Stein lacked probable cause to make a warrantless arrest of Winarske or even take him into custody beyond the limits of *Terry*.

Again, the key is to confront the facts of the precedent and show how they differ from the present case. The best briefs fully lay out that comparison, thus demonstrating confidence in their analysis. Here is an example of an argument in a case involving whether an attorney's fee provision in a contract's arbitration clause would support an award of attorney's fees for a judicial proceeding. As you will see, the argument distinguishes an earlier case, *Ajida*, on the ground that the provision at issue in that case was quite different:

Moreover, permitting appellate attorney fees in *Ajida* made sense given the broad attorney fee provision in the arbitration award that explicitly permitted fees "in any dispute" arising under the arbitration award. But here, the parties' attorney fee provision contained no language resembling the "in any dispute" clause justifying an award of fees for judicial proceedings in *Ajida*. Rather, the parties' narrow fee provision permitted only those attorney fees incurred during arbitration and awarded as part of a final arbitration award. For these reasons, *Ajida* does not factor into the calculus here.

7. Applying Statutes

An argument that applies a statute requires a slightly different approach than using a case. The goal is the same — to reach an outcome based on the case or statute. With statutes, however, you are applying the facts in your case to the specific wording in the statute. No comparison of facts is involved.

Still, the overall approach is similar. You must identify the issue that the statute will resolve and the relevant facts in your case. You then apply the facts to the statute and reach a conclusion. Once again, as with cases, do not leave the application to the reader; set it forth specifically in your argument.

Here is another example from a brief filed by the Solicitor General of the United States:

As in any case of statutory construction, this Court's analysis "begins with the language of the statute." *Hughes Aircraft Co. v. Jacobson*, 525 U.S. 432, 438 (1999) (internal quotation marks omitted)....

As relevant here, the INA [Immigration and Nationality Act] bars any person who "ordered, incited, assisted, or otherwise participated in the persecution of" any person on account of "race, religion, nationality, membership in a particular social group, or political opinion" from obtaining asylum or withholding of removal. 8 U.S.C. 1101(a)(42), 1158(b)(2)(A)(i), 1231(b)(3)(B)(i). The question in this case is whether there is an exception to that persecutor bar for an alien who claims that he did not act out of malice or that his conduct was coerced. The statutory text directly answers that question: there is no such exception. . . .

The language of the persecutor bar is broad and categorical. It denies eligibility for asylum and withholding of removal to "any person" who has participated in the persecution of "any person" on account of a protected ground. 8 U.S.C. 1101(a)(42); *see* 8 U.S.C. 1158(b)(2)(A)(i) (bars "the alien" who participates in the persecution of "any person"), 1231(b)(3)(B)(i) (bars "an alien" who participates in the persecution of "an individual"). "[T]he word 'any' has an expansive meaning," and it suggests that Congress intended no limitation on the statute's reach other than that apparent from the text. *Ali v. Federal Bureau of Prisons,* 128 S. Ct. 831, 835-836 (2008).

Moreover, Congress chose comprehensive language to describe the conduct that triggers the persecutor bar, barring those persons who "ordered, incited, assisted, or otherwise participated" in persecution. Those verbs encompass a wide range of conduct, from taking a leadership role in persecution ("ordered" or "incited") to providing aid ("assisted") or otherwise furthering ("participated in") acts of persecution. The breadth of the words used thus demonstrates Congress's intent to reach *all* aliens who participated in persecuting others, regardless of their role.

The quoted passage illustrates several features of a good argument applying a statute. First, it identifies the specific language of the statute at issue and then applies the statute to the facts. The relevant statutory language bars persons who persecuted individuals on the grounds of race, religion, etc., from obtaining asylum or preventing removal from the country. The brief then concludes that the statutory language cannot support an exception to its reach.

Second, the brief builds on that conclusion by emphasizing specific words in the statute. Here, it focuses on the word *any* as indicating that Congress intended the statutory language to reach broadly. And it emphasizes the array of language — "ordered, incited, assisted, or otherwise participated" in persecution — as demonstrating an intent to reach all individuals who persecute.

Third, it cites other cases that dealt with the meaning of words found in this statute. One of those cases talked about the meaning of the word *any,* and the brief folds that authority into its argument.

8. Policy or Intent Arguments — Know Your Audience

A final type of argument contends that a policy or settled purpose of the law would support a particular decision by the court on the issue posed. Given the emphasis on policy in some law school classes, one can easily conclude that this type of argument is always central to the appellate process. Depending on the appellate court, however, policy may have little effect on the outcome. Because intermediate appellate court review is circumscribed and generally limited to reversing for prejudicial error, a policy argument is rarely decisive. Rather, advocates in the intermediate appellate courts should emphasize legal authority that courts must apply in given situations, such as case precedents and statutes. In contrast, in the courts of last resort both at the state and federal level, policy arguments may play a greater role in assisting the court to discern the intent of the legislature or the framers of the Constitution.

A policy argument cannot persuade a court where a case on point, or a statute, specifically calls for a different result. Such an argument might, however, tip the scales in a close case. Here is an example of a policy argument in a case applying the federal Speedy Trial Act:

B. Excluding Additional Time Granted at a Defendant's Request To File Pretrial Motions Furthers the Purposes of the Speedy Trial Act

Interpreting Section 3161(h)(1) to exclude additional time for filing pretrial motions granted at a defendant's request furthers the purposes of that provision and the Speedy Trial Act as a whole. As discussed above, Section 3161(h)(1) is designed to exclude delay arising from proceedings that advance the defendant's case towards trial or other resolution, particularly procedures of which the defendant might legitimately take advantage to pursue his defense. *See United States v. Mobile Materials, Inc.,* 871 F.2d 902, 913 (10th Cir.) (per curiam), *opinion supplemented on other grounds on reh'g,* 881 F.2d 866 (10th Cir. 1989) (per curiam), *cert. denied,* 493 U.S. 1043 (1990); *Jodoin,* 672 F.2d at 238. Grants of additional time to explore whether to file and to prepare pretrial motions, like pretrial motions themselves, serve those goals.

Pretrial motions — such as motions to suppress evidence or to dismiss the indictment — advance the case towards resolution because they shape the content or structure of the trial and may even eliminate the need for trial altogether. The same is true of additional time granted at a defendant's request to research, prepare, and file pretrial motions. Motions cannot be resolved fairly and accurately if a defendant has insufficient time to prepare them. And if the additional time leads a defendant to conclude that he should not file any motions, that result too promotes efficient resolution of the case.

The first prerequisite for an effective policy argument is to identify the specific policy that will serve as the basis for the argument. This task is not an exercise in ingenuity; rather, counsel must locate the policy in statutory language, previous case law, or legislative findings in the statute or in the legislative history. In the excerpt above, the argument cites two previous appellate decisions that determined the purpose of the Speedy Trial Act. The argument then logically details how a decision in the client's favor will promote the specific purpose in question.

Even when cases are clear, keep in mind that it is critical for the writer to tell the court not only that the writer's side should win, but *why* the writer's side should win. Policy arguments speak directly to that point. In fact, one of the values of making policy arguments, even at the intermediate appellate courts, is that they allow the court to view the case before it in a broader context. Reaching a conclusion that is supported by a public policy also reassures judges that the conclusion is not only legally required, but it is also reasonable and fair.

Nonetheless, remember the overall point: A policy analysis will not substitute for the use of cases and statutes to convince a court of a position.

9. Using Quotations in Making Arguments

At some point, you will have to choose whether to use a quotation from a case. Start by asking yourself where the quote would fit into your analysis. If you are using a case, the quote is most helpful as part of your explanation of the court's holding. A quote can explain the court's reasoning. For an issue involving the interpretation of a statute, the quote from a case is best used to help explain the meaning of a word or phrase in the statute.

In general, you should use quotes sparingly, only after carefully deliberating their usefulness to you in the specific context. Most importantly, and strange as it may seem, you can generally express the point better and more directly by putting it in your own words. *You* get to choose the words to use (within the limits, it goes without saying, of accuracy). In contrast, when you use a quote, you are inserting someone else's writing into your brief. Further, the use of long quotes from the law is not a substitute for thoughtful analysis. In fact, over-reliance on quotations suggests to the reader that the writer does not understand the law. In addition, the writing style of the precedent simply may not fit well with the other parts of the brief. Finally, if the quote is too long, it is tiresome to read.

Still, a quote can powerfully make a point that helps you. So follow this rule: Use a quote when the wording in the precedent is both sharp and directly to the point. But keep it short — no more than half a dozen lines. Also, consider whether to use an introductory phrase or sentence summarizing what the quote will say.

Finally, keep in mind former Circuit Judge Kozinski's warning: "Let's face it, if the block quote really had something useful in it, the lawyer would have given me a pithy paraphrase." Alex Kozinski, *How You Too Can Lose Your Appeal*, 23 MONT. LAW. 3 (1997).

10. To Footnote or Not?

Lastly, we take up another point that inevitably arises: When should a brief use a footnote? As discussed in Chapter Two, the perspective principle can answer this question. You must consider the mental tasks that a footnote requires of the reader. First, the reader must decide whether to read the footnote at all; after all, it's just a footnote and thus, by definition, not as important as the text of the brief. If the reader opts to read it, the reader then must decide whether to read the footnote now or at some other time, say, after reading to the end of this page. At either point the reader looks to the bottom of the page and reads the footnote. After finishing, the reader must come back to the text and find the particular point where the reader left off in the text.

At a minimum, this entire effort is distracting. It will divert the reader's attention — a precious commodity, from your standpoint — away from the main thread of the argument.

So keep your footnotes to an absolute minimum. Do not put anything important in a footnote. The reader should be able to read the entire brief and should think that the brief is complete and convincing without referring to any footnotes. Refraining from using footnotes requires self-control. If, in writing, you find that certain points are relevant but do not fit well into the main argument, the natural tendency is to include those points in a footnote. One set of authors has termed this type of footnote as a "cameo footnote" — "a discussion that addresses a nice, little point, perhaps even an interesting point in one sense, but one that is not integral to the flow of the argument to which it is appended." Philip A. Lacovera (ed.), FEDERAL APPELLATE PRACTICE 311 (2008).

Most such footnotes should be discarded as unnecessarily distracting. Just ask yourself: Do you *really* need this footnote?

It is appropriate to include a footnote in your brief in only a small handful of situations. For example, a footnote may be helpful to provide the full context for a statement in the text — to quote extensive language of a rule, statute, regulation, will, contract, or other essential document where the text of the brief refers only to an excerpt.

Finally, if you put a footnote in, try to locate it at a point in the argument that will allow the reader to make an "easy return" to the text. The best place is at the very end of a paragraph. In second place — but a distant second — is the end of a sentence within a paragraph.

C. TRANSITIONS

At this point we can visualize the argument as addressing a series of issues and using precedents. But the various arguments on the issues are not connected; for now, they simply exist. How do we connect them and build them into a coherent, overall structure?

The connection occurs through the use of transition devices. A transition can be a word, a phrase, a sentence, or a paragraph. The purpose of a transition is to send a signal to readers telling them where the discussion is going next, or to summarize where the discussion has just gone. Transitions are road signs.

The importance of transitions stems from the perspective principle. Put yourselves in the shoes of the reader. Even the simplest appellate case requires a judge to master a large body of material: the facts of the case, the outcome below, the use of many cases and statutes, etc. While this material may seem obvious to you (the expert, with your expertise acquired after hours of work), it may seem quite complicated to the appellate judge, someone new to the case. That judge must constantly be able to follow your argument if you are going to persuade.

Transition devices help the writer make sure that the judge "stays with" the argument as it progresses through the brief. Even if you think the judge could stay with you without that transition device, you do not want to take the chance that you are wrong.

Transitions are critically important and often underused by inexperienced (or ineffective) legal writers. Why are they so important? Think of it this way: There should be *no* mystery about the outcome in good legal writing. Instead of leaving the outcome of the analysis to the very end, the reader needs to be told the outcome from the beginning. Then, as the brief sets out each step of the legal analysis, the reader needs to be carefully brought along to reach that outcome.

The transitions tell the reader whether the next case used will reach the same outcome as the previous case, or whether that precedent case will be distinguished. The transition tells the reader when the argument is changing to a new issue. The transition tells the reader that the analysis is turning to a discussion of policy. At the end of a discussion, the transition reminds the reader about the outcome of the analysis of that specific issue. You get the idea.

In sum, transitions accomplish the task of signaling to the reader where the discussion is going. They are a kind of glue that joins together the groups of "building blocks" in a legal argument: the blocks that applied cases and statutes. Transitions can accomplish this task in various ways.

1. The Structure of Transitions

What do transitions look like? They come in different forms. Some transitions are complete paragraphs, although they will be short. Other transitions are the first sentences in paragraphs. These are often known as "topic sentences," and they set out the principal idea found in the paragraph, or next couple of paragraphs. They tell the reader the "conclusion" — where the argument is leading them — before it does so. A transition can be the last sentence in the paragraph summarizing the points made above. Finally, the transition can be a single word, usually at the beginning of a sentence but sometimes even in the middle.

Whatever their form, however, transitions have a common feature. They inform the reader in some fashion about the progress of the analysis. In reading the following example, in a case that involves the statute of limitations, ask yourself what information the transition gives you:

> The trial court erroneously relied upon two prior decisions by this Court: *Plaza Speedway, Inc. v. United States*, 311 F.3d 1262 (10th Cir. 2002) and *Cannon v. United States*, 338 F.3d 1183 (10th Cir. 2003). Neither of these cases, however, can reasonably be read to suggest that the mere suspicion of a lay individual about a medical condition suffices to trigger the statute of limitations, especially when reliable medical evidence discredits that suspicion. In *Plaza,* . . .

You can see from this transition that the argument will address two cases upon which the trial court relied. In doing so, however, the transition also tells

the reader where the discussion will come out. Finally, a last small transition—
"In *Plaza*, . . ." — informs the reader that the brief will proceed directly into a discussion of that case.

Here is another example, a transition sentence at the beginning of a new paragraph:

> The court applied the same rule in *Sierra Club v. Young Life Campaign, Inc.*,
> 176 F. Supp. 2d 1070 (D. Colo. 2001). . . .

The sentence acts as a kind of roadmap, telling the reader that the discussion will continue on the same rule that was just examined in the previous paragraph. It allows the reader to anticipate where the discussion is going in light of the previous paragraph — to connect the thread of the argument.

The same transition may look both forward and backward. For example, the reader may be reminded that the discussion previously dealt with two parts of a given test and is now going on to the third part of the test. Or a transition may inform the reader that, if the previous argument failed, then the appellant (or appellee) still cannot prevail for another reason. Here is an example of that type of transition, which deals with an express release in a tort suit:

> Even if the Court were to conclude that the release unambiguously applies
> to the facts here, the release would still be unenforceable as against public policy. A release cannot exculpate a violation of law.

This "two-headed" transition tells the reader that (1) the discussion is over with respect to the application of the release, but (2) even if the court found that the release did apply, it would be unenforceable as against public policy.

As should be clear by now, argumentative legal analysis is a very specific type of writing. It is designed to persuade, and it uses cases or statutes to do so. All briefs share these features. As a consequence, certain kinds of transition words and phrases often recur in briefs. These specific transitions are particularly useful in transmitting information about the application of a case precedent. As you read the following, think about when each of these particular transitions would be useful:

1. Transitions that enumerate or indicate order: *first, second, finally, lastly*, etc.
2. Transitions that indicate additions to what has gone before: *moreover, in addition, additionally, furthermore, also*
3. Transitions that indicate exceptions or negations to what has gone before: *but, however, nevertheless, yet, on the contrary*
4. Transitions that indicate a conclusion from what has just been said: *therefore, thus, accordingly, as a result, consequently*
5. Transitions that indicate a specification of what has just been said: *for example, in particular*

But you are not limited to this list; other formulations are possible. Here, for example, is a list of transitions that can you use to keep the flow of the writing:

along the same lines; in that respect; in short; indeed; in all events; in contrast; in the same way; in any event; in spite of; all of that may be true, but; for instance; to that end, quite the contrary; what is more; the bottom line; if anything; to be sure and that is why.

2. Caution and Precision

Two final warnings in using transitions:

Caution No. One: You cannot simply insert transitions into your writing without thinking about them. The words *tell* your reader something; they convey information. If they convey false information, the reader is betrayed.

For example, if you are analyzing a case and want to distinguish it, you will not want to use the transition word *similarly*. This word indicates to the reader that the cases are alike, when you mean exactly the opposite. You will have a confused and, ultimately, unhappy reader on your hands.

Caution No. Two: Be as precise and informative as possible in using your transitions. The more information that you can convey to the reader in a transition, the better. For example, you could use the phrase *Another issue is . . .* as a transition from one issue to another. But that transition does not link the new issue to the previous issue, even if just to tell the reader that they are unrelated, or give any other context to the new issue. You are not misleading the reader, but you are hurting yourself by forgoing the opportunity to offer a navigational aid to your reader. The reader gets to swim when you could have thrown a rope and pulled them along.

So something like this is much better: "While the statute of limitations bars Robinson's action, even if it did not, the defendant Akers owed no legal duty to Robinson under settled law." This "topic sentence" transition fully situates the reader on where the argument stands at that point.

Summary

- To apply a precedent to the facts of the case on appeal, the court must first identify the issue to be decided. It then must examine the facts and holding of the precedent, and determine the relevant facts of the present case. It then compares the facts of the precedent case to those of the present case and reaches a conclusion. These steps are the core of the legal analysis.

- A court does not always need to go through all these steps. But on the central issues of the case, it must apply the precedent in this manner.

- Applying a statute is similar. The court applies the facts of the present case to the text of the statute and reaches a conclusion about the statute's applicability.

- You must give the court the background legal information needed to set up the issue that you are raising.

- Under your point heading, but before the first subheading, you can summarize the argument you are making under that heading, thus "previewing" the argument for the court.

- Comparing the facts of the precedent case to those of the present case is quite difficult. You must avoid the tendency to leave that comparison to the court by using phrases like "as in the *Smith* case" and then not actually showing why the two cases are analogous. Instead, you must specifically explain why the facts are comparable.

- Applying statutes requires you to identify the issue that the statute will resolve and then apply the relevant facts to the pertinent statutory language. Again, you cannot leave the actual application to the court; instead, you must explain precisely what outcome you reach, and why. Be careful to apply all the pertinent words in the statute and use the various other tools of statutory construction.

- A policy argument will not substitute for use of actual legal authority, but it can bolster the argument that you made with that legal authority.

- Use quotations from cases sparingly, and do not use long block quotes. Use footnotes sparingly as well and locate the footnote in the text where it will minimize the distraction to the reader.

- Transitions link the various parts of the argument together. They tell the court where the argument is going, and sometimes point to what part of the argument came previously. Transitions are words, sentences, and even short paragraphs.

Appendix B contains exercises that ask you to evaluate two arguments in light of the principles discussed in this chapter.

CHAPTER 9

The Introduction or Summary of Argument

A. PREVIEWING THE CASE TO THE COURT

When judges first turn their attention to an appeal, they might desire to obtain an overview of the matter. To do so, a judge could examine the point headings, which encapsulate the arguments made in the brief. Another possibility is to look at the statement of the issues to see what lies ahead.

There is, however, another option. Almost every brief will contain either an introduction, sometimes known as a preliminary statement, or a summary of argument. Some briefs (relatively few) have both. In a couple of pages, these sections lay out what the appeal is about and synopsize the arguments about to be made.

1. The Perspective Principle (Once Again)

If you place yourself in the shoes of the judge, you can see how important this part of the brief is. The judges will read it early in their consideration of the case. Moreover, they will do so expecting that in it the lawyer for the party will present the appeal in a manner that quickly allows the judge to get a "handle" on the issues.

In short, the introduction or summary offers the appellate lawyer a critical opportunity to present an overview of the case. Initial impressions of a case are important, and the judges will form impressions from this part of the brief. So the appellate lawyer must pay close attention to it.

2. Differentiating an Introduction from a Summary of Argument

While there is a large overlap between an introduction and a summary of argument, differences exist. The phrase *summary of argument* accurately states its content. In short form, the summary will set forth the series of arguments—or, at least, the principal arguments—found in the argument section of the brief. The summary thus acts as a specific synopsis of what is to come.

An introduction likewise will summarize the main arguments found in the brief. But its charter is a bit broader. The introduction allows the advocate to establish themes in the brief, to emphasize certain key facts, and to paint a more comprehensive picture of the case from that party's standpoint. If relevant, it also briefly describes the procedural history so the reader understands how the case arrived at the appellate court. In contrast, a summary of argument should not stray much past the "summarizing" line, particularly if a rule of court prohibits a more expansive approach.

Put another way, an introduction can be more artful and informative than a summary. It can go beyond the summary by placing the actual legal argument in a broader factual and procedural context. That context can be human, emphasizing the fairness of ruling in favor of the party. Or it might be legal, showing the court how a ruling for the party will be consistent with the overall development of the law. Thus, the introduction adds to the arguments, while the summary narrowly encapsulates them.

In the discussion that follows, references to an "introduction" apply to both an "introduction" and "summary of argument," except where the discussion indicates otherwise.

3. Checking the Court's Rules

As with much of appellate practice, the rules of court are the place to start in determining the content of this part of the brief. In the federal system, Federal Rule of Appellate Procedure 28(a)(7) requires the brief to include "a summary of the argument, which must contain a succinct, clear, and accurate statement of the arguments made in the body of the brief, and which must not merely repeat the argument headings." The Seventh Circuit's *Practitioner's Handbook for Appeals* goes on to recommend that, "[f]or longer summaries it is useful to the court that the summary include references to the pages of the brief at which the principal contentions are made." http://www.ca7.uscourts.gov/rules-procedures/Handbook.pdf, at 158.

Many court rules, however, are silent about the introduction or summary of argument. This silence, of course, means that a brief is not required to contain these parts. The introduction and summary of argument, however, play essential roles in briefs and are important tools for the advocate to employ. For that reason, you will want to include an introduction or summary even if the individual court rules do not call for it.

Finally, some briefs include *both* an introduction and a summary. In such briefs, the writer must ensure that the introduction clearly performs a different function than merely summarizing. Otherwise, the two parts will be duplicative, an outcome the court will not appreciate.

4. Purposes: Summarizing and Persuading

As explained above, the fundamental purpose of both the introduction and the summary is to inform the court of the legal arguments that the party is making. Yes, the introduction is somewhat broader in focus; it can take a bit more leeway in setting forth themes. But both parts center on the arguments.

Accordingly, keep in mind that the overall goal of the brief is to persuade, and that this goal pervades all parts of the brief. Thus, even though the summary of argument is just that, a *summary*, the goal of persuading the court is always in the advocate's mind. You must craft your summary accurately; it must honestly reflect the arguments that the court will read later. But even as you summarize, you can try to persuade through your word choice and by emphasizing certain key points.

Put another way, a summary does not have to be dry. It can be lively and should begin to persuade the reader. Below, Section C explores how persuasion can be achieved in a summary of an argument and introduction.

B. COMMON QUESTIONS FOR THE BRIEF WRITER

Before the writer has decided which elements of the case to feature in the introduction and summary of the argument to achieve persuasive aims, some additional matters must be considered. We discuss those in this section.

1. Location in the Brief and Its Consequences

The introduction and summary of argument are situated in different places of the brief. The summary of argument is almost always located in the brief just before the actual argument. Thus, the statement of facts and procedural background precede it, as does the statement of jurisdiction.

By contrast, introductions often appear at the very beginning of the brief. Their location here implicitly recognizes that introductions are broader than mere summaries of argument, often emphasizing factors such as the equities of the case. Lawyers choose to place the introduction at the beginning to take advantage of the fact that, at this place in the brief, the court's attention is likely at its peak.

The location has consequences. If a part of the brief is situated at the very beginning of the brief, everything in it will be new to the court. By contrast, if the summary is located just before the argument, the court will probably have read the statement of facts and procedural background first. So a summary at this location might rely on those facts and background in making its points.

A word of caution, however. A particular judge may well decide to read a summary of argument *first*, even though the summary is not the first section of the brief. Thus, if the summary assumes knowledge of facts from the statement of facts, or knowledge of the procedural background, then the summary will make less sense to the judge. So, in the end, you should make sure that your summary (or introduction, if placed just before the argument) reads well on its own and does not depend on previous knowledge. Test it for yourself: If the court were to read this section first, would the court completely understand it?

2. Deciding the Length

You must decide how long your introduction or summary should be. Of course, you remain subject to the overall word or page limits for briefs set forth in the rules of court. Furthermore, to some degree the number and complexity of the legal issues dictates the length of the summary. A long, complex antitrust case needs a longer summary, and a longer introduction, than a "one-issue" criminal appeal.

But the advocate must consider an important additional factor. By nature, a reader does not *expect* an introduction or a summary to be lengthy. If the introduction or summary runs long, readers will begin to get antsy and their attention may wane.

You must balance these considerations and exercise sound judgment. A good rule of thumb is that, unless the legal issues are unduly complicated, an introduction or summary should be no more than four pages, and if the appeal has only one issue, the introduction should really be no more than two pages in length. If you greatly exceed these limits, the introduction will be less effective because you can easily lose the reader's attention. Indeed, if the summary runs very long, the court might just give up mid-read, figuring that it is easier to read the actual argument below.

3. Sources of Material

The practitioner has an array of source material to choose from in crafting an introduction. The specific legal issues raised in the appeal can, of course, be discussed in a straightforward manner, and the key facts from the case are obviously available for use. Also, in some cases counsel should mention important parts of the procedural background to provide context.

However, in deciding what might begin to persuade the court, other materials can be summoned for use. An overarching legal principle might apply to the case, or there might be a key policy that the outcome will conflict with or support. The equities of the case might be particularly striking, or there might be consequences that will occur if the court decides the case in a certain way. Counsel will examine all the possibilities and choose the combination of these source materials that most persuasively advances the client's cause.

4. When to Write the Introduction or Summary: A Debate

You might think that because the introduction or summary is located before the argument in the brief you will want to write it before drafting the argument. That conclusion, however, is debatable.

Writing it first certainly seems logical. You have already done your research and drafted your point headings; thus, your arguments appear relatively settled at this point. Summarizing them, or writing an introduction that includes a summary, can help ensure that you are certain about your arguments. If you cannot summarize an argument easily, the argument likely has not sufficiently crystallized. Furthermore, by this point you have a good idea of the key themes that you wish to emphasize, and you can use them in an introduction, if you are writing one.

Nonetheless, there are strong reasons for writing the summary or introduction after you have written at least the first draft of the entire brief. Perhaps the most important reason is that your arguments are likely to change as you write them. You may drop an argument that is too weak, significantly alter an argument as you get into it, or even identify a new argument. These changes are a natural part of the brief writing process. Because they cause delay and involve wasted effort, you will try to minimize them by writing an outline. Nonetheless, thinking about an argument is not the same as writing it, and the weaknesses of an argument may not become fully apparent until you actually write it.

In short, the brief writing process is inevitably a process of discovery, and that discovery can change the focus and emphasis of the arguments you make. As two Supreme Court specialists put it, "Experienced brief writers know that the summary of argument is usually written after the argument itself. . . . [T]he structure of the argument tends to evolve over the course of drafting and editing." Andrew L. Frey & Roy T. Englert, Jr., *How to Write a Good Appellate Brief*, 20 LITIGATION 6, 12 (1994). Novice lawyers in particular are likely to find that their arguments have changed substantially in the process. Thus, if you write your introduction or summary first, it may become outdated or inaccurate by the time that you have finished refining and editing the argument.

So you have a choice about when to write the introduction or summary. For the attorney just learning the craft, however, the better option is to write the introduction or summary after completing the argument itself.

C. TECHNIQUES

Often the summary of the argument and the introduction are the shortest sections of the brief. While remaining focused on the key legal points and the dispositive facts, the writer must also keep certain matters in mind in drafting this section, including capturing the reader's attention and asking for relief. The writer must also use the opportunity presented by the summary and introduction to present themes, summarize their client's story, and frame their opponent's argument. Therefore, summary and introductions must accomplish a lot with limited space.

1. Capturing the Court's Attention

At their core, appeals are about people. Counsel often tries to quickly attract the court's attention by describing the people in the case, what happened to them, and, if appropriate, the theme of the case. In the following first paragraph of an introduction, the brief quickly encapsulates the key facts about the appellant that underlie the appeal:

> In this action, plaintiff, a steelworker, seeks to recover for damages he sustained when he fell through an unguarded opening in the floor of a building under construction and landed on a temporary metal structure, roughly ten feet below. The proof was undisputed that the opening had not been covered and that plaintiff had not been provided with a safety belt or harness for his work. Also undisputed was the fact that no lifelines or stanchions had been erected in the area of plaintiff's fall as anchorage points.
>
> Nevertheless, a divided Appellate Division concluded that plaintiff was not entitled to summary judgment . . . .

The paragraph sets forth the circumstances of the accident in which the plaintiff was injured, emphasizing the lack of safety measures. At the same time, the paragraph also emphasizes to the court the unsafe nature of the area in which the plaintiff was working.

The next example from an introduction takes just a bit longer to summarize the facts that gave rise to the appeal:

> On June 26, 2004, Jane Thompson was found beaten to death in her Laguna Niguel home. Sam Nelson, Thompson's fifteen-year-old neighbor, was subsequently identified as having made some purchases with her credit cards. On June 29, he was transported from his home to the sheriff department's headquarters in Santa Ana, advised of his *Miranda* rights, and then questioned over a six- to seven-hour period regarding Thompson's homicide and two neighborhood burglaries.
>
> A little over halfway through the interrogation process, and facing increasingly pointed questions about Thompson's murder and pressure to take a lie detector test, Nelson asked to call his mother. He wanted to tell her what was happening, talk to her about it, and see what he should do. He repeated this request to the officers several more times before being given a phone. Although he contacted other family members, he was unsuccessful in reaching his mother and eventually confessed to Thompson's murder and two neighborhood burglaries.
>
> The Court of Appeals reversed Nelson's murder conviction and two burglary convictions....

By the end of the first two paragraphs, the court has the people and the story firmly in mind. You should note that this introduction appeared in the brief before the statement of facts. Otherwise, the information would have duplicated what appeared in the statement of facts.

2. Telling the Story

The two examples set forth just above summarize the key facts in a relatively straightforward manner, without embellishment. In some cases, however, counsel may feel that the client's circumstances are particularly sympathetic. In the following example, counsel for a criminal appellant tries to use the opening paragraphs of the introduction to shed light on why the appellant acted as he did:

> On November 6, 1999, at the age of 23, petitioner Raymond Carrasco was struck by a railroad train while walking on the tracks. He was in a Class 3 coma, rated as a severe head injury, for two weeks, and was hospitalized for almost four months. In addition to severe injury to his right leg and right arm, he suffered permanent organic brain damage, rated as moderate to severe.
>
> As a result of the brain injury, he suffered wide mood swings, frustration, and increased irritability. People with this kind of injury have difficulty controlling

themselves, engage in behavioral problems, and are often verbally or physically abusive and short-tempered.

In a two-week period from August 1-15, 2000, Mr. Carrasco threatened to kill his wife on two occasions, threatened to burn down a neighbor's house, and threatened to kill his mother-in-law. He never took any steps to carry out any of these threats.

Mr. Carrasco was charged with making criminal threats in violation ...

The next introduction is from the opposite perspective, that of the prosecution:

In April 2007, appellant, a gang member, shot two complete strangers. He shot the first victim because that victim was "walking tough" in appellant's neighborhood, and he shot the second victim for "staring" at appellant and appellant's girlfriend. When officers arrested appellant days after the second incident, they found him hiding in the closet of his house wearing a bullet-proof vest and armed with two weapons and ample ammunition. He was apparently preparing for a gun battle with police.

On appeal, appellant argues that his conviction for active participation in a criminal street gang must be reversed pursuant to Penal Code Section 657 because ...

Did the prosecution effectively portray the defendant in its opening paragraph? What was your reaction?

3. Employing Themes

Conventional advice for appellate lawyers is to weave a theme into the brief and to introduce the theme early. A theme is a unifying idea that ties the argument together and that, at the same time, places the party's case in a favorable light. Themes are an essential part of appellate advocacy, and they should appear first in the introduction and sometimes in the summary of argument.

The theme might concern the unfairness of the statutory interpretation sought by the opponent. It could touch on the adverse consequences to others from a particular holding. It might concern the tactics used in the litigation. There are many variations.

Here is the first paragraph of the brief filed by states challenging the federal health care legislation, the Patient Protection and Affordable Care Act, in the Supreme Court:

The individual mandate rests on a claim of federal power that is both unprecedented and unbounded: the power to compel individuals to engage in commerce in order more effectively to regulate commerce. This asserted power does not exist. If Congress really had this remarkable authority, it would not have waited 220 years to exercise it. If this power really existed, both our Constitution and our constitutional history would look fundamentally different.

We would not have a federal government with limited and enumerated powers, or States that continue to enjoy dignity and residual sovereignty. The extraordinary power that the federal government claims here is simply incompatible with our founding document.

Were you able to identify a theme in this paragraph? Notice some of the key words and phrases used to characterize the Act: "unprecedented," "unbounded," "remarkable authority," "extraordinary power." Then look at the phrases used in addressing the relationship of the Act to the Constitution: "asserted power," "really existed," "look fundamentally different," "simply incompatible." The theme jumps out: The Act is unprecedented and without bounds, and it is fundamentally incompatible with the Constitution.

Themes, of course, often necessarily involve key facts from the case. Next, an example from an introduction to a United States Supreme Court brief (slightly edited) emphasizes two points: (1) the incompetence of counsel for a defendant convicted of murder, and (2) the passing of a critical appeal deadline without the defendant's fault:

> This case tests when events beyond an inmate's control may bar federal court review of the merits of serious constitutional claims on habeas. The petitioner, Cory Maples, is on death row in Alabama. The jury recommended death based on the slimmest margin allowed under the law. The trial and sentencing were also tainted by gross ineffectiveness on the part of Maples's court-appointed counsel. Those counsel themselves admitted that they were "stumbling around in the dark" given their inexperience in handling capital cases. *Infra* at 8-9.
>
> Maples seeks federal habeas review of the merits of his claim that he was convicted and sentenced to death in violation of the Sixth Amendment. The courts below, however, held that Maples lost the opportunity even to raise that claim to a federal court due to a missed deadline for which all agree that Maples himself bears no blame.

Here is a third example from a personal injury appeal. Do you see a theme in the first two paragraphs?

> Jessica Gregorie died too young. While carrying a snowboard in icy conditions along an ungroomed slope—which substantial evidence indicates was mismarked as being within the boundary of Alpine Meadows Ski Resort—she slipped, fell, and slid hundreds of feet to her death. She plunged over a hidden cliff and came to rest in a wilderness area adjacent to the resort. She was 24 years old.
>
> Jessica's parents, Daniel and Margaret Gregorie, filed this lawsuit out of a desire to prevent this sort of tragedy from happening again. This outcome can be easily accomplished with accurate signage that warns when a trail or traverse is located or leads outside the boundary of a ski resort. Signage of this type

allows patrons to make an informed decision whether to assume the increased risks of skiing or snowboarding in the backcountry.

Themes are useful persuasive devices. When placed in the opening sentences of an introduction, they can serve as a call to arms for the reader that evokes support for your client's position. Consider for example, the first two sentences of the Respondent's summary of the argument from *Bowers v. Hardwick*, 478 U.S. 186 (1986):

> The State of Georgia would extend its criminal law into the very bedrooms of its citizens, to break up even wholly consensual, noncommercial sexual relations between willing adults. And the State contends before this Court that it may freely do so without giving any good reason.

These sentences are evocative and effective. They cast the respondent's case in a favorable light. And they introduce a theme—the state's abuse of its police powers in violation of fundamental privacy rights—that appeals to the reader's sense of justice and fairness. Thus, the best themes are those that get the reader on board with your client's cause irrespective of ideology or worldview.

Developing a powerful and effective theme is not easy, however, and beginning appellate writers have to approach deploying them with care. Not only are persuasive themes difficult to identify, they must then be carefully employed in the brief. Using a theme effectively involves judgment; counsel must have a clear understanding about how the reader—here, the judges—will react to the theme. If a theme fails, that failure will reflect on the lawyer who used it and may affect how the entire argument is perceived. So the best advice for new lawyers is to use themes conservatively until you accumulate more experience.

4. Requesting Relief

Most importantly, in both an introduction and summary of argument, you want to tell the court what you want it to hold. As California Court of Appeal Justice Arthur Gilbert put it, "[Y]ou are not writing a mystery novel, so you should immediately tell the reader that the butler did it. In some cases, you may want to state the holding in the very first sentence."

Here is an example from the opening paragraph of an appellee's introduction that immediately gets to the point:

> The principal question in this appeal is whether business travelers, who live and work out-of-state, became covered by the State of California's wage-and-hour laws when they visit California on business trips. The trial court held that business travelers are subject to the wage-and-hour law of the state in which they are *based,* and that the applicable law does not vary when business travel occurs. This Court should affirm.

Note that in three sentences, the court knows what the appeal is principally about and the party's view as to how it should come out.

Here is another example from the first paragraph of an appellant's summary of argument:

> The district court erred in dismissing Ms. Velez's claims under the Alien Tort Statute and the Fair Labor Standards Act, and state law for breach of contract. The court also erred in holding that the Trafficking Victims Protection Reauthorization Act applies and preempts her claims.

The summary then went on to describe the district court's holding in more depth and to explain why, in the appellant's view, the district court erred.

A third example from an appellant's summary of argument uses a little more space to elaborate the central arguments:

> Appellant pleaded guilty to four counts of bank robbery, was found to be a Career Offender under the Sentencing Guidelines, and was sentenced to 188 months in prison. To be considered a Career Offender, he had to have two prior convictions for violent offenses that were counted separately under the Guidelines.
>
> He had two 1997 convictions for bank robbery, which the district court counted separately. The court erred for two separate reasons. First, the government was precluded from relitigating the factual issue whether these robberies were part of a common scheme or plan. Under the doctrine of collateral estoppel, that factual issue has been resolved against the government in a 2007 bank robbery case. Second, the district court erred in holding that the two bank robberies were not part of a single common scheme or plan, and thus would be counted separately under the Sentencing Guidelines.

Again, the approach here is straightforward: Tell the court what the issue on appeal is and why you should prevail. A summary of argument necessarily performs this function, and an introduction must do so as well.

5. Framing the Opponent's Argument

The responding brief in a case presents different considerations than the opening brief. In writing this brief, counsel has already read the opposing arguments. Now, in the introduction or summary of argument in the responding brief, counsel has the opportunity first to describe the opponent's argument, and then to immediately explain why that argument is wrong. Here is an example of that strategy taken from a summary of argument:

> Appellants contend that the order authorizing the wiretap of Jones's cellular phone violated Title III's "necessity" requirement because the government failed to fully exhaust other methods of investigation (Appellants' Brief at 21). On the contrary, the government's affidavit described the nature of the task force's drug

investigation, explained the need for the wiretap, recounted specific evidence, and stated reasons why other nonwiretap investigative techniques would be inadequate. This Court's decisions make clear that is all the government's affidavits needed to do to support the district court's wiretap authorization order.

Appellants also claim that the district court erred in refusing to hold an evidentiary hearing under *Franks v. Delaware*, 438 U.S. 154 (1978), to investigate alleged defects in the affidavit of FBI Special Agent Stephanie Yanta supporting the wiretap authorization order, and the extension of that order (Appellants' Brief at 18, 27-35). The district court did not clearly err in concluding that the challenged affidavits contained no statements that were intentionally misleading or made with reckless disregard for the truth, and that, in any event, any alleged misstatements or omissions were immaterial to the probable-cause finding.

The pattern employed here is to summarize the appellant's argument and then immediately confront it by explaining why it is wrong. Notice how the introduction includes citations to the appellant's brief, adding specificity to the quick counterattack.

Here is another example of this type of introduction, which starts by emphasizing key facts:

The Chief of Police of the City of Chula Vista (Chief) terminated the employment of police officer Moises Rodriguez (Rodriguez) for slamming the head of a nonviolent, handcuffed citizen into the hood of a police car and dishonestly reporting about his use of force thereafter. (AA 2, 4; RA 3.) The violence was captured on a security video camera of a convenience store. (AA 3; RA 3.) Rodriguez appealed the Chief's decision to the City of Chula Vista Civil Service Commission (Commission). (AA 4; RA 4.) It affirmed the termination. (AA 60-64.) Rodriguez petitioned for a writ of mandate in superior court. (AA 1-10.) The superior court denied the petition (AA 85-88.), and Rodriguez appeals. (AA 89-90.)

Rodriguez's primary contentions are that neither the Commission nor any court can believe what they see on the video and that the Chief can rely only on the video to sustain the Commission's decision. Rodriguez errs in both contentions.

Rodriguez also failed to brief an express independent ground on which the superior court denied his petition. The court may affirm the judgment on that ground alone.

A final possibility is to emphasize the tactics used by the opposing party as a theme. But bear in mind that characterizing opposing arguments is dangerous and can easily look unprofessional. Courts do not like parties "calling each other names." Still, in a small number of instances, if a party is convinced that its opponent *has* acted badly, the introduction might make use of those actions. Consider this first paragraph:

This appeal by the Indonesian Daily News is little more than an effort to escape responsibility for its failed litigation tactics and ill-guided efforts to intimidate its employees from participating in the litigation. Indeed, many of the rulings about which the News now complains are of its own making.

For example, Defendant claims that the trial court's orders ...

Themes like this one should be used only rarely, and only when you are certain that you can "make good" on such claims in the brief itself.

Summary

- Because judges often read the summary of argument or the introduction early in their consideration of the appeal, these parts of the brief present an important opportunity to affect the judges' first impression of the case.

- The summary of argument and introduction overlap, but there are differences. The summary acts as a synopsis of the overall argument, although it does not simply repeat that argument. An introduction paints a somewhat broader picture of the equities of the case, while also encapsulating the arguments made.

- Court rules may dictate that a summary or introduction must be used. If they are silent, however, the effective advocate will include one of them in any event.

- Experts debate whether to write the summary or introduction before or after writing the main argument. Younger lawyers or law students learning the craft will find it easier to write it after they have completed a solid draft of the argument.

- The introduction may be located at the beginning of the brief, while the summary is likely to be located within the brief just before the argument. The location will affect how they are written.

- In the first paragraph or two, both the summary and introduction should immediately state the basic premise of the appeal and the outcome sought. At the same time, the first paragraphs need to capture the court's attention.

- Finally, the summary and introduction may tell a story and employ themes that place the party's position in a favorable light.

Appendix B contains exercises that ask you to evaluate several introductions in light of the principles discussed in this chapter.

Basic Writing Rules and Other Mechanics

A. GOOD WRITING IS NOT A MATTER OF "STYLE"

We now turn to the mechanics of actually writing the brief. The importance of good writing skills to appellate work cannot be overestimated. The appellate brief "has become the preeminent feature of the appellate process . . . the main source of communication with the appellate court." Nancy Winkelman, *"Just a Brief Writer"?*, 29 LITIGATION 50 (2003).

One risk of bad writing, of course, is simply that the court will not understand your arguments. That much is obvious. "[J]udges must understand and remember your position before they can agree with it." Andrew L. Frey & Roy T. Englert, Jr., *How to Write a Good Appellate Brief,* 20 LITIGATION 6, 14 (1994).

But there is another risk. Even if the judge understands your positions, a badly written brief can lead a judge to suspect that those positions are wrong. Chief Justice John Roberts warns: "You don't have a lot of confidence in the substance if the writing is bad." Bryan A. Garner, *Interview with John G. Roberts Jr.,* 13 SCRIBES J. LEGAL WRITING 5, 6 (2010). The late Justice John Paul Stevens said much the same thing: "[I]t's perhaps unfair, but if someone uses improper grammar, you begin to think, well, maybe the person isn't as careful about . . . his or her work as he or she should be." Bryan A. Garner, *Interview with John Paul Stevens,* 13 SCRIBES J. LEGAL WRITING 41, 49 (2010).

Everyone exhibits some defensiveness about their writing, and law students may feel that criticism of their writing by law professors is simply a disagreement over "style." In the worst case, they view the criticism as arbitrary; the professor either "likes" or "does not like" the student's writing. After all, most students assume that they must be very good writers, or at least good ones. Otherwise, they never would have been admitted into law school.

Let's start with the last point. Most students *are* good writers, if the pool of overall writers is considered as either college students or, more generally, the public. But outstanding appellate lawyers must be excellent writers; their success depends upon their written product. The best appellate lawyers possess the ability to craft convincing legal arguments that flow seamlessly such that the reader is not really conscious of anything other than the reasoning. Law students must aspire to reach that level of writing. They are not nearly there yet.

If a brief at any point does not convey the information or point desired, even just slightly, the advocacy fails. For example, if a judge has to read a sentence twice before understanding its meaning, the advocate has lost an edge. And, of course, if the reader still cannot understand the sentence after rereading it, the writer has lost the battle to persuade.

As for the idea that criticism of student writing just reflects differences in "style," that assertion is theoretically possible. Legal writing does leave some room for creativity, and in an individual case, the criticism could center on the student's creativity rather than on the technical writing. However, over the last 40 years the legal profession has focused a significant amount of attention on what constitutes good legal writing, and out of that effort a consensus has emerged on methods to improve legal writing. These are *not* just stylistic points; they are empirically verified, concrete principles. If students diligently follow them, their writing will markedly improve. They will produce clear, readable briefs.

So the goal of the material below is to set forth a limited set of essential writing principles. There are many more, of course. The legal literature is rife with advice — much of it quite good. But too many principles will overwhelm you, so here we concentrate on the "basics."

A number of the most important principles are found in Richard C. Wydick's seminal work, PLAIN ENGLISH FOR LAWYERS (6th ed. 2019 with Amy E. Sloan). Others derive from research on how people read, from admonitions by judges, or from settled understanding about sentence structure. They are common sense principles, and their origin lies in detailed examinations of how good legal writing is constructed. At their base, all of them are fundamentally concerned with conveying information — the essential goal of any brief.

Failure to follow these principles scrupulously does not necessarily lead to disaster. For example, you can write briefs that contain excessive passive voices and make yourself understood. If you do overuse the passive voice, however, your writing will not be as effective as it could be. So if the principles improve your writing, why would you ignore them?

One final point: The news here about the writing principles is part "good" and part "bad." Let's take the good news first. The principles set forth below are relatively simple and few in number. They are not hard to understand. Now for the bad news: You need to internalize the principles so that you *automatically* follow them, and getting to that point takes a long time. So what do you do in the interim?

You attempt to comply with the principles in writing your first draft, but you do not overly focus on them. In your first draft, your goal is to get your ideas down on paper (or, more accurately, on the computer). Then, when you edit, you spend the time needed to conform to each one of the writing principles. In other words, editing is absolutely crucial to good legal writing, and your best work will emerge through the editing process. A critically important function of editing is to ensure compliance with the writing principles, so you must know them.

B. TEN WRITING PRINCIPLES TO FOLLOW

Working through these principles can sometimes seem tedious, and some of them are difficult. So here is one idea to keep in mind as you begin: If you assimilate and then implement the principles, you *will* write clear, readable briefs. You want to be a successful professional, so achieving that skill should motivate you as we go on.

1. Sentence Length

Read the following sentence[1]:

In decisions concerning the sentencing and correction of individual offenders, the general purposes of the law ought to be to render punishment within a range of severity sufficient to reflect the gravity of the offense and the blameworthiness of the offenders, and where there is a realistic prospect of success, to serve the goals of offender rehabilitation, general deterrence, incapacitation of dangerous offenders,

---

[1] Taken from Richard Wydick, PLAIN ENGLISH FOR LAWYERS 37 (5th ed. 2005).

and restoration of crime victims and communities, but to impose sentence no more severe than necessary to achieve the foregoing purposes.

Did you understand the sentence? If you did, was it easy to read? What was the problem with it? The answer is obvious. The sentence is simply too long.

Think of the mental process of reading a sentence as analogous to holding your breath. As the sentence gets longer and longer, it becomes more uncomfortable as you wait to exhale. You concentrate less on the sentence and begin thinking, "When will this sentence end?" Finally, you exhale, simply glad that you are done. In that situation, reading the sentence has become an ordeal and, in the end, the effort to read has increasingly drawn your focus away from the meaning of the sentence.

If you wrote that sentence, you have made reading the brief unpleasant or, even worse, you may have simply lost the reader. Long sentences tend to entangle thoughts so that the reader cannot easily follow them. If you are trying to persuade, that outcome obviously is not good. Thus, the late Judge Harry Pregerson — a very experienced federal appellate judge — wrote in his "Checklist for Writing," "Use short, declarative sentences." Harry Pregerson & Suzianne D. Painter-Thorne, *The Seven Virtues of Appellate Brief Writing: An Update from the Bench*, 38 Sw. L. Rev. 221, 232 (2008). So says Judge Randy Smith. Robert H. Thomas, *Preparing an Effective Appellate Brief—The Expert View*, Council of Appellate Lawyers, Appellate Issues 26 (Spring 2012) ("Judge Smith stressed: 'short sentences, paragraphs, quotes and citations'").

So how long should sentences be? The literature on reading comprehension offers a rough answer: Any sentence over 40 words in length runs an increasing chance of losing the reader's comprehension. As the late Supreme Court Justice Ruth Bader Ginsberg put it, "We simply don't have time to ferret out one bright idea buried in too long a sentence." Mark Rust, *Mistakes to Avoid on Appeal*, 74 A.B.A. J. 78, 79 (1988). To avoid that situation, follow this rule: No sentence should be longer than 40 words in length. The only exception is a situation in which a reader is given an aid that, in essence, breaks up a sentence over 40 words. The principal kind of aid is the use of a numbering system of (1), (2), (3), etc.

Are you supposed to actually count the words in your sentence? Absolutely. You can easily use the Word Count function in your writing software to do so. And the 40-word limit is a *maximum*. Shorter sentences are better.

Maybe the long sentence that you just wrote in your draft was capable of being understood. It does not matter. If the sentence goes over 40 words, find some way to break it up into two or shorten it. You are concerned about the *risk* that the judge will lose the meaning of the sentence, or will become uncomfortable getting through it, and you do not want to take that risk.

There are a couple of easy ways to break up a long sentence. First, the sentence may have connectors in it ("and" or "but," for example) or another convenient place to break the sentence up. Consider the following sentence:

In response to questioning by counsel, the defendant acknowledged that he wanted to plead guilty to misdemeanor larceny, that he had discussed this plea with his lawyer, that no one had forced him to plead guilty, and that he was giving up his right to a jury trial, his privilege against self-incrimination, and his right to confront adverse witnesses.

The sentence is readable at 59 words. But it's a slog to get through. You can easily break it into two sentences and, in the process, render your brief more readable:

> In response to questioning by counsel, the defendant acknowledged that he wanted to plead guilty to misdemeanor larceny and had discussed this plea with his lawyer. He admitted that no one had forced him to plead guilty and recognized that he was giving up his right to a jury trial, his privilege against self-incrimination, and his right to confront adverse witnesses.

Now you have two sentences of 26 and 35 words. However, maybe you can do even better by breaking up the second sentence at a connector:

> In response to questioning by counsel, the defendant acknowledged that he wanted to plead guilty to misdemeanor larceny and had discussed this plea with his lawyer. He admitted that no one had forced him to plead guilty. He also recognized that he was giving up his right to a jury trial, his privilege against self-incrimination, and his right to confront adverse witnesses.

Compare this paragraph to the initial 59-word sentence above. You can readily discern the difference.

The second possibility is to shorten the sentence by striking out unnecessary words. Here, the first two sentences in an introduction are 55 words each:

> This appeal raises the issue whether a fired executive formerly employed by a corporate parent under an express written contract with only the corporate parent can choose that he will not sue the corporate parent but instead will sue one of the subsidiary companies for breach of an alleged implied employment contract with the subsidiary. It also presents the question whether that executive can sue a troubled bank, which is operating pursuant to an Administrative Order issued by the State Department of Banking, for breach of an alleged implied employment contract, where such a contract would violate the Administrative Order and state banking regulations applying to insufficiently capitalized banks. The answers to both of these questions are "no," and this Court should affirm the judgment of the trial court.

The sentences are readable, but shortening them will make them flow better:

> A parent corporation formerly employed a now-terminated executive under an express written contract with only that corporate parent. The principal issue in this appeal is whether, instead of suing the parent corporation, that employee may sue a subsidiary of the parent for breach of an alleged implied employment contract with the subsidiary. A second question involves the Seaman's Bank, which is operating

under an Administrative Order issued by the State Department of Banking. The question is whether the employee may sue this bank for breach of an alleged implied employment contract where that contract would violate the Administrative Order and state banking regulations. The answers to both questions are "no," and this Court should affirm the judgment of the trial court.

Here we have sentences of 19, 34, 21, 30, and 18 words.

So let's assume that you are convinced of the risk posed by long sentences. As a believer, you decide to carry the reasoning a bit further: "I want to make sure that the reader *always* understands me. So I will always write in short sentences." Consider this paragraph:

> The evidence showed that police officer Lawrence Maines stopped a car driven by defendant Oates. Maines placed Oates in his squad car for the duration of the stop. After completing the stop, Maines first told Oates that he could leave. Maines then began questioning Oates about whether the car contained drugs. Oates consented to a search of the car. Maines then told Oates to stand in front of the car. He ordered a passenger in the car, Paula Quintera, to stand behind the car. Maines searched the car for five minutes and found no drugs. Maines then asked Oates if he could search the car's trunk, and Oates agreed. The search of the trunk by Maines revealed a bag of marijuana. Maines then arrested Oates.

Was the text understandable? Yes. But was it enjoyable reading? No. Take a look at the sentence length: What do you see? A series of 11 sentences of much the same length: 15, 13, 12, 11, 8, 11, 14, 11, 14, 12, and 4 words.

Writing that does not vary the sentence length is called "choppy." If all the sentences are roughly the same length, the reading becomes monotonous. Once again, if you are boring the judge, then her attention may wander, and you've lost the persuasive edge that the appellate advocate seeks.

How to avoid choppy writing? Vary your sentence length (and also your paragraph length, which is discussed immediately below). You should *average* around 20 to 25 words. If you do, the reader's attention will not flag:

> The evidence showed that after police officer Lawrence Maines stopped a car driven by defendant Oates, Maines placed Oates in his squad car for the duration of the stop. After completing the stop, Maines first told Oates that he could leave but then began questioning Oates about whether the car contained drugs. As a result, Oates consented to a search of the car.
>
> Maines then told Oates to stand in front of the car and ordered a passenger in the car, Paula Quintera, to stand behind the car. After Maines searched the car for five minutes and found no drugs, Maines asked Oates if he could search the car's trunk. Oates agreed. After the search of the trunk by Maines revealed a bag of marijuana, Maines arrested Oates.

The sentence lengths? 29, 23, 11, 25, 22, 2, and 16 words. Average: 18 words.

2. Paragraph Length

Apply the perspective principle: Pretend you are an appellate judge and just look at — do not yet read — the paragraph set forth below. Do you *want* to read this paragraph? What goes through your mind as you contemplate reading it? The answer is obvious — you think that this paragraph is long and that you will struggle to get through it. The appellate judge knows that reading it cannot be avoided (after all, reading is part of the job) but the judge is not looking forward to this task. Or, in the worst case, maybe the judge just refuses to read it and moves on.

Now go ahead and read the paragraph:

Plaintiff Alan Adams was arrested for public drunkenness at approximately 12:30 a.m. in the small town of Pleasant. After leaving a local saloon, Mr. Adams observed Pleasant County Deputy Sheriff Bart Baker arrest an acquaintance of Mr. Adams for public intoxication. Mr. Adams took umbrage at this and decided that the appropriate thing to do was to immediately call the Sheriff Department's dispatch operator and demand to speak with the elected Sheriff of Pleasant County, Cathy Cleaver. Not surprisingly, Sheriff Cleaver was not available at 12:30 a.m. Mr. Adams nonetheless insisted that he needed to speak with Sheriff Cleaver "now." When approached by Deputy Baker, Mr. Adams admitted he had been drinking. In this litigation he also admits that his breath smelled of alcohol at the time. He refused to answer Deputy Baker's questions as to how much he had been drinking, insisting instead on speaking with the dispatch operator. When told to go home by Deputy Baker — home for Mr. Adams being less than a mile away — Mr. Adams chose instead to follow the Deputy back to his patrol vehicle to demand that Adams's friend be driven home rather than taken to jail. When he finally did comply with multiple requests of the Deputy to go home, instead of walking the short distance to his house, Mr. Adams got into his vehicle and started it — apparently intending to drive away. Rather than let Mr. Adams drive in his condition, Deputy Baker placed him under arrest for public intoxication in violation of Columbia Penal Code section 123.

Having read it, what do you think now? The paragraph is understandable; there are no overly long sentences, and the sentence length is relatively varied. But the paragraph just contains too much material. You accurately predicted that it would not be pleasant getting through it.

Moreover, from the advocate's standpoint, the paragraph fails for a second reason: It's hard to retain all the knowledge in that single paragraph. If the paragraph had been broken up, the reader would have stood a much better chance of remembering the information. Consider also that the escapade described in the paragraph is somewhat interesting. Imagine how much worse reading a paragraph like this one would be if it concerned technical issues about a patent or a complicated contract.

So you need to worry about paragraph length. The rule: The paragraph should be a maximum of six sentences or two-thirds of a page, whichever is shorter.

Below, this principle was used to edit the long paragraph that you just read:

Plaintiff Alan Adams was arrested for public intoxication at approximately 12:30 a.m. in the small town of Pleasant. After leaving a local saloon, Mr. Adams observed Pleasant County Deputy Sheriff Bart Baker arrest an acquaintance of Mr. Adams for public intoxication. Mr. Adams took umbrage at this action.

Mr. Adams decided that the appropriate thing to do was to immediately call the Sheriff Department's dispatch operator and demand to speak with the elected Sheriff of Pleasant County, Cathy Cleaver. Not surprisingly, Sheriff Cleaver was not available at 12:30 a.m. Mr. Adams nonetheless insisted that he needed to speak with Sheriff Cleaver "now."

When approached by Deputy Baker, Mr. Adams admitted that he had been drinking. In this litigation he also admits that his breath smelled of alcohol at the time. He refused to answer Deputy Baker's questions as to how much he had been drinking, insisting instead on speaking with the dispatch operator. When told to go home by Deputy Baker — home for Mr. Adams being less than a mile away — Mr. Adams chose instead to follow the Deputy back to his patrol vehicle. He then demanded that Adams's friend be driven home rather than taken to jail.

When Mr. Adams finally did comply with multiple requests of the Deputy to go home, instead of walking the short distance to his house, Mr. Adams got into his vehicle and started it. He apparently intended to drive away. Rather than let Mr. Adams drive in his condition, Deputy Baker arrested him for public intoxication in violation of State of Columbia Penal Code section 123.

Notice how much easier it is to read these four separate paragraphs rather than the original single paragraph. Each of the paragraphs centers on one part of the sequence: (1) the incident that triggered the problem as Adams left the bar, (2) the attempt by Adams to call the Sheriff, (3) Adams's encounter with Deputy Baker, and (4) the arrest. You can certainly improve the paragraphs with other editing, but they are much better.

One last point on the paragraph length rule: Is it ever appropriate to use a one sentence paragraph? The answer is yes, but only in two very limited circumstances: (1) to emphasize a key point that you wish to make stand out to the reader, or (2) as a transition sentence. Here is an example of the latter:

In summary, appellant has failed to demonstrate that the trial court erred in applying the Jones Act to appellant's injury.

Do the first two principles involving sentence and paragraph length work? Here are two paragraphs from a complicated appellate brief prepared by leading Supreme Court advocates. Read them:

1. *AFMC's account at CoreStates.* AFMC maintained several demand accounts at CoreStates. The account at issue in this case, although denominated a "settlement

account," was a general deposit account, not a special or restricted one. Pursuant to a "zero balance account agreement" between CoreStates and AFMC, cash accumulated in any of AFMC's accounts could be used to cover checks drawn on the other accounts. Nevertheless, over time, AFMC ran up a series of overdrafts in its accounts and became indebted to CoreStates for the amount of those overdrafts, totaling approximately $4.5 million.

2. *The Pioneer loans and purported security interest.* RNG was a company that "originated" mortgages — i.e., loaned money to home buyers. It then sold the resulting notes and mortgages to investors. As a "warehouse lender," Pioneer advanced money to RNG to fund loans that RNG made. In May 1997, Pioneer and RNG entered into a loan and security agreement governing the grant of a line of credit from Pioneer to RNG. The agreement gave Pioneer a security interest in the notes and mortgages obtained by RNG (the "Collateral") and in any proceeds obtained therefrom.

Andrew L. Frey & Roy T. Englert, Jr., EFFECTIVE BRIEF WRITING IN FEDERAL APPELLATE PRACTICE 81 (2008).

Both paragraphs smoothly lead the reader through complex facts. Now go through them and apply the principles. Check the sentence lengths and note how they vary. Then count the sentences in each paragraph. Again, it's not that longer sentences, or longer paragraphs, are always unintelligible. However, sentences and paragraphs that follow these principles *are* easily readable. Another aid is the short subheading in italics that begins each paragraph and acts as a transition for the reader, a subject we discussed in Chapter Eight.

3. Minimize Use of the Passive Voice

A third basic rule involves using the passive voice. Law students have varied reactions when considering the subject of the passive voice. Some think: "Not this subject again; I got enough of it in eighth grade." Others think, "I am in law school. Why am I paying this exorbitant tuition for something that I could get for $100 at a junior college?" Still others — more than you realize — will admit to themselves, "I am still not sure what a passive voice is."

So, if you fall into one of these three categories, you need to face reality. After sentence and paragraph length, the single, easiest change that you can make to improve your writing *and* to take a large step toward becoming a good legal writer is recognizing and eliminating unnecessary passive voices. You should use the passive voice strategically, not automatically.

Most individuals instinctively choose verbs in the active voice rather than the passive voice. A person would probably say, "I threw the ball" (active voice), rather than, "The ball was thrown by me" (passive voice). However, in the process of legal writing, too many writers often forgo clear, active verbs and instead use the passive voice.

Here is an example of the distinction between active and passive voice in the legal context:

The <u>court</u> <u>entered</u> a <u>judgment</u>. (active)
  (subject) (verb) (object)

A <u>judgment</u> <u>was</u> <u>entered</u> by the <u>court</u>. (passive)

In the passive voice, three changes occur:

1. The object (judgment) of the first sentence — the active voice sentence — becomes the subject of the sentence.
2. The verb changes from active voice ("entered") to passive voice ("was entered").
3. Finally, the former subject ("court") becomes the object of a preposition ("by the court").

Frequently, in the passive voice the subject of the active voice sentence drops out entirely, a change that can create ambiguity. For example, consider this sentence in the passive voice: "The prisoner was shot." Shot by whom? A guard while escaping? Somebody else? The reader doesn't know.

Here are some additional examples of active and passive voice constructions:

Active Voice

The court decided the motion for a new trial.
Today the judge will postpone the trial.
The defendant's attorney argued that the statute of limitations had expired.
No limitation on agency power prohibited Rule 40.

Passive Voice

The motion for a new trial was decided by the court.
The trial will be postponed today by the judge.
The argument that the statute of limitations had expired was made by the defendant's attorney.
Rule 40 was not prohibited by any limitation on agency power.

The writing principle that you must follow is to minimize use of the passive voice. Using the passive voice has several downsides. First, the passive voice employs more words. As you will see below, appellate lawyers are always on the lookout to prune unnecessary verbiage.

Second, the passive voice asks more of your reader. The reader's mental "eye," which tracks the action in the sentence, must move backwards because the actor of the sentence receives the action, rather than causes the action. As a result, the passive voice forces the reader to stop at the end of the sentence to reconsider the information and mentally sort out "who did what."

That extra mental effort on the part of the reader — the appellate judge — is wasteful and unnecessary. The active sentence is shorter, clearer, and more logical. It keeps the reader's eye moving forward and clarifies both the subject and the action. It allows the verb to take its crispest, liveliest form. The actor comes first (court), the verb second (decided), and the object third (motion):

Example: The court decided the motion for a new trial.

You do not, however, have to avoid the passive voice completely. Once you can recognize the passive voice and know the reasons for being wary of it, you will employ the passive voice strategically in your writing, rather than mindlessly utilizing it. Use the passive voice for the following three reasons:

1. To mask the identity of the actor and thus de-emphasize who the actor is:

A decision was made to cut the plaintiff's salary. (passive)

Or:

The rate for filing pleadings in court will be increased. (passive)

2. When the object of the verb in your sentence is more important than the subject:

When John Lennon was killed, newspaper headlines proclaimed, "Lennon murdered!"

Here, the object of the action taken (John Lennon) is more important than the actor (the person who killed John Lennon).

3. To de-emphasize unfavorable facts or law. For example, the attorney for the defendant might want to write the following:

The plaintiff was assaulted by the defendant. (passive)

The "de-emphasis" occurs because the subject of the sentence (the plaintiff) is not the actor. In contrast, the attorney for the prosecution might write:

The defendant assaulted the plaintiff. (active)

Why is minimizing use of the passive voice so important? Remember that in an appellate brief you are conveying information to someone who has no previous information on the subject. That person will find it easier to assimilate information presented in the active voice, because the active voice is linear — it describes the action in a "who did what" fashion. Furthermore, the active voice makes maximum use of power verbs. As a California judge puts it in recommending use of the active voice, "Active verbs deliver more punch than passive ones" and "provide the muscle to carry your ideas forward." Julie Brook, *A Brief Browse on Briefs: Writing Tips from a Judge (Part 3),* http://blog.ceb.com/2011/09/28/a-brief-browse-on-briefs-writing-tips-from-a-judge-part-3/.

If you are writing in a complex area, you need to take advantage of every opportunity to ensure that you convey the information in a way that the reader understands. The active voice helps greatly in this effort.

That said, as discussed above, the passive voice *is* strategically appropriate in some instances. So, given that using the passive voice is sometimes the right choice, what do you do? Your first task is to *recognize* the passive voice. You cannot decide whether to use the passive voice until you are aware of it. Look especially for this combination: verbs ending in *ed* together with a version of the verb *to be* (for example, *is* or *was*). The latest versions of word processing programs can also help you find passive voices, but you cannot totally outsource this task to your computer.

Excellent legal writers automatically write in the active voice in most instances. But even the best of them sometimes will use the passive without thinking. That initial usage in a first draft, however, does not mean that the passive voice will end up in the final brief. In the editing process, the writer will affirmatively look for inadvertent uses of the passive voice and then decide whether to change those uses.

You must put yourself in a position where you are able to make this choice. To reach that point, you have to recognize the passive voice. You have no other option.

4. Keep Subjects Near Verbs and Verbs Near Objects

As the discussion of passive voices taught you, the verb is always at the heart of any sentence. The subject performs the action described by the verb, and the object receives the action from the verb. This core information — how the subject acts upon the object — is what the reader needs to know above all.

To maximize the possibility that the reader will receive this information, you should keep the subject near the verb of the sentence, and the verb near the object of the sentence. Often, you can accomplish this result simply by rearranging clauses:

> The plaintiff, who sought damages for personal injuries two years after the accident, filed her complaint.

The subject is "plaintiff"; the verb is "filed." But the two are separated. Try:

> Seeking damages for personal injuries, the plaintiff filed her complaint two years after the accident.

Here is another example:

> Lawyers who understand that they must be highly ethical in all instances, particularly in transactions in which they take part, will avoid ethical lapses.

The subject is "lawyers" and the verb is "will avoid." But 19 words keep them apart. Try:

> Lawyers will avoid ethical lapses if they understand that they must be highly ethical in all instances, particularly in transactions in which they take part.

The key here is being able to identify the subject, verb, and object in your sentence. You have that skill.

5. Omit Surplus Words

This principle is simple to state and hard to apply. Writers find it difficult to edit out words or phrases that they have previously inserted into a sentence. They tend to assume, perhaps even unconsciously: If I put the words in the sentence to begin with, they must be important.

That conclusion misses the point. You may be able to keep the *idea* that was in the phrase; you just change it so that you use fewer words. Alternatively, you can edit out certain words that are not central to the point.

In the end, though, you have little choice about whether to omit surplus words. Modern courts impose stringent rules on the length of briefs, most of them framed in terms of word limits. If your draft brief is too long, you *must* cut parts of it out. You have two choices in doing so: (1) cut out paragraphs or sections of the brief as a whole, or (2) cut out individual surplus words. The second method is better, for it does not sacrifice any part of the substantive argument.

In deciding whether to take out a word, phrase, sentence, or paragraph, you ask a simple question: Do I need this word (or phrase, sentence, or paragraph) to make my argument? Keep in mind, again, that the reader has no knowledge of the issue that you are arguing and is looking for help. Thus, the little "side point" that you are making in this paragraph may, indeed, be sophisticated and worthwhile, but it may be less than central to the overall brief. You may be better off taking the point out and shortening the brief so that it now focuses only on more critical points.

One important place to look for surplus words is the use of adjectives or adverbs. These are words that modify other words, usually nouns and verbs, and they can certainly be useful tools in writing. However, beginning legal writers sometimes use them because they think it makes the brief sound more "lawyerly" or adds emphasis to their argument. Thus, instead of an argument being "erroneous" or "wrong," it will be "clearly erroneous" or "utterly wrong." Or they may couple an adverb with a verb to make sure the point is obvious: "lying" becomes "obviously lying," or "asserted" becomes "unbelievably asserted."

Not all adverbs or adjectives are bad; some add needed information. ("The legislature *just* passed a law outlawing . . . ."). Many, however, are unnecessary, so you confront them in a two-step process. First, you identify them. A key is to look for words that end in "ly": very, extremely, really, obviously, undoubtedly, patently, etc. Second, just ask yourself: Does this word add to the meaning of the sentence? If not, get rid of it.

Another way to shorten is by substituting words. Can you take out three words and insert one in their place? If so, you have made a net gain in the persuasiveness of your brief. Here is an example:

> Rather than explaining how a grainy 1996 map merely showing the "approximate" extent of the location of the house could have demonstrated such a precise figure, Respondents' briefs remain characteristically silent.

Now, an edited version:

> Respondents never explain how a grainy 1996 map could demonstrate such a precise figure when the map showed only the "approximate" location of the house.

The edited version is 25 words, 6 words less than the first sentence, yet it loses no meaning.

Be aware, though, that this type of editing is hard to do. It will take time, and much discipline, to become good at it. Nonetheless, it is a vital skill, and you must begin to acquire it. And the need to eliminate surplus words again shows you how the editing of a brief is crucial. Your first draft will inevitably include words that could be eliminated.

6. Do Not Turn Verbs Into Nouns

The sixth principle is to avoid nominalizations. A nominalization takes a verb and transforms it into a noun. For example: "The defendant took action by . . . ." The word *action* is a nominalization of the verb *act*. Much better to say: "The defendant acted by . . . ."

Sometimes nominalizations attract law students because they seem to make the writing sound more "legal." After all, wouldn't a real lawyer "make an assumption" (a nominalization) rather than merely "assume" something? And doesn't it sound more "legal" to "take action" rather than just to "act"?

Throw away any such preconceptions about how lawyers ought to sound and go back to what you originally learned about verbs in grade school: They are *action words*. The verb injects life into a sentence. The use of strong, descriptive verbs in the active voice enlivens factual situations. By contrast, nominalizations stultify the writing. As one writer put it, "I call them 'zombie nouns' because they cannibalize active verbs . . . ." Helen Sword, *Zombie Nouns*, N.Y. Times (July 23, 2012), https://opinionator.blogs .nytimes.com/2012/07/23/zombie-nouns/.

So, instead of having the agent "give careful consideration to the policy," have the agent "carefully consider the policy." And instead of having the court "render a decision," just have it "decide."

7. Avoid Noun Chains

In legal writing, it is tempting to string together nouns as a means of particularizing a legal term. For example, start with the word *rights*. Now, particularize it: "free speech First Amendment rights." And put the phrase in a sentence: "States cannot prohibit free speech First Amendment rights."

Does the sentence read well? No. You can figure out why by identifying the subject and the verb. They are *states* and *cannot prohibit*. What do you expect next after the subject and verb? You can expect an object — say *speech*.

When you read these two words, "free speech," you now believe that you understand the basic part of the sentence. But then you are immediately surprised, because it goes on. You read more nouns: *First Amendment* and *rights*. Now, all the nouns before "rights" have suddenly turned into modifiers, narrowing the type of "rights." So by the end, you have to rearrange your thoughts to take those modifiers into account.

These are called noun chains, or noun strings. Here are two more examples:

The pollution rules regulated public transport gasoline engine vehicles.

Defendant introduced into evidence the asbestos exposure risks analysis report.

Once again, you have noun chains: "public transport gasoline engine vehicles" and "asbestos exposure risks analysis report."

You can quickly fix noun chains by breaking them up. You do so by moving to the front the noun that actually is to perform the function of a noun. Then, you add prepositional or other phrases to qualify the noun.

States cannot prohibit speech protected by rights under the First Amendment.

The pollution rules regulated vehicles used for public transport that have gasoline engines.

Defendant introduced into evidence the report that analyzed the exposure to risks from asbestos.

8. Avoid Vague Referents

Here is a lesser-known rule: Do not use "vague referents." You may not even know what a "vague referent" is, so we will start with that concept. Consider the following:

The court held that these circumstances supported a finding that actual knowledge on the part of the landlord existed. *This* was based on the fact that the landlord had ample opportunity to view the dog's vicious nature.

The lease here, just as the lease in *Smith v. Jones*, was month-to-month and terminable upon notice to the tenant. *That* satisfies the control element of the *Smith* test.

The defendants were playing a practical joke on the plaintiff, *which* shows that they intended a battery.

The key words are, respectively, *this, that,* and *which.* Each is used to refer back to a concept revealed earlier. But to properly carry out this assignment, the words must refer back to a *specific word or clause.* In other words, the reader should be able to (mentally) go back to the preceding sentence or clause, find a specific word or clause, and replace *this, that,* or *which* with that word or clause.

In these three examples, the reader cannot make that replacement. Instead, the words *this, that,* and *which* refer sort of generally to *something* that came previously. But the reader is not sure what that "something" is.

Use of vague referents is unacceptable in good legal writing. Discussions of legal issues require precision; the reader must know exactly what a word is referring to and cannot be left guessing. Consider the following rewrites:

> The court held that these circumstances supported a finding that actual knowledge on the part of the landlord existed. *This holding* was based on the fact that the landlord had ample opportunity to view the dog's vicious nature.

> The lease here, just as the lease in *Smith,* was month-to-month and terminable upon notice to the tenant. *That ability to terminate* satisfies the control element of the *Smith* test.

> The defendants were playing a practical joke on the plaintiff, and *their action* shows that they intended a battery.

So look for *this, that,* or *which* standing alone in your draft and ask whether you can find the precise words to which *this, that,* or *which* refers. If you cannot, you probably have a vague referent. If so, fix it.

9. Do Not Assume Knowledge by the Reader

Hearken back yet again to the perspective principle: Put yourself in the shoes of the reader. Remember that when you are using a case in a brief, you cannot assume knowledge on the part of readers that they do not have.

Now consider the following:

> The key case is *Jones v. Kiely,* 456 P.3d 678 (Wash. 2012). In that case, a mother was not actually present during *the explosion* that injured her son.

Or:

> In *Laffer v. Mole,* 123 F.3d 456 (12th Cir. 2007), a landlord leased property to the Coles. Prior to *the attack* on the plaintiff, *the dog* had attacked one other adult.

The reader is proceeding nicely through the first paragraph until the text refers to "the explosion." The reader then thinks: "The explosion? What explosion? I do not know anything about 'the explosion.' Did I miss something?" The writer of the paragraph knows about the explosion, having researched and read the case. But in conveying that information, the writer wrote in a way that assumed the reader knew as well. The same problem occurs in the second paragraph: The reader thinks, "Prior to *what* attack? And *what* dog?"

Assumptions like these violate the perspective principle. If you put yourself in the shoes of your reader, you can see how they would be confusing. Fortunately, you can easily avoid improper assumptions. The use of the articles *the* or *that* often precedes them. Just make sure that, in writing, you lay out facts in a way that does not assume the brief has already discussed them:

> The key case is *Jones v. Kiely*, 567 P.3d 789 (Wash. 2020). In that case, a mother was not actually present when *an explosion* injured her son.

> In *Laffer v. Mole*, 123 F.3d 456 (12th Cir. 2020), a landlord leased property to the Coles. Two months later, *the Coles' dog attacked the plaintiff.* Prior to *that attack*, the Coles' dog had attacked one other adult.

10. Use Topic Sentences and Stress Locations

This last rule addresses techniques used in paragraphs and sentences that are more difficult to implement. They can, however, add both clarity and persuasiveness to your argument.

The first part of the rule may sound familiar: Use topic sentences to introduce a paragraph. You learned about topic sentences in your basic English courses. But topic sentences are particularly important in legal writing because they act as a transition device by telling the reader where your argument is headed. One professor describes the topic sentence as a "jurisdictional statement for that paragraph." Noah A. Messing, *The Art of Advocacy* 253 (2013). Legal writing expert Bryan Garner says a good topic sentence "announces what the paragraph is about," while the other sentences in the paragraph "play supporting roles." Bryan A. Garner, *The Winning Brief: 100 Tips for Persuasive Briefing in Trial and Appellate Courts* 116 (2d ed. 2004).

Here are some examples of topic sentences:

> The court of appeals gave three reasons for rejecting the Commission's explanation of its change in policy. First . . . .

> The courts of appeals have repeatedly found that copyright owners may refuse to license a copyrighted work or do so only on terms the copyright owner finds acceptable, without engaging in misuse of the copyright. . . .

> Centuries of Anglo-American law have recognized monetary bail as an accepted mechanism for preserving the traditional right to freedom before conviction. . . .

> Statements of opinion by sellers about their product are mere "puffery" and do not create express warranties actionable by buyers. . . .

After reading each of these topic sentences, you know where the discussion in the paragraph will lead you. And topic sentences are not merely useful in discussing cases. They can preview material in the statement of facts and are useful in implementing the "inverted pyramid" that proceeds from broader law down to the specific issue.

Writing topic sentences is hard; it will take time and practice for you to master the technique. At first, you are likely to start with weaker topic sentences, such as:

> Another case that discusses sentencing under the guidelines is *O'Toole v. United States,* 789 F.3d 123 (12th Circuit).

This sentence does tell the reader that you are about to discuss the *O'Toole* case, and in that sense performs a transition function. But your topic sentence should tell the reader more about what the upcoming paragraph will do. Compare the sentence above with this variation:

> The Court in *O'Toole v. United States*, 789 F.3d 123 (12th Circuit), likewise found that the trial judge relied on the impermissible factor of a defendant's upbringing in imposing a sentence.

Here, this topic sentence (1) links to a discussion above ("likewise found"), and (2) tells the reader exactly how the case will be used (to show error in relying on an impermissible factor).

This example also gives you a hint about how to create a topic sentence. In Chapter Eight, we discussed the method for using a case. A core feature of that method was the conclusion after a precedent's facts were compared to those of the present case. That conclusion can often be re-worded and used as the topic sentence to begin the discussion of the case.

Another method is to ask yourself what you are trying to accomplish in the paragraph. Let's say the paragraph is about a case. You will ask yourself: Why am I using this case? Or: How does the point I am making here contribute to the overall analysis? *See* Anne Enquist, *Topic Sentences — Potentially Brilliant Moments of Synthesis*, 14 No. 3 Perspectives: Teaching Legal Research and Writing 139 (2006). You can put a topic sentence to a broader use, not just to introduce a paragraph but to preview what will happen in several paragraphs.

You need to have patience. Writing excellent topic sentences takes both practice and deeper analytical thought. You will work on your topic sentences while editing brief, for good topic sentences rarely appear in a first draft.

Now we drill down a little deeper into the individual sentence. The parts of a sentence — the beginning, middle, and end — do not affect a reader equally. Rather, readers naturally give more attention to material at the end of a sentence. For that reason, the end of a sentence is known as the "stress position." Readers expect that this part of the sentence will contain the most important information.

If you present the same information to a reader in two different sentences, alternating the stress position, you leave the reader in a different place. Consider the following sentences, which use the same words:

> While it was a close case, the jury found for the plaintiff.

> While the jury found for the plaintiff, it was a close case.

The first sentence leaves the reader with the thought that the plaintiff won. The second leaves the reader with the thought that the case was close.

Here is another example:

> The judge will likely exclude the evidence because the police did not have probable cause to search.

> Because the police did not have probable cause to search, the judge will likely exclude the evidence.

Do you see the difference in emphasis?

The lesson here for legal writing is that you should place your most important information — the information you would like to *stress* — at the end of a sentence. If you can control the emphasis in your sentences, your writing will become much more persuasive. One renowned expert in legal writing even goes so far as to opine that not using the stress position "remains the number one problem in legal writing." George D. Gopen, *A Once Rogue Punctuation Mark Gains Respectability: What You Can Now Accomplish with an Em Dash*, 45 LITIGATION 13, 14 (2019).

Using the stress position is not an easy principle to implement. You will need to do so in your editing when you are examining individual sentences. Read a sentence and ask yourself: Which words or phrases in the sentence would you highlight if you could? If they are not at the end of the sentence, edit that sentence to put them in the stress position. Using the stress position may require you to begin a sentence with the word "Because," but that use is fine.

You won't be the first lawyer to use the stress position effectively, but you will follow in some large footsteps. What thought did the lawyer place in the stress position when he wrote the following first sentence of his oration?[2]

> Four score and seven years ago our fathers brought forth on this continent, a new nation, conceived in Liberty, and dedicated to the proposition that all men are created equal.

C. A SHORT LIST OF USAGES TO AVOID

The ten principles stated above are important but not easily put into practice. You will have to work hard to internalize them over a period of time and to

---

[2] Noted in Nancy Lawler Dickhute, *The Writer's Block: Writing Better Sentences*, NEB. Law. 15, 16 (April 2001).

implement them in your work. Other usages, however, are more readily avoided. Here is a list of them:

1. **Contractions:** Legal writing has a formality and certain dignity to it. It does not include the use of contractions. Consider:

   Mr. Brantingham returned home after finding his daughter *wasn't* there.

   Do not say "wasn't" (or "isn't" or "can't"). Say "was not" (or "is not" or "cannot").

2. **Slang:** Slang is also out. You will not write: "The dog was driving everyone nuts."

3. **Legalese:** Just a reminder here, because your legal writing course taught you not to use legalese. Do not use "aforementioned" or "heretofore."

4. **Acronyms:** Except in circumstances where an acronym is universally known ("FBI"), do not use acronyms. The Pension Benefit Guaranty Corporation should not become the "PBGC" throughout your brief. A judge on the Sixth Circuit Court of Appeals explained why: A brief filled with acronyms is "a short-term memory test." Raymond M. Kethledge, *A Judge Lays Down the Law on Writing Appellate Briefs*, GP SOLO, Vol. 32 No. 5 (Sept.-Oct. 2015).

5. **Feelings:** As a beginning legal writer, do not use "We feel" or "We think." Your feelings and thoughts are not relevant to the court.

6. **Name calling:** You may feel strongly that your opponent has acted improperly. Nonetheless, use restraint in your reply. Judges hate name calling or personal attacks. Do not describe an opposing argument or an opponent's brief as "idiotic," "stupid," "ridiculous," "imbecilic," or "blatantly wrong." Instead, let your argument speak for itself by *demonstrating* what was wrong with the opponent's argument.

Finally, you must think about one last usage: the question of gendered pronouns. In legal writing, you will have to refer to unspecified individuals who have no specific gender.

For example, you may be talking about what "a judge" must do in a specific case. You use the term "judge" in your first sentence: "The judge must decide the sentence after considering the probation report." Then you go on: "In passing the sentence . . ." — what comes next? How do you refer back to the judge? Do you simply repeat the word "judge"? Do you say "he or she"? Do you use "she" the first time the issue comes up, and "he" the second? Or do you avoid the problem by using the word "they"?

Certainly the one usage you must avoid is only using the pronoun "he." Among the other choices, each has drawbacks. If you keep repeating "the judge," you can avoid the use of the pronoun, but it sounds repetitive. The phrase "he or she" (or "she or he") works but seems a bit clunky. Use of "they" is confusing and poses a grammatical problem: The singular "judge" has now turned into a plural "they." Perhaps using "she" and then, later, "he" may be the safest choice.

No consensus has yet emerged on gendered usage. *See* Greg Johnson, Esq., *Welcome to Our Gender-Neutral Future*, 42 Vᴛ. B.J. 36-37 (2016) (discussing the various pros and cons). You will have to make your own choice. But *think* carefully about that choice, and if possible, rewrite the sentence to avoid the problem.

D. CITATIONS: A FEW WORDS OF WARNING

Your brief will include a multitude of citations, and they must conform to a consistent style. Normally, following the well-known Bluebook will fulfill that requirement. Alternatively, some individual states have a particular style manual that the rules of court require counsel to follow. If you are familiar with the court rules governing appeals, you will know about such a manual.

Whatever the citation system used in a jurisdiction, your citations must be consistent throughout the brief. If they are not, the court may assume that the *brief* is likely to be inconsistent in other areas. You do not want the court to adopt that skeptical attitude toward your brief.

Aside from the form of the citation, several problems recur in citing cases. We deal with those now. As we go through them, again consider the perspective principle. The discussion below is fully consistent with that principle.

Generally, you have two goals in citing authority: (1) to appear professional and competent, and (2) to make it easy for the court to check your authorities. Initially, consider the obvious: Every time that you make a statement about the facts or the holding of a precedent case, the court must be able to check your reference. So you must include a citation to that case.

You must always use a "pin" cite — a cite to a specific page in an opinion — whenever you are citing a case for its content, and not just informing the court of its existence in an initial cite. You are directing the court to information within the case, and that information will not appear on the first page of the opinion. So pin cites to cases are needed.

A single citation should not direct the court to more than two pages in a case. You do not want a citation that reads: 88 N.W.2d at 113-119. That citation would require the court to read seven pages to find the points that you have referenced. Instead, your cite must be more specific. For example, consider the following paragraph:

> The holding in *Smith v. Jones*, 123 A.2d 456 (R.I. 2012), controls the present case. In *Smith*, the plaintiff Smith was driving down Main Street within the speed limit. As she went through an intersection with a green light in her direction, defendant Jones did not stop his truck at the red light. The truck smashed into the side of Smith's car, severely injuring her. 123 A.2d at 458-459.

Here, all the summarized facts can be found on pages 458 and 459 of the case. However, if the facts are found on more than two pages of the opinion, then you should add more citations after the two middle sentences. Otherwise, if the court wants to verify a fact, it must look through too many pages to find it. So, if the facts were spread over four pages of the precedent, your paragraph would read:

> The holding in *Smith v. Jones*, 123 A.2d 456 (R.I. 2012), controls the present case. In *Smith*, the plaintiff Smith was driving down Main Street within the speed limit. *Id.* at 458. As Smith went through an intersection with a green light in her direction, defendant Jones did not stop his truck at the red light. *Id.* at 460. The truck smashed into the side of Smith's car, severely injuring her. *Id.* at 462.

Remember also that you can never include a page cite without a volume cite. Thus, the following citation is improper:

> In *Jones*, *supra* at 26, the court held that the Environmental Protection Act required the agency to prepare an environmental analysis of the pollution.

The reason should be obvious: To check this cite, the court must go back in your brief and find the place where you gave a full cite to the *Smith* case. You have placed an unnecessary and annoying burden on the court. Instead, your citation should read:

> In *Smith*, 160 F.3d at 26, the court held that the Environmental Protection Act required the agency to prepare an environmental analysis of the pollution.

One final word about cases and citations, and their use in sentences. You may see a brief containing a sentence that starts out as follows: "*Abel v. Baker*, 400 U.S. 300 (2012), applies in the present case." To increase the readability of the sentence, do not start a sentence with the case name and citation as the subject matter. Instead, use normal words: "The decision in *Abel v. Baker*, 400 U.S. 300 (2012), applies in the present case." It's a subtle change, but increasing readability is about such small changes.

E. WRITING IMPROVEMENT IN PERSPECTIVE

Improvement in your writing will not occur in large leaps and bounds. Instead, it will occur gradually. As the court recognized in *Briganti v. Chow*, 42 Cal. App. 5th 504, 512 (2019), "Good brief-writing requires hard work, rigorous analysis, and careful attention to detail."

As you follow the principles set out here, you will start to see small improvements in your writing. Then, as you get better at using the principles and start to internalize them, the improvements will continue. In the end, if you are diligent, you can greatly improve your writing by following the principles. But that improvement will only occur gradually as you get used to following them.

Adhering to the principles set forth in this chapter is no easy task; you are dealing with habits ingrained in your writing for years. To improve, you will need discipline and a strong desire to become an outstanding legal writer. But always keep in mind that good writing is by far the most important skill needed by appellate lawyers.

Summary

- Good legal writing is at the core of effective appellate advocacy. Writing is not just a matter of "style." You can take specific steps to improve your writing.

- Avoid sentences over 40 words in length unless you use an ordering device (for example, (1) . . . ; (2) . . .) and vary your sentence length so you average 20 to 25 words. Paragraphs generally should be no more than six sentences or two-thirds of a page long, whichever is shorter.

- You must learn to readily identify the passive voice in your writing. Then, use the passive voice with caution and for strategic purposes.

- When looking at sentence structure, keep your subject near the verb, and the verb near the object. Also, ruthlessly edit out surplus words that you do not need.

- Verbs are critically important to your writing, so avoid nominalizations, which turn verbs into nouns. Do not use "noun chains," in which nouns are strung together. Also avoid vague referents — that is, the use of words like *it* or *that* which do not refer back to specific words in the sentence.

- Be careful not to assume knowledge of facts or law by your reader.

- Use topic sentences that preview the information in a paragraph. In sentences, put the idea you want emphasize at the end in the stress position.

- Slang, contractions, legalese, and name calling have no place in briefs.

- Avoid obvious citation problems such as citing multiple pages and including a page cite without a volume number. Almost every citation must include a pin cite.

Appendix B contains exercises that test your understanding of the principles discussed in this chapter.

CHAPTER 11

Editing and Finalizing the Brief

A. THE PROCESS OF EDITING

You have finished the first draft of your brief. You sit back with a satisfied smile and take a breath. You think that the worst is behind you.

You are right, at least to a certain degree. Most of the *hardest* work is behind you, but the work ahead is critically important to a successful brief. That work involves editing your draft. The editing that you will undertake will make or break the entire brief-writing effort.

1. The Importance of the Editing Function

Editing is vitally important for several reasons. First, even the best lawyers rarely can turn out a first draft that is even close to being ready for the court. When you write a brief, you are truly "multitasking," even after you have already completed a detailed outline. As you write you are trying to (1) write coherent sentences, (2) craft the actual argument, (3) focus on having good transitions, (4) choose individual words and phrases that place the client's case in the best light, and (5) follow the various "good writing" principles.

Accomplishing these goals alone is a very large task, but they are only part of the story. As you write your first draft, you are also evaluating your argument as you go. You are deciding whether the argument "works" or whether changes are needed—say, by modifying the order of the issues that you are presenting. You are also determining whether the cases work well when you actually use them. It may turn out that an argument is simply weaker when put on paper than you envisioned. You know that you will need to strengthen it.

In short, your first draft cannot accomplish everything you need to do in writing a good brief. You have the chance to make the necessary changes in the editing process. At the same time, you have the opportunity to make those modifications that, on a cumulative basis, greatly improve a brief. They include changing a sentence to the active voice, choosing a better adverb, editing out unnecessary words, etc.

Given the complexities involved in legal writing, good legal writers *must* be good editors. One recent article put it well: "Revision, editing, and rewriting are what make mediocre writing good and good writing great." Wayne Schiess, *Legal Writing Is Not What It Should Be*, 37 S.U.L. REV. 1, 16 (2009). Indeed, good writers generally must be good editors. In an interview, Ernest Hemingway said that he wrote the last page of *A Farewell to Arms* 39 times. Apparently astonished, the interviewer followed up: "Was there some technical problem there? What was it that had stumped you?" Hemingway's response?: "Getting the words right."

2. Creating an Approach to Editing

So how do you become a good editor? You begin by making sure that you have sufficient time to edit. You must recognize that the process of editing is time-consuming. So you set an early deadline for completing a sufficient first draft of your brief. Then you *meet* that deadline. If you are writing a first draft of your brief a couple of days before the brief is due, you will not produce a superior final product.

Now, on to the actual editing. From the discussion of editing above, it should be apparent to you that, just like writing the first draft, the editing function also requires you to multitask. You must look for passive voices, check the transitions, make sure all the information needed to use a precedent is set forth in the brief, check the sentence and paragraph lengths, re-examine your topic sentences, etc. You simply cannot do all these tasks well at once.

So you don't. Instead, you break up the editing function so that each "round" of editing carries out discrete tasks. In doing so your editing moves on a continuum beginning with "macroediting" and ending with "microediting."

Here is an example of how the editing might proceed sequentially.

Editing Round No. One: Cohesiveness of the Argument. The purpose of your first round of editing is to test the cohesiveness of the argument. You are examining the draft's use of the basic steps in applying cases and statutes, and whether the argument on a specific issue fits together as a whole. So you will read full paragraphs at one time, because you are examining the overall flow of the argument.

Perhaps you discover that, in two places, the comparisons of the facts of the present case to the facts of a precedent were not set out as precisely as they should be. So go fix them.

In this first round of editing, you might find yourself taking out sentences or even paragraphs of the brief. If you do, open up a separate document and save these "trimmings" in that document. You probably won't reconsider your decision to cut this material, but if you do decide later to add something back, you know where to locate the excised material.

Editing Round No. Two: Structure. Your second round of editing might focus on structure, centering in particular on transitions and point headings. You will want to check the beginning of your discussion of each issue to confirm that the appropriate transitions into the issue are present. You will ensure that you have adequate internal transitions within your arguments. You will look for individual words used as transitions and ask: Can I make this transition more effective, perhaps by adding words or expanding the transition into a sentence? You will also examine your topic sentences to determine if they are sufficiently robust. Finally, you will want to check your headings to see that they accurately describe the arguments below them.

Editing Round No. Three: Technical Writing. Your next round of editing hones in on the individual sentences. You will examine the draft to see if you have correctly and consistently used good writing techniques. The focus is on sentence and paragraph length, use of the active voice, keeping the subject near the verb, eliminating unnecessary words, proper use of the stress position, etc. In doing so, you are not focused on the coherence or structure of the argument; your previous two rounds of editing examined those questions. Now you are editing at a technical level, trying to elevate the writing.

Editing Round No. Four: Micro Improvements. Finally, your last round of editing can be at the "micro" level. Are you satisfied with individual words? You will focus especially on verbs. Can you replace a verb in your draft with another verb that has more "life" or vitality? Look also at individual adverbs and adjectives: Do you need them? Are there better ones that you could use?

If you break the editing down to these discrete tasks, the actual editing process becomes easier and more focused. Furthermore, you need to consider whether you should do all the editing on the computer. Some lawyers certainly do so. But remember that what you see on the computer is not the same as what prints out on paper and, although some judges read briefs on screen, many do not. So perhaps the third and fourth editing rounds should be done with a pen and paper.

All of these steps count as good news, for they break the overall task of brief-writing down into quite discrete, manageable tasks. Now for the bad news: Good editing requires considerable discipline, takes considerable time, and is much harder than it looks. Beginning editors have a tendency to simply read the draft and change it at random as thoughts or edits occur to them. Plenty of those will occur in editing the first draft. And the end product might well be quite good after three or four general rounds of this type of editing. But that product will not be *as good* as it could be if the editing was carried out more systematically.

The key is taking control of the editing by looking for specific items as you edit, not just reacting to what you read. For example, if you make yourself look specifically for passive voices, you will recognize more of them than if you just read through the draft and make changes as they occur to you.

3. The Need to "Break Away"

Editing is tiring, and the editor may well lose focus as time passes. When you are down to the "micro" level of editing, your mind has narrowed to small details, as it should. The risk, however, is that you may overlook some much larger problem. For example, maybe you made an editing change in one part of the brief that requires an analogous change in another part, but you have overlooked this connection between the two parts of the brief.

So, after you have completed the editing described above, and before you do the final edit, you need to clear your mind. You do so by taking some time away from the brief. You put the brief aside, do something else, and then come back to it later.

How much later? If you have planned right, you should be able to put the brief aside for a significant period, preferably three to five days. Then, when you come back to it, you have put your previous thoughts aside and you can read the brief with an open mind. It won't be like reading it for the first time, of course, because you remember the brief (having written it!). However, the brief *will* appear different because you have put it aside. And you can almost be certain that you will find one mistake that seems obvious now but was not obvious when you last edited the brief.

4. Developing Editing Skills Through Practice

Lastly, here are two final thoughts to keep in mind about the editing process. First, editing presents a considerable opportunity for the legal writer. Many individuals are not particularly skilled at writing first drafts; they just do not have as much facility at initial "wordsmithing" as others. But these individuals *can* be excellent legal writers. They simply need to improve their editing skills and apply those skills systematically.

Second, do not get discouraged. Becoming a good editor requires much practice. The principles set forth in this book are numerous; there are principles about writing, about various parts of the brief, about transition words and phrases, about steps for using case precedents, etc. Mastering all of these principles is hard, and you will not do so quickly.

But if you work at editing long enough, and use sequential editing, you *will* internalize the tasks of good editing. You will automatically start to see passive voices, lack of transitions, inadequate or inaccurate headings, etc., and you will gradually internalize the overall principles. Developing the skills of editing will take time, but the effort is worth it. Editing is crucial to excellent briefs.

B. FINALIZING THE BRIEF

You are near the end of the editing process. After much work, the brief is looking good! But you are not done yet. A couple of important tasks remain.

1. Cite Checking

You must carefully verify the citations in the brief. A citation represents to a judge that a specific point will be found at the specific reference. The judge must be able to rely upon that representation.

If the citation is inaccurate—say, the volume where the case is found is actually 53 A.2d, not 52 A.2d—your mis-citation will set in motion certain repercussions. The judge now must find the correct cite, either by looking at the table of authorities of the brief (which, in the worst case, repeats the mis-citation) or by doing separate research. The judge is not happy about this waste of time. *See, e.g., Federated Mutual Insurance Co. v. Anderson,* 277 Mont. 134, 145, 920 P.2d 97 (1996) (sanctioning lawyers for, among other errors, inaccurate citation of authorities).

Second, and even more important, the judge has now learned that she cannot trust your citations. Inevitably, she will then wonder whether she can trust the substantive representations in your brief. As a former Illinois Supreme Court justice put it, "An inaccurate cite 'makes you wonder if the whole case is weak.' . . ." Mark Rust, *Mistakes to Avoid on Appeal,* 74 A.B.A. J. 78 (1988). You must avoid that cloud on the persuasiveness of your work by making sure that all your citations are accurate.

The best cite checker is someone who is not involved in the brief writing and who will not bring any preconceptions to reviewing the citations. In legal practice, paralegals often act as cite checkers. But, as a law student, you do not have a paralegal, so you will have to do it yourself.

As part of the cite checking, you must determine whether the cases used are still "good law." A new, relevant precedent may have been handed down since you first read the cases during your legal research. If you are citing a very recent case, you must be particularly careful that a higher court has not agreed to hear the case and vacated the opinion upon which your draft brief now relies.

In sum, you want completely accurate cites. No exceptions.

2. Double Checking Compliance with Rules

Next, do one last check of whether the brief complies with the rules of court. Of course, you examined those rules *before* you began writing the brief. Hopefully, no problem will arise.

Still, the rules can be quite precise, and you might easily overlook something. Indeed, a publication issued by the Seventh Circuit Court of Appeals states that "nearly two dozen jurisdictional statements are rejected each month" because of rule violations. U.S. Court of Appeals for the Seventh Circuit, Practitioner's Handbook for Appeals 168 (2020 ed.). So take the small amount of time needed to make certain that you have met every requirement.

3. Final Proofreading

Lastly, you need to do a final, complete proofreading of the brief. Your goal is basic and non-negotiable: The brief is to be perfect. No typographical errors, no misspellings, no computer glitches. Moreover, you cannot entirely rely on the "spell check" function of your word-processing program. As you may have learned already, if the misspelling in your brief actually *correctly* spells another word—the wrong word—the program probably will not pick up your mistake.

Proofreading is far more important than beginning lawyers often realize. Consider carefully the following statement from the late Judge Patricia Wald, formerly Chief Judge of the District of Columbia Circuit Court of Appeals:

> You cannot imagine how disquieting it is to find several spelling or grammatical errors in an otherwise competent brief. It makes the judge go back to square one in evaluating counsel. It says—worst of all—the author never bothered to read the whole thing through, but she expects us to.

Patricia M. Wald, *19 Tips from 19 Years on the Appellate Bench*, 1 J. App. Prac. & Process 7, 22 (1999).

You should not entirely delegate the proofreading task to others, for some problems may appear in the brief that only you, the brief writer, can spot. This "nondelegation" principle, however, does not mean that you need to be the *only* proofreader. In fact, having an additional person proofread the brief is an excellent idea. Two heads are, indeed, better than one.

The biggest problems in proofreading arise from those individuals who fall into the category of "fast readers." Their eyes tend to automatically read groups of words at once, and in doing so, they may mentally insert a word on the page that is not actually there. Additionally, their speed in reading can easily cause them to gloss over misspelled words and typographical errors.

So all proofreaders need to slow down when they read the brief this one last time. To meet this goal, we highly recommend that you finish the editing process by reading the brief out loud. This process will take some time, of course. However, reading it aloud allows you to assess the sound and beat of the writing. Then, add a "fail safe" to this oral reading: Put your finger on each word that you read. The finger will slow you down.

A well-written brief will sound good to the listener. On the other hand, if the brief still has problems, reading it can bring them to the surface. As the manual prepared for law clerks to federal judges summarizes, "Read the material to be edited aloud; this may disclose previously unnoticed problems." *A Handbook for Law Clerks to Federal Judges* (3d ed.), 2017 WL 2911771.

In proofreading, pay special attention to the table of contents in the brief. This page will be the first one that a reader sees, and first impressions are important. Furthermore, the table is compiled rather than written, and it is often put together at the last minute. Consequently, the table can easily include mistakes of one sort or another. Indeed, some appellate specialists believe that more mistakes are found in the table of contents than anywhere else.

The suggestions made above (reading aloud and using a finger) may seem a bit foreign to you, but typos have a way of springing up at the worst times. Consider a former colleague of the authors who, while in practice with a very large, national law firm, was working on a mammoth, extremely important filing for a large airline. A team of 15 lawyers worked around the clock for days on the pleading. They pored over the document, making small changes up until the end. Finally, it was ready to go, and the president of the airline came to the firm's office to sign it.

He found a typographical error on the first page.

Summary

- Editing is vital to good brief writing.

- You must have an editing "plan" so that you undertake multiple editing rounds with specific goals in mind.

- Give yourself enough time to edit, and step away from the brief for a period of time before completing your final edit.

- To finalize the brief, you must cite check it and carefully proofread it. You must also, once again, ensure that the brief complies with the applicable rules of court.

CHAPTER 12

Oral Argument

A. AFTER THE BRIEFING IS COMPLETE

1. The Waiting Period

The parties have completed the briefing of your appeal. You know the record, the law, and the arguments. You can't *wait* for oral argument to be calendared.

Yet, in the real world, waiting is exactly what you will probably do. Some appellate courts are relatively current in keeping up with their caseload. If your appeal is in such a court, you might expect to be calendared for oral argument within a couple of months after the completion of the briefing. The delay in many other courts, however, can be much longer. For planning purposes, counsel must find out. The court's clerks can be helpful in giving counsel some idea about when the court will calendar a case for argument.

Another possibility is that you will not have an opportunity for oral argument. Nationally, courts are increasingly deciding cases without benefit of oral argument. *See* FED. CT. APP. MANUAL § 33:1 (6th ed.) (noting that more than 87% of all federal appeals are decided without oral argument). That statistic should reinforce what you learned above in this book: The brief is the most important part of appellate practice. Still, in important cases, or those before supreme courts, oral arguments will be scheduled. Meanwhile, in the intervening period before the argument, events are occurring at the court.

2. The Court's Internal Analysis

Before the oral argument, the court will analyze the appeal to prepare it for decision. If an intermediate appellate court is hearing the appeal, a panel of judges (usually three in number) will be assigned to the case. If the appeal is docketed in a state supreme court or the U.S. Supreme Court, the full court hears the matter.

Before the case is set for oral argument, the court will initiate an internal procedure for analyzing the issues. The procedure varies somewhat from court to court, but the main process is uniform. Some person—either an individual judge or a research attorney supervised by a judge—will be assigned to prepare a memorandum on the case. Often the memorandum will take the form of a draft opinion. That memorandum will then circulate to the other judges who will hear the appeal.

In some courts the judges do not talk with each other about an appeal before oral argument, while in other courts the panel may have a pre-argument conference. In either case each judge comes to the argument independently prepared, often with an idea as to how the court should decide the appeal

The internal procedure followed by the court demonstrates, once again, the decisive role that legal writing plays in the appellate world. Before oral argument and based solely on the briefs, judges will reach tentative (and, likely, quite strongly held) conclusions about how to decide the appeal. A party may have the "better" side of the legal issues raised on appeal, but if that party's briefs do not adequately argue those issues, oral argument is unlikely to save the day. Still, oral argument can be important. As federal appellate judge Joel Dubina recounted: "I confess that I have seen cases where a good oral argument compensated for a poor brief and saved the day for that particular lawyer's position. I have also seen effective oral argument preserve a victory in a deserving case." The Honorable Joel F. Dubina, *How to Litigate Successfully in the United States Court of Appeals for the Eleventh Circuit*, 49 CUMB. L. REV. 297, 304 (2019).

After the court's preparatory work is complete, counsel will receive a notice that the court has now calendared the appeal for oral argument. In a few courts the panel may even send the parties the "tentative" opinion before the argument. Appellate counsel will then proceed to prepare for oral argument.

B. PREPARING FOR ORAL ARGUMENT

1. "Hot" and "Cold" Benches

In thinking about the oral argument, we will first skip ahead and see if we can draw any general conclusions about what will occur at the argument. Of course, if you could somehow predict the argument's flow, your preparation would be much easier. That sort of prediction, however, is not usually possible.

Some courts will pepper counsel with questions, sometimes interrupt answers to those questions with new questions, demand authority for positions, and generally inquire animatedly into the issues. These are known as "hot" benches — perhaps because they make the lawyers feel "the heat" as they try to answer the questions.

In other situations, the court can be quite passive. The judges will listen to the argument but will ask only a handful of perhaps uninspired questions. They may even look bored as you argue before them. Even worse, the few questions that they ask may seem to demonstrate some ignorance about the issues raised on the appeal. These are known as "cold" benches.

If the highest court in a jurisdiction is hearing the appeal, you can generally assume that the court will be fully prepared and will ask numerous questions. At the lower appellate level, however, oral argument practices vary among individual courts. Furthermore, a lower appellate panel may act as a "hot" bench for one case and a "cold" bench for another. Accordingly, the practitioner has no choice but to prepare for both types of argument.

Lawyers arguing cases will research the panel of judges who will hear the case to find out about their backgrounds and previous decisions that they authored. If possible, the lawyers also will observe a session of oral arguments in the court held before the panel of judges scheduled to hear their argument. Visiting the court before you are scheduled to argue also gives you an opportunity to note the logistics and layout of the parking, the courthouse, and the courtroom. Doing this "homework" beforehand will reduce your stress on the day that you are set to argue.

If you are arguing in a moot court competition during law school, you will not be able to research the judges. However, you might be able to visit the moot court room and any classrooms where the arguments will be held. Familiarity with their features may likewise ease your nerves on argument day.

2. Refamiliarizing Yourself with the Case

You start your preparation by thinking about where you want to be at the *end* of that preparation. You have a number of objectives:

- To be fully familiar with the legal arguments in the briefs
- To have responses ready to the legal arguments of your opponent
- To know the key cases
- To be fully familiar with the facts and with the record of your case
- To present an argument that does not just repeat what is in your brief
- To be able to respond to the most difficult questions that a court can ask you

Overall, the oral advocate wants to be comfortable and confident presenting the case at argument.

Accomplishing these tasks is a tall order. So you break the preparation down into smaller, logical steps.

You start by carefully rereading the briefs. Apply the perspective principle and try to see them as an appellate judge would read them for the first time. What issues would stand out? Is your position consistent with the overall trend of authority on an issue, or are you asking the court to decide an issue of first impression? Is this a case where the equities seem to favor one side? Additionally, are there themes that you want to emphasize in your argument?

As you consider these questions, take notes so you won't forget the points that come to your mind. Your thoughts here will form a key part of your oral argument.

Next, review the important parts of the record. You may not have to reread every page of the entire record, but be careful. You must be familiar with all the pertinent facts and the procedural history of the case. If a judge at the argument asks you about a factual or procedural matter, you do not want to reply, "I am not sure, Your Honor."

A logical next step is to reread the cases. In doing so, however, you must keep in mind a key difference between written and oral arguments. Written argument affords an advocate the opportunity to be extremely precise in applying a precedent. In a brief you can discuss in depth both the facts and the intricacies of the court's legal reasoning, for written argument lends itself to micro-analysis.

Oral argument is quite different, for lawyers arguing before a court will discuss cases in more general terms. This type of argument certainly does not absolve you from in-depth knowledge of the cases. It means, however, that instead of referring to minute facts in the case, you will describe it more generally and likely discuss it with a much "broader brush" during the argument. Accordingly, as you reread the cases, you will want to make a one- or two-paragraph summary of each case.

Finally, you will want to update your research to make sure that no new relevant authorities have been handed down since you filed your briefs. Moot court rules in law school competitions generally have a "cut off" date for the authorities that you may cite. In the real world, however, courts are vitally interested in getting the most current authority. If you find new relevant cases, the appropriate procedure is usually to write the court, with a copy to opposing counsel, informing them that you intend to cite certain new cases at oral argument.

3. Outlining Your Argument

You are now ready to begin outlining your argument. You will not write out your argument verbatim, for a simple reason: You will not be reading it. So do not tempt yourself to read; instead, put your argument in outline form.

In creating an outline, you have a specific goal: to create usable notes that you can bring with you to the podium on the date of oral argument. One popular method is to use only two pages of notes. You may feel more comfortable with a slightly longer outline. However, keep in mind that you will need to refer quickly to the outline during argument, so you need to keep the outline as succinct and short as possible. Furthermore, the longer the outline is, the more difficulty you will have finding the "right spot" in it during an argument — particularly if you have to flip pages.

So a two-page outline is usually best. Make sure that you do not cover the entire page with a large "blob" of words that is hard to read. You need to glance down and be able to quickly access the material. So the outline cannot be too dense; you want "headlines," not paragraphs of material.

When you are done, print the pages out and paste them inside a folder. Alternatively, punch three holes in them and insert them in a binder, so they face each other.

4. Taking Control of the Beginning and the Conclusion

As discussed above, it is hard to predict whether the bench will be relatively silent or will ask you a multitude of questions, so you must prepare for both situations. Ultimately, you must have the ability to adjust to the "flow" of the argument, whether you encounter a "hot" bench pressing you with questions or a "cold" bench content to sit back and listen to you.

However, while you cannot predict how the argument will play out as a whole, you can be relatively certain about two parts of it. First, most courts will allow you to begin the argument uninterrupted for some period of time. It could be just a minute, but it could be longer. Indeed, until recently, justices on the United States Supreme Court were likely to quickly interrupt lawyers with questions.

However, the Court has changed its approach. Now the Court "generally will not question lead counsel for petitioners (or appellants) and respondents (or appellees) during the first two minutes of argument." *Guide for Counsel in Cases to Be Argued Before the Supreme Court of the United States,* at 7, https://www.supremecourt.gov/casehand/Guide%20for%20Counsel%202019_rev10_3_19.pdf. You can also usually count on having a brief period (a minute or even less) to conclude when your argument is over.

So you can prepare the beginning and conclusion in advance. Outline them in some detail, and then practice them. Get the beginning and the conclusion down cold, and your preparation will produce benefits. You will appear polished and prepared at the two times of the argument during which you probably can speak without interruption.

5. Confronting the Hardest Questions

In the *Star Wars* movie *The Empire Strikes Back*, Luke Skywalker trains under the Jedi master Yoda on the planet Dagobah. At one point in the training, Luke goes into a kind of hole where he is forced to confront his worst fears.

You want to undergo the equivalent experience in your preparation for oral argument — confronting your worst fears about the argument. So what is the worst event that can happen? The most common "worst fear" is that you will be asked a very difficult question and be unable to answer it. You can see it now: You will stand there, mumbling incoherently when pressed to answer, obviously unable to give the judge an appropriate response.

But you can avoid this dismal prospect by confronting your fear. You have the ability to do so simply by (yet again) putting yourself in the judge's shoes.

You already know the weaknesses of your case; you identified them when you wrote the brief. Now write a list of the ten or so hardest questions for your party to answer. Then take the time to think through the best answers that you have to the questions, and write them out as well.

Not all of the answers will be completely persuasive. Hard questions are just that — hard. But you *will* have an answer for the court when the questions come up. Equally important, because you have confronted the questions during your practice, they will not catch you off guard at the argument. Familiarity with the questions, and the time that you spent thinking through answers, will give you confidence. Finally, this process may even suggest some new approaches to answering the difficult questions.

6. Practicing the Argument and Properly Using Notes

In an increasing percentage of all appellate arguments, appellate counsel now engage in a "mock" or "moot" practice arguments before the actual oral argument. In cases before the United States Supreme Court, almost every lawyer who argues participates in several of these "moots."

Obviously, students find it much harder to undertake this type of preparation. In all probability, the only people that you can round up to participate in a practice argument are the other members of the class or close friends and relatives, and they might not have much time. But one moot can be a big help, even if it just consists of a person unfamiliar with the case asking you questions that you have provided. If nothing else, you will become comfortable standing at and speaking from a podium.

If a moot is not possible, you want to practice your argument again and again, making changes to smooth out "rough spots" as they appear. The more practice that you do, the more comfortable you will be at the time of the actual argument. You can practice before a mirror to get used to standing on your feet. You can also practice before family and friends, as advocated by Supreme Court Justice

Stephen Breyer: "Know your case and explain it to your spouse, teenaged daughter, somebody prepared to listen. When they understand it, you've got it." Margaret D. McGaughey, *May It Please the Court — or Not: Appellate Judges' Preferences and Pet Peeves About Oral Argument*, 20 J. APP. PRAC. & PROCESS 141, 159 (2019).

A very useful tool is to record your practice argument on a smartphone. You can see how you will appear to a panel of judges and adjust your presentation accordingly.

Finally, students and lawyers who are doing their first oral arguments are often nervous, a reaction that is perfectly normal. However, one response to a case of nerves is for the student or lawyer to seek comfort from their notes. Thus, nervous students and young lawyers may constantly veer back and forth between looking at the court and looking down at their notes. Of course, it goes without saying that this type of "back and forth" is not an effective way to retain the attention of the court.

So how do you avoid over-reliance on notes? The best way is to practice your argument without *any* notes in front of you. It will be difficult the first time, but it will go better than you expect. Then, each time that you argue without notes, you will gain confidence in your knowledge of the case. Soon, you will be maintaining continual eye contact with the bench and consulting your notes much less frequently.

7. Knowing and Using the Record

If certain critical parts of the record play a central role in the appeal, be ready to use them. Citing a specific page of the record in your argument is effective if done sparingly. You might say: "As the record states at page 250, . . ."

C. THE MECHANICS OF ARGUING

1. The Formal Decorum of Oral Argument

As the day of oral argument approaches, use some common sense. Make sure you get enough sleep before the argument; arriving in court tired is never a good idea. Also make sure you are hydrated and have eaten sensibly.

Appellate courts are decorous environments. Many oral arguments in state appellate courts are available for viewing online, and you should watch some of them. You will see that the courtrooms tend to be stately. Furthermore, the procedures followed are quite formal.

You must respect that decorum. You will dress as a professional for oral argument. You want to give the court the impression that you are prepared and competent, and slovenly dressed lawyers do not give that impression.

You will give your oral argument standing behind a podium. In doing so, you must avoid postures or actions that are out of place or even disrespectful. Competent, prepared advocates will not rock back and forth, walk around, squirm, put their hands in pockets, gesture wildly, roll their eyes, or otherwise appear out of control. Instead, professionals stand calmly at the podium, perhaps using their hands once in a while to emphasize a point.

2. Engaging in a Conversation

From the advocate's standpoint, the overriding aim of oral argument is to *engage* the court. You want the judges to pay attention and, most importantly, to ask questions if something is bothering them. You do not want to make a speech or presentation; instead, you want to have a conversation with the court about the case.

To do so, you must talk directly to the judges, so you make eye contact with them. And, to repeat, you *never* read your argument. Not only is reading to the court unprofessional, it is entirely counterproductive. As one federal appellate judge put it, the purpose of oral argument is to engage the court in "the same type of robust discussion one would have around a dinner table . . . ." Margaret D. McGaughey, *May It Please the Court — or Not: Appellate Judges' Preferences and Pet Peeves About Oral Argument,* 20 J. App. Prac. & Process 141, 161 (2019).

Engaging in that type of discussion is hard for law students in moot court competitions and for young lawyers. But you need to keep it mind as you practice.

3. Using a Moderate Tone

Use a normal, moderate tone in your argument. There is no "special" voice for oral argument. Never raise your voice, and never get angry. Don't be indignant or whine; just be firm and convincing. You can show measured passion and demonstrate to the court that you care about the case, but an appellate court is not a place for histrionics.

4. Avoiding the Speed Trap

Last, but certainly not least, is the question of the speed at which you speak. Arguing before an appellate court is a stressful, "high wire" act. You must think on your feet, answer questions, and reorganize your thoughts "on the go." It is exhilarating but difficult to do well.

The stress commonly leads students and young lawyers presenting their first arguments to exhibit one characteristic: They speak too fast. Some think that they have to speak quickly to get the answer out before another question from the court stops them. Others just get nervous and respond by speaking rapidly.

The problem is that speaking quickly inhibits the "conversation" that you wish to have with the court. Judges find it harder to follow fast speech. Moreover, speaking rapidly gives the appearance that the advocate is nervous, not fully in control, and (perhaps) worried about being able to answer. If your purpose is really to convince someone, you will speak slowly.

You can take steps beforehand to address the problem. First, write "Slow Down" in big letters at the top of your argument outline. Second, train yourself in answering questions to pause for two beats ("one thousand one, one thousand two") before answering. Third, if you have talked too fast in answering a question during your practice argument, immediately answer the question again in a slower voice. The repetition will help you speak more slowly.

Fourth, record some of your practices and listen to the recording. It will give you valuable feedback on whether your argument is sufficiently "conversational."

If you still have trouble speaking slowly, sit down at a desk with a friend. Looking across at him or her, make your argument. In doing so, talk as you would to a friend while having a cup of coffee. Keep practicing until your speed has slowed. Then stand up and try it from a podium.

In addition to conveying your argument in a more convincing fashion, speaking slowly has one other important advantage. You may end up dealing with a "hot" bench, where the judges interrupt your answers with other questions and speed up the tempo. You can get into a fast "back and forth" with the court that can easily prevent you from fully making the points that you need to make. However, if you learn to respond by speaking slowly, this type of slower response in turn may cause the court to slow down a bit. In effect, you may be able to exercise some control over how the argument proceeds.

D. ARGUMENT PROCEDURE

Now we turn to the procedures used at the actual oral argument.

1. Introducing Yourself and Reserving Time for Rebuttal

The clerk will call your case. If you are the appellant, you will argue first. You will proceed to the podium and get settled. Then, when the court indicates that you may proceed, you begin by introducing yourself. You might say:

> May it please the court. My name is Ashley Binghamton. I represent appellant John Smith in this matter.

Counsel for the appellee will make the same type of introduction at the beginning of the appellee's argument.

In the real world, oral arguments on a single side are rarely split between counsel. However, if you are arguing in a law school moot court, the convention is that two students argue each side, so in this situation you will also want to tell the court how the argument will split the issues. After introducing yourself, you would say something like:

> Your Honors, I will be arguing the Fourth Amendment issues regarding the validity of the search. My co-counsel, Ms. Perez, will argue the Eighth Amendment issues concerning the right to a jury trial.

If you are the appellant, you argue first but have the right to "reserve" some of your time for rebuttal. The rebuttal will occur after the appellee's argument. Normally, you will want to reserve a brief amount of time for rebuttal argument. Since the usual argument is 10 or 15 minutes long, reserving two or, at most, three minutes for rebuttal would be right. After you introduce yourself, you will say:

> May I please reserve two minutes of my time for rebuttal?

If you are splitting argument time with co-counsel, you would say:

> May I please reserve two minutes of time for rebuttal, with the time split evenly between myself and my co-counsel?

When the court grants your request, you respond:

> Thank you, Your Honor.

If you forget to reserve time for rebuttal, you will forfeit that right. Likewise, do not "waive" your rebuttal time. Always reserve the chance to have the proverbial "last word" before the court.

2. Creating a Roadmap for the Argument Ahead

After the introductory statements just discussed, you should give the court an overview, or "roadmap," of the argument that you will make. It should be very brief: "This is a case about . . . . Appellant Smith contends . . . ." Another acceptable beginning is to outline the issues before the court: "This appeal concerns the applicability of the statute of limitations for a tort claim where the symptoms of the malpractice were hidden for years. Appellant submits that the statute of limitations does not bar appellant's claim for three reasons. First . . . ." After that brief roadmap, you immediately launch into your principal argument.

Some older books on appellate argument suggest that counsel ask the following question at the beginning of the argument: "Would the court like a recitation of the facts?" Almost all courts will decline this offer. After all, they have read the briefs and the bench memo, so they don't *need* such a recitation. In fact, some can be offended by the question. So this type of offer to the court is outmoded.

3. The Appellee's Argument

There are, of course, differences between presenting an argument for an appellant and one for the appellee. For one thing, the appellant may reserve time for rebuttal, while the appellee may not. More basically, the burden is on the appellant to demonstrate that the lower court erred.

For oral argument purposes, however, a critical difference is that the appellee argues *after* the appellant. Thus, the appellee has an opportunity to capitalize on what went on during the appellant's argument. For example, perhaps a judge asked a question of the appellant's counsel that was not answered well. The appellee's lawyer might want to answer that same question during the argument. Alternatively, perhaps the court was particularly interested in a certain case and raised it during the appellant's argument. The appellee's lawyer might decide to address that case as well.

However, to take advantage of the fact that the appellee argues after the appellant, the appellee must be flexible. While the appellee's counsel will have a prepared argument to give, after listening to the appellant's argument, counsel may want to change the order or emphasis of the argument. To do so, you must anticipate this possibility before the argument. During your preparation, force yourself to rearrange the order of your presentation in some of the practice arguments. You "shuffle the deck" of your main arguments, giving them in different orders.

The more that you practice this rearranging, the easier you will find it to reorder your argument "on the fly." Your ability to do so can bring great rewards.

4. The Concluding "Time Crunch"

If you have a "hot" bench, you may be in the middle of an answer when your time expires. You can be informed that the time is up in one of several ways. The chief judge may interrupt you and say, "Your time is up, counsel." Alternatively, some courts have electronic timers at the podium, and they start to run in the negative when you exceed your allotted time. In moot court competitions in law school, the bailiff may hold up a sign with a zero on it.

If your time is up, you have no right to continue. You could simply stop in mid-sentence, say, "Thank you, Your Honor," and sit down. However, if you run out of time because you have been trying to answer a question (as opposed to just arguing without interruption), you may wish to say to the court: "I see that my time is up. May I briefly conclude?" Most courts will give you a short time — maybe 30 seconds — to finish the answer. You cannot abuse this privilege. If you go on too long, you are asking for the court to interrupt you and tell you to sit down.

Other times, you are simply arguing when the court interrupts you and says that your time is up. Once again, you could ask: "May I briefly conclude?" Here, though, it was not the judge's question that caused you to go over; it was the length of your argument. So the answer may be "no." Accordingly, you must be aware of the time. If you are in your last minute and are not interrupted by questions, you want to complete your argument before your time runs out.

Your overall goal is to finish your argument by giving the brief conclusion that you have practiced in your preparation. Doing so will allow you to vacate the podium in a polished and professional fashion, leaving a good impression.

5. Using Rebuttal Time Effectively

If you are doing a rebuttal as the appellant, you will want to make only two, or at most three, very specific points. Make them clearly and succinctly. You want to avoid opening up large issues that take time to explain or that are controversial. If you raise such an issue, you are inviting the court to start questioning you about it again, and you will then use up the little time that you have available without being able to accomplish anything.

The best rebuttal arguments respond directly to a relatively narrow point made by opposing counsel. For example:

> Counsel for Appellee cites the case of *Cedar v. Dogwood* as holding that no proximate cause exists here. That case, however, is about actual cause, because it concerns whether the injury would have occurred if the defendant was not negligent. It provides no authority for the issue of proximate cause.

One final point about rebuttals: Just because you reserved a short time for rebuttal, you are not required to use that time. If the argument has gone well, and you have nothing effective to say, you can just submit the case. Better to quit while you seem to be ahead. There are instances in which lawyers gave an effective opening argument but then blundered into real trouble with an ill-considered rebuttal.

In moot court competitions, however, you should exercise your right to give a rebuttal argument. You want the last word before the panel of judges.

E. ANSWERING QUESTIONS

1. The Initial Response: A Full Stop

As an appellate advocate, you *hope* for questions. They indicate what topics or issues are of interest to or bothering a judge. Questions are an opportunity to reinforce the judge's thinking, or to try to turn the judge around on a point. If you are not asked questions, you do not have this opportunity; instead, you are left to guess what interests or bothers the court.

Because of the importance of questions, and because the court is in control of the argument, a fundamental rule of appellate advocacy is *never* to talk "over" a judge. As soon as a judge starts to speak, or even makes a noise, you stop — instantly. You stop even if you are in the middle of the most profound or important point of your entire argument. You stop and listen respectfully to the question.

2. Answer, Then Explain

Then, you answer the precise question. You never put off the answer by saying, "I'll get to that later in my argument." You never respond by saying something like, "That isn't the issue."

The best answer to a question is "Yes, Your Honor" or "No, Your Honor." You *then* explain your reasoning for the "yes" or "no." Or, if a simple "yes" or "no" is impossible, start with a short, one-sentence answer: "In that instance the statute of limitations would bar the action, Your Honor."

Sometimes inexperienced advocates will begin their answer by trying to set forth the assumptions behind their answer or by explaining the conditions on which it rests. They might say: "I assume, Your Honor, that the injury remains the same, and that no other actions are on file in the matter. In that situation, Appellant would then agree to the transfer. So the answer to your question would be yes." The problem here is that, if the bench is hot, you may get interrupted before you get to the end of your answer. Furthermore, this kind of answer can irritate the court, which has to wait patiently for you to get to the ultimate point.

So experienced advocates will answer the question fully but quickly. After doing so, they can then elaborate on the reasoning behind the answer, or the background or exceptions to it. If they get interrupted at this point, they still have answered the question.

If you are not interrupted when you are answering a question from a judge, do not rush through your answer so that you can move on to another topic. Rather, stay on this topic until the judge seems satisfied. If the judge is still interested in the topic, then by definition *you* are still interested. Only when you feel that you have satisfied the judge's interest will you move on.

One final, important point about questions: They can serve different purposes. Certainly, judges can ask questions because they disagree with, or at least have serious questions about, the advocate's position on an issue. Most law students and many young lawyers assume that such disagreement is behind any question directed to them, and they offer an answer that assumes they have to win the judge over on the point. That may indeed be the case.

However, judges (including those on moot court panels) also ask questions for other reasons. Perhaps one judge agrees with you but knows another judge on the panel has problems with your position, so the judge's question may be designed to provide information to that other judge. Maybe the judge doesn't know the answer to the question and simply wants information. Or maybe the judge agrees with you. As one judge on Maryland's highest court put it, "[A] judge may give you a friendly or helpful question—a 'softball.'" The Honorable Patrick L. Woodward, *Effective Oral Argument Before the Court of Special Appeals*, MD. B.J. 28, 31 (Jan./Feb. 2017).

The point is that, as an advocate, you cannot automatically assume that a judge's question is hostile to your position. One law clerk to a judge observed this negative attitude in oral arguments that she witnessed: "Sometimes, I saw attorneys so fixated on making their arguments that they failed to recognize when a judge's question was actually calculated to guide the attorney toward an argument helpful for the client." Emily R. Bodtke, *Arguing at the Appellate Level: A Judicial Clerk's Perspective*, BENCH & B. MINN. 34, 36 (April 2017).

So you need to listen carefully to the question and try to ascertain its purpose. Don't rush your answer. Instead, while you are thinking, pause for a few seconds to mentally categorize the question as hostile, information-seeking, helpful, etc. Then tailor your answer accordingly. An answer to a question that seriously challenges your position will be quite different than an answer to one that is actually friendly to that position.

3. Always Respect the Court

The proper response to a question or statement by the court is "Yes, Your Honor." Not, "Yes." You are not the court's equal. Also, do not use slang ("OK," "sure"), for such usage is disrespectful. Finally, generally avoid the use of the pronoun "I" in your argument, for the argument is not about you.

Summary

- The court will analyze the case before argument, often preparing a draft opinion for its internal use.

- In many instances you must prepare "two" arguments: one before a "hot" bench, the other before a "cold" bench. As part of your preparation, you will also update your research to see if you should bring any important new cases to the court's attention.

- You will bring an outline of your argument to the podium with you. The outline should not be lengthy and should be easy to reference when you are at the podium.

- You can practice a set beginning and conclusion to your argument. Avoid relying excessively on notes when you make your argument. Practice your argument without notes.

- Write out the hardest questions that the court can ask you, as well as answers to those questions. Then practice them.

- At oral argument your goal is to engage in a conversation with the court. You do this by talking slowly and using a moderate tone.

- At the beginning of the appellant's argument you will reserve some time for rebuttal. The appellee does not get rebuttal. However, the appellee can take advantage of the fact that the appellant argues first by addressing those points of most concern to the court during the appellant's argument.

- In answering questions from the court, give a "yes" or "no" answer if you can. Otherwise, give a full answer in one sentence, then go on to more fully explain the answer. Avoid a long "windup" to the actual answer; you might be interrupted by another question before you complete that answer.

- Always be respectful to the court by saying, "Yes, Your Honor" or "No, Your Honor," and never talking "over" a judge.

- All questions from a court are not hostile; they may serve various purposes. So listen carefully to the question and pause for a few seconds to tailor an answer that responds to the nature of the question.

A NOTE ON THE FORMAT OF APPENDIX A

Appendix A is a sample opening brief by an appellant in a federal court of appeals. It models the various principles discussed in this book.

The brief uses a set of facts modified from a real case. However, the appeal in Appendix A is situated in a fictional federal circuit court of appeals, so that the brief would not have to concentrate on prior decisions in one circuit. This methodology allowed the authors more flexibility in choosing cases with facts that best illustrate the application of the principles in the book.

Except for those case cites to the standard of review in the "12th Circuit" (which cites are fictional), all decisions and other legal materials cited in this brief could be used in an actual appeal. However, because the brief is intended as a teaching tool that illustrates the key principles set forth in the book, it does not attempt to comply with all aspects of the Federal Rules of Appellate Procedure.

Docket No. 20-3456

UNITED STATES COURT OF APPEALS
FOR THE TWELFTH CIRCUIT

ANN ARNOLD,
Plaintiff-Appellant,

v.

THE UNITED STATES OF AMERICA
Defendant-Appellee

Appeal from the United States District Court
for the District of Caledonia
Case No. 17-89

APPELLANT'S OPENING BRIEF

Erin A. Rogers, Esq.
ROGERS, SHOWELL, AND TAYLOR
400 A Street, Suite 600
Springfield, Caledonia 01234
ERogers@RSTLaw.com
(980) 765-4321
Attorneys for Appellant Ann Arnold

TABLE OF CONTENTS

TABLE OF AUTHORITIES

Statutes

Rules

STATEMENT OF JURISDICTION

Appellant Ann Arnold initiated this action against the United States under the Federal Tort Claims Act ("FTCA"). *See* 28 U.S.C. §1346(b)(1). Jurisdiction was proper in the district court under 28 U.S.C. §1331.

The district court granted summary judgment in favor of the United States on October 17, 2019, disposing of Ms. Arnold's claims. Appellant's Appendix, page 478. Pursuant to Federal Rule of Appellate Procedure 4(a)(1)(A), Ms. Arnold filed a Notice of Appeal within 60 days after entry of the district court's judgment. Appellant's Appendix, page 490. Accordingly, this Court has jurisdiction under 28 U.S.C. §1291.

STATEMENT OF THE ISSUES

1. Did the district court misapply the "discovery rule" when it determined that Ms. Arnold's claim for damages accrued under the FTCA before any doctor correctly diagnosed her medical condition and its cause?
2. Did the district court err in holding that the doctrine of equitable tolling is limited to timely filed but defective pleadings and to fraudulently concealed information, and that, in any event, appellant failed to meet the doctrine's requirements?

STATEMENT OF THE CASE

Ms. Arnold initiated this litigation in January 2017 under the Federal Tort Claims Act, 28 U.S.C. §2671 *et seq.* The parties conducted discovery and then filed cross-motions for summary judgment. They stipulated to the facts. Appellant's Appendix, page 450. After holding an oral argument, the district court filed a written opinion granting the motion of the United States and denying Ms. Arnold's motion. The district court held that the FTCA's statute of limitations barred Ms. Arnold's action. Appellant's Appendix, page 505.

Thereafter, on December 2, 2019, the district court entered judgment for the United States. Fifteen days later, Ms. Arnold filed a notice of appeal. Appellant's Appendix, page 531.

STATEMENT OF FACTS

A. Ms. Arnold's Work Near an Army Facility and Her Unknowing Exposure to the Toxic Nerve Agent Sarin

Born and raised in Pennsylvania, Ann Arnold graduated from Ohio State University in 2007 with a degree in conservation biology. Appellant's Appendix, page 2 (hereafter referred to as "App. at 2.") After graduation, Ms. Arnold took a summer job with the State of Caledonia Division of Wildlife as a member of a "range crew." *Id.* From April through early October 2007, Ms. Arnold participated in wildlife studies at remote sites throughout Caledonia. App. at 5.

The range crew spent approximately six weeks in Caledonia's Moon Desert during July and early August 2007. This period included work at a location less than two miles from Fort Forester, a United States Army installation. App. at 6. Ms. Arnold did not know that the Army was then secretly testing chemical and biological weapons at Fort Forester. The testing included the open burning of those weapons. *See* App. at 567, 575.

Ms. Arnold has alleged that, during the time that she spent near Fort Forester, she suffered significant exposure to toxic chemicals and nerve agents. These included the extremely dangerous nerve agent known as sarin. App. at 8.

B. The Medical Symptoms After the Exposure and Ms. Arnold's Initial Treatment

After completing her summer duties as a range technician in late 2007, Ms. Arnold returned to Pennsylvania where she accepted a position with the Pennsylvania Department of Conservation. App. at 22. Approximately one month after moving there, Ms. Arnold began to develop mysterious physical and neurological symptoms. App. at 26. Ms. Arnold's lip and face became numb at times, and she suffered blurred vision. *Id.* The numbness was episodic, and she initially thought that the blurred vision might be attributable to excessive hours spent on a computer at work. *Id.*

However, when the symptoms remained after several months, Ms. Arnold sought medical help. App. at 28. In early February 2008, an ear, nose, and throat specialist ordered a magnetic resonance imaging ("MRI") test. App. at 31. The MRI came out normal. *Id.* Nonetheless, later that month, Ms. Arnold felt her entire left side go numb on two occasions. App. at 36.

Understandably alarmed, Ms. Arnold immediately consulted a neurologist, Dr. Christopher Columbus, who reviewed her MRI and conducted a neurological examination. App. at 45. Although the MRI and examination revealed nothing abnormal, the numbness soon intensified, spreading intermittently to Ms. Arnold's right foot and right arm. *Id.* Then, in April 2009, Ms. Arnold suffered a sudden and extreme dizzy spell, and paramedics transported her to a hospital emergency room. *Id.* Her treating doctors suspected that the dizzy spell was due to a sudden restriction in her blood supply; accordingly, they discontinued her use of asthma pills. App. at 47.

Failing to improve, Ms. Arnold sought treatment that fall from yet another neurologist, Dr. Daniel Diaz of the Eastern Neurological Center in Pittsburgh, Pennsylvania. Dr. Diaz ordered a new set of imaging studies, including a brain and cervical-spine MRI, and performed a spinal tap. App. at 57. Again, the tests read as normal, and Ms. Arnold's symptoms remained undiagnosed as of December 2009. *Id.*

C. The Erroneous Diagnosis of Multiple Sclerosis and Further Complications in Ms. Arnold's Condition

By March 2010, Dr. Diaz began to suspect that Ms. Arnold's symptoms were related to multiple sclerosis ("MS"), so he referred her to two neurologists at the

University of Pennsylvania. App. at 64. They conducted further testing and then sent Ms. Arnold to Dr. Evelyn Eder, an MS specialist at the university. *Id.* Dr. Eder formally diagnosed Ms. Arnold with MS in April 2010. *Id.* Dr. Eder prescribed the drug Copaxone. App. at 65.

Although Ms. Arnold's symptoms temporarily improved during the second half of 2010 and early 2011, her condition turned significantly and permanently worse in March 2011. She began to experience severe difficulty walking and breathing, and she quickly deteriorated "from functional to nonfunctional." App. at 74. She was unable to care for herself and depended on her husband for assistance. *Id.* Ms. Arnold also experienced muscle tightness and spasms, lost feeling below her chest, and had difficulty feeding herself. *Id.* Steroids prescribed by Dr. Eder only exacerbated her symptoms. App. at 75. Nonetheless, a new MRI read normal. App. at 77.

In July 2011, Ms. Arnold traveled to Peck Medical Center in Chicago, Illinois, to see another neurologist specializing in MS, Dr. Frances Wong. App. at 83. After a normal MRI and a neuropsychology test, Dr. Wong decided that Ms. Arnold had been incorrectly diagnosed with MS. App. at 86. In September 2011, Dr. Wong concluded that Ms. Arnold's physical and neurological symptoms were psychosomatic. App. at 92.

Given this diagnosis, Ms. Arnold did not immediately seek additional medical assistance. *Id.* However, when her condition remained unchanged through September 2012, Ms. Arnold began to explore the possibility that her symptoms might relate to neck issues. App. at 98. She began treatment with a chiropractor, Dr. Gale Gordon, who specialized in chiropractic care that focused on neurologic issues. *Id.* In filling out paperwork for Dr. Gordon, Ms. Arnold mentioned that she had once worked in Caledonia near an army base. App. at 102. In response, Dr. Gordon casually mentioned the possibility that some type of heavy metal might have poisoned Ms. Arnold. *Id.*

D. Ms. Arnold's Continued Investigation into Her Debilitating Illness and Two Negative Tests for Chemical Exposure

In early 2013, Ms. Arnold happened to read a magazine article about a Texas woman, Rena Rutnick, who suffered from unusual neurological symptoms somewhat like those of Ms. Arnold. App. at 112. Still searching for answers, Ms. Arnold contacted Ms. Rutnick, who said that she had become sick after visiting an Army base in Texas. *Id.* Ms. Rutnick revealed her suspicion that exposure to chemical weapons at the Texas base had caused her symptoms. App. at 114. Thereafter, Ms. Arnold undertook internet research into chemical and biological weapons. From a few blogs, she learned for the first time of stories about the testing of such weapons at Fort Forester. App. at 122, 123. The stories reported that the Army refused to confirm any such testing. App. at 124.

Following up on this research, in September 2013 Ms. Arnold decided to consult Dr. Steven Vu of the Institute of Poison Medicine. Dr. Vu informed Ms. Arnold of a specific test for exposure to chemical weapons, known as the polymerase chain reaction or "PCR" test. App. at 130. At the same time, Ms. Arnold continued to explore other explanations for her symptoms, including whether an anti-seizure medicine that her mother took during her pregnancy might have caused them. App. at 145.

In October 2013, Ms. Arnold underwent the PCR test suggested by Dr. Vu. App. at 148. The test results were negative. *Id.* Nonetheless, Ms. Arnold continued her ongoing research, and in December 2013 she learned of a former government employee who had worked at Fort Forester and who believed that he had been exposed to nerve agents there. App. at 160. Ms. Arnold located and then spoke to that employee, who told Ms. Arnold that the Army had tested sarin and other nerve agents at Fort Forester. *Id.* He described his symptoms, which were like those suffered by Ms. Arnold. App. at 181.

Armed with this new information, in early 2014 Ms. Arnold followed up with her medical professionals, "trying to explore my belief that something at Fort Forester could have caused my symptoms" because "I didn't know." App. at 201, 202. She consulted Dr. Robin Rupert, a physician in Salt Lake City, who tested her acetylcholine levels, and Dr. Rupert indicated that this test would reveal whether Ms. Arnold had been exposed to nerve agents. App. at 205. The test, however, came out negative. Consequently, Ms. Arnold discontinued seeing Dr. Rupert. *Id.*

By the end of July 2014, no physician had diagnosed Ms. Arnold with symptoms stemming from exposure to a nerve agent.

E. The Diagnosis of Sarin Exposure

By February 2015, Ms. Arnold's symptoms were still unchanged. App. at 214. In desperation, Ms. Arnold decided to inquire again into the possibility that exposure to biological or chemical weapons might have caused her symptoms. To pursue her theory, Ms. Arnold consulted Dr. Warren Wrede, a national expert on neurotoxicity at the Environmental Health Center in Boston, Massachusetts. App. at 222. Though prior tests had seemingly ruled out sarin exposure, Dr. Wrede ordered tests of Ms. Arnold's cholinesterase levels. These tests are more sensitive and more accurate indicators of that type of exposure. App. at 224.

The tests came out positive in June 2016. App at 225. Accordingly, Dr. Wrede immediately diagnosed Ms. Arnold with toxic encephalopathy, chronic fatigue, fibromyalgia, autonomic nervous system dysfunction, and immune deregulation resulting from exposure to sarin gas. App. at 228. Dr. Wrede began treating her for those medical conditions. App. at 231.

F. The Army's Denial of the Administrative Claim

As required by the FTCA, counsel for Ms. Arnold filed an administrative claim with the Army on August 5, 2016. The claim sought damages from the United States for negligently exposing Ms. Arnold to the nerve gas sarin. App. at 345. Five months later, the Army denied the claim as untimely. App. at 350.

SUMMARY OF THE ARGUMENT

Appellant Ann Arnold spent eight years fruitlessly searching for the cause of her serious medical symptoms. Over that time, she saw 11 doctors, and she suffered through one misdiagnosis of multiple sclerosis immediately followed by another misdiagnosis that dismissed her symptoms as psychosomatic. In the middle of this period, Ms. Arnold began to suspect that her symptoms might relate to exposure to chemicals in 2007, when she worked near the Army's Fort Forester. However, two tests that she then took for such exposure were negative. Furthermore, the government would not even confirm that it had tested nerve gas at Fort Forester.

Finally, in 2016, a nationally recognized expert in neurotoxins diagnosed Ms. Arnold's symptoms as originating from exposure to the nerve gas sarin. Shortly thereafter, Ms. Arnold filed a claim with the Army for damages, which was denied, and she then filed suit. The district court, however, rejected the suit, reasoning that Ms. Arnold's cause of action had accrued in 2013, when she first "suspected" exposure to chemicals from Army testing. The court held that the two-year statute of limitations for federal tort claims, 28 U.S.C. §2401(b), had expired.

In so holding, the district court erred. Under the "discovery rule," which applies to the FTCA, a cause of action does not accrue until an injured party has knowledge of both her injury and its cause. Here, no doctor correctly diagnosed Ms. Arnold's injury until 2016, and she then promptly filed a claim. Under the discovery rule, a plaintiff's cause of action does not accrue before her physicians correctly diagnose her ailment, as a contrary rule would elevate a plaintiff's suspicions above professional medical opinion. Yet the district court held that Ms. Arnold's action had accrued before any doctor diagnosed the true nature of her condition.

The discovery rule also requires that a plaintiff know the cause of her injury before a cause of action can accrue. In the case of the FTCA, this requirement is grounded in common sense. A plaintiff obviously cannot determine whether her injuries resulted from negligence without knowing what caused those injuries. Equally important, without that knowledge, a plaintiff cannot find out whether a federal employee was involved, a prerequisite to suit under the FTCA.

Here, while Ms. Arnold speculated that testing at Fort Forester might somehow relate to her injuries, she could not investigate her suspicion for a simple reason: The government refused to release *any* information about testing there. Absent that information, Ms. Arnold had no way of ascertaining the source of her injuries, and thus her cause of action did not accrue under the discovery rule.

The district court also erred in refusing to apply the doctrine of equitable tolling to Ms. Arnold's situation. That doctrine allows a court to toll the running of a statute of limitations if circumstances warrant equitable intervention. The district court erroneously found that the doctrine was limited to timely but defective pleadings or fraudulent concealment, and also that plaintiff otherwise did not meet its requirements.

Once again, Ms. Arnold submits that the district court erred. The doctrine is not limited to defective pleadings and fraudulent concealment. Rather, it applies to any situation in which "extraordinary circumstances" prevent an individual from filing a claim or otherwise acting within the time established by the statute of limitations. Here, the nature of the injury and the government's concealment of its source constitute those extraordinary circumstances. Ms. Arnold could not discover the cause of her symptoms because the government decided to hide its activities at Fort Forester. The government cannot classify the critical information as secret and then deny claims on the basis that the plaintiff did not act quickly enough on that with-held information.

Finally, the doctrine of equitable tolling requires a plaintiff to exhibit "due dil-igence" in seeking a diagnosis of her injuries. In this respect, Ms. Arnold's actions were remarkably diligent over a long eight-year period. She saw 11 doctors in var-ious parts of the country, pursuing further answers when those doctors could not diagnose or misdiagnosed her symptoms. If Ms. Arnold's actions were not diligent, then no individual's actions will ever meet that standard.

The parties in this appeal stipulated to the facts on the motion for summary judgment. Based on those facts, Ms. Arnold prevails as a matter of law. The Court must reverse the district court's judgment and instruct it to enter judgment for Ms. Arnold.

ARGUMENT

I. The De Novo Standard of Review Applies to the District Court's Grant of Summary Judgment

This Court reviews *de novo* a district court's grant of summary judgment and its legal conclusions. *Garnett v. Howell,* 205 F.3d 1210, 1216 (12th Cir. 2006). Furthermore, as the Court held in *Hitchcock v. United States,* 485 F.3d 939, 945 (12th Cir. 2012), whether a plaintiff has filed her FTCA claim within the two-year statute of limitations is also subject to *de novo* review. Accordingly, the Court should review *de novo* the issues presented in this appeal. *See Dunaway v. Smith,* 753 F.2d 789, 792 (12th Cir. 1988). Under that standard, the Court extends no deference to the district court's ruling or to its reasons, but decides the matter anew. *Id.* at 794.

II. The District Court Erred in Applying the Discovery Rule When It Concluded That Ms. Arnold's Claim Accrued in 2013 Even Though No Doctor Correctly Diagnosed Her Condition Until 2016

The well-known discovery rule operates to toll the running of a statute of lim-itations where plaintiffs possess insufficient facts to know that they have a claim for damages. Appellant Ann Arnold found herself in exactly that situation. Until just before she filed her claim, she did not know either her true medical condition or that the government caused this condition. Her facts fulfill the requirements of the discovery rule.

A. The Discovery Rule Applies to Ms. Arnold's Claim Because She Did Not Learn of a Connection Between Her Medical Symptoms and the Army's Testing of Chemical Weapons Until Years After Her Exposure

The FTCA requires a plaintiff to present a tort claim "in writing to the appropri-ate Federal agency within two years after such claim accrues. . . ." 28 U.S.C. §2401(b). Under normal circumstances, an FTCA claim accrues at the time of a plaintiff's injury. *United States v. Kubrick*, 444 U.S. 111, 120 (1979). However, in some situations "the fact or cause of an injury is unknown to (and perhaps unknowable by) a plaintiff for some time after the injury occurs . . . ." *Rakes v. United States*, 442 F.3d 7, 19 (1st Cir. 2006).

In those situations, the so-called "discovery rule" applies to the claim. For a claim to accrue under that rule, a plaintiff must know, or in the exercise of reasonable diligence should know, the factual basis of the cause of action. Those facts include "the existence of an injury and its probable causal connection to the federal government." *Dominguez v. United States*, 799 F.3d 151, 153 (1st Cir. 2015); *see Kubrick*, 444 U.S. at 120-21.

The purpose of the discovery rule is to protect plaintiffs who, through no fault of their own, "do[] not learn that a defendant has caused [them] harm until the limitations period has already run. . . ." *United States v. Spectrum Brands, Inc.*, 924 F.3d 337, 350 (7th Cir. 2019). While the discovery rule is often applied in malpractice actions, the courts of appeals have employed the rule in many other circumstances. *See, e.g., Stoleson v. United States*, 629 F.2d 1265, 1269 (7th Cir. 1980) (discovery rule is not limited to the malpractice context but also applies to occupational safety cases).

The circumstances of the present case fall squarely within the discovery rule. Ms. Arnold was exposed to undetectable neurotoxins released into a remote Caledonia location when the Army secretly tested weapons. *See* App. at 3, 224. Because of the government's secrecy about its testing program, Ms. Arnold did not know of the exposure at the time and afterwards had no means available to learn about it. Thus, she did not know about the nature of her injury or its cause. *See Skirwa v. United States*, 344 F.3d 64, 77 (1st Cir. 2003) (outside the context of medical malpractice, the "factual basis" for an FTCA claim is "(1) the fact of injury and (2) the injury's causal connection with the government").

Furthermore, her symptoms for years baffled numerous, highly qualified medical professionals. Indeed, even the district court concluded that in the immediate aftermath of Ms. Arnold's exposure to sarin, she could not have conceivably connected her symptoms with her work in Caledonia. App. at 3.

Accordingly, because the facts about the nature of Ms. Arnold's injury and its cause were hidden at the time of the injury, the discovery rule governs the accrual of her claim under the FTCA.

B. The District Court Misapplied the Discovery Rule by Equating Ms. Arnold's Mere Suspicion About Her Injury and Its Possible Cause with the Required Knowledge of Her Injury and the Specific Cause of It

When the discovery rule applies, a claim accrues only when a "reasonably diligent plaintiff would have known of the injury and its cause." *Cannon v. United States*, 338 F.3d 1183, 1190 (10th Cir. 2003); *see also Osborn v. United States*, 918 F.2d 724, 731 (8th Cir. 1990) (claim accrues when the plaintiff "actually knew, or in the exercise of reasonable diligence should have known, the cause and existence of his injury") (quoting *Wehrman v. United States*, 830 F.2d 1480, 1483 (8th Cir. 1987)). The "reasonable diligence" part of this test is an objective one. *Donahue v. United States*, 634 F.3d 615, 624 (1st Cir. 2011), *cert. denied*, 566 U.S. 1004 (2012).

Here, the District Court misapplied that test.

1. Ms. Arnold Did Not Acquire the Knowledge of Her Condition Needed for Her Cause of Action to Accrue Until a Doctor Finally Diagnosed Her Symptoms as Resulting from Exposure to the Nerve Gas Sarin

The district court concluded that Ms. Arnold's claims accrued when she had "any reason to suspect that her symptoms might have been caused by exposure to toxic agents near Fort Forester." App. at 3. According to the court, as of early 2013 she had reason to suspect that chemical exposure caused her injury. The court cited three events that occurred by this date: (1) her chiropractor mentioned the possibility of metal poisoning; (2) Ms. Arnold had spoken with a Texas woman who "suspected" that exposure to biological weapons at a base caused her symptoms; and (3) Ms. Arnold had engaged in internet research and found stories about the testing of weapons at Fort Forester.

In focusing only on this evidence, the district court ignored the uncontested fact that, well after this time, medical professionals could not confirm that chemical exposure had caused Ms. Arnold's symptoms. After the date of accrual found by the district court, Ms. Arnold took two tests — the "PCR" and acetylcholine level tests — that her doctors recommended to detect exposure to chemical weapons. The tests came out negative. Not until June 2016 did Dr. Warren Wrede, a national expert on neurotoxicity, correctly diagnose the exposure and begin the appropriate treatment.

Numerous Circuit Court decisions have held that a patient's claim does not accrue when medical practitioners cannot confirm the patient's suspicions about the cause of an injury. The Ninth Circuit stated the general rule in *Rosales v. United States*, 824 F.2d 799, 805 (9th Cir. 1987): "Ordinarily, a plaintiff cannot be expected to discover the general medical cause of his injury even before the doctors themselves are able to do so."

The decision in *Winter v. United States*, 244 F.3d 1088 (9th Cir. 2001), exemplifies the application of this rule in a situation much like the present case. The plaintiff Winter participated in an experimental program in which electrodes were implanted into the legs of paraplegics. In 1989, six years after receiving the electrodes, Winter was hospitalized for cellulitis, an infection in his left leg. *Id.* at 1089. When Winter suspected that the implanted electrodes might be causing his problems, his treating doctor contacted the doctor who directed the implant program. This directing doctor, however, explained that only two of his patients experienced cellulitis and that neither case related to the implantation of electrodes. Accordingly, the doctor treating Winter six years later did not further pursue the matter. *Id.*

In 1994, Winter's infections became more severe, and he underwent numerous operations to remove the electrodes. *Id.* He filed an administrative claim under the FTCA with the Veterans Administration that same year. *Id.* at 1090. The government argued that the cause of action had accrued in 1989 when Winter first suspected that the electrodes caused the infection.

The court disagreed. It explained that decisions have "consistently held" that a cause of action does not accrue under the FTCA when a plaintiff "has relied on statements of medical professionals with respect to his or her injuries and their probable causes." *Id.* That principle, said the court, applied to Winter's situation:

At no point did any doctor tell Steven Winter that the electrodes implanted by Dr. Marsolais caused, or might have caused, his cellulitis. When Winter suggested in 1989, based on his lay suspicion, that the electrodes might have been causing problems, he was clearly told that the electrodes were not the cause of his infection. . . . Yet the government asks us to hold that Winter, a layman with no medical knowledge, knew or should have known the cause of his injuries at this point. . . .

Id. at 1091. Consequently, the cause of action did not accrue at the time of the plaintiff's unconfirmed suspicion. *Id.* at 1092.

In the present case, the government presses the same argument that *Winter* rejected. Both the plaintiff in *Winter* and Ms. Arnold only held suspicions about the causes of their injuries. In both situations, no medical doctor confirmed those suspicions until the end of a long series of consultations. Accordingly, just as the cause of action in *Winter* accrued when doctors confirmed that the implants caused the cellulitis, here the cause of action accrued only when a specialist in 2016 diagnosed exposure to sarin as causing Ms. Arnold's injuries.

Another decision, *Nicolazzo v. United States,* 786 F.2d 454 (1st Cir. 1986), reached the same conclusion regarding the accrual of a cause of action under facts like those in the present case. The plaintiff Nicolazzo was injured in a 1969 helicopter crash while serving in the Army. When he was discharged in 1971, his symptoms included a constant ringing in his left ear, chronic infection in that ear, some hearing loss, and loss of balance. *Id.* at 454.

Thereafter, Nicolazzo suffered through a long series of fruitless medical attempts to diagnose his symptoms. For example, in both 1972 and 1974, a doctor for the Veterans Administration diagnosed his condition as fluid on the ear, but the doctor did not prescribe antibiotics or take x-rays. *Id.* In 1977, another federal doctor diagnosed profound hearing loss dating back to the accident in 1969 but did not recommend surgery. In total, between 1972 and 1980, Nicolazzo saw Veterans Administration doctors on ten occasions with various diagnoses. *Id.* at 454-55. Not until 1980 was his condition correctly identified as a chronic infection at the site of a skull fracture from the helicopter crash. Surgery then corrected the condition. *Id.* at 455.

Nicolazzo filed an administrative claim under the FTCA and then sued, alleging that competent doctors would have tested him for his chronic infection at a much earlier date. *Id.* The district court found that the claim had accrued in 1977, when Nicolazzo was first aware that his treatments were not aiding him. The court of appeals reversed, holding that the claim did not accrue until 1980 because "the factual predicate for his medical malpractice claim could not have become apparent to him before receiving a correct diagnosis" in that year. *Id.* at 456.

Ms. Arnold's situation closely resembles that of Nicolazzo. Just as Nicolazzo saw a number of doctors and received a series of erroneous diagnoses, Ms. Arnold likewise consulted numerous doctors and received two wrong diagnoses — multiple sclerosis and psychosomatic symptoms. Neither she nor Nicolazzo discovered the "factual predicate" for their causes of action until new doctors correctly diagnosed their conditions at the end of long searches. Accordingly, just as Nicolazzo's cause of action accrued only at the time of the correct diagnosis, so did Ms. Arnold's cause of action, and she timely filed her administrative claim. *See also Schnurman v. United States,* 490 F. Supp. 429, 435 (E.D. Va. 1980) (link between plaintiff's maladies and earlier exposure to toxic gases "was supplied . . . by Dr. Smith, who . . . diagnosed plaintiff's problems as the direct result of exposure to the toxic war gas").

The holdings in *Winter* and *Nicolazzo* are part of a uniform line of federal appellate decisions addressing the time when a claim accrues under the FTCA. These decisions hold that, where the plaintiffs are uncertain about the nature of their injuries, their claims do not accrue until expert medical advice diagnoses those ailments. *See Osborn,* 918 F.2d at 733 (rejecting the government's argument that "Shawna's mother should have known the cause of Shawna's difficulties when the doctors, including specialists in pediatrics and pediatric neurology, had not yet reached a conclusion"); *Brazzell v. United States,* 788 F.2d 1352, 1356 (8th Cir. 1986) (affirming finding that "appellee could be charged with the ability to discover the cause of her injuries only after her doctor had concluded that the vaccination was the culprit"); and *Tunac v. United States,* 897 F.3d 1197, 1207 (8th Cir. 2018), *cert. denied,* __U.S.__, 139 S. Ct. 817 (2019) (citing cases that an FTCA cause of action does not accrue where plaintiffs reasonably rely on doctors' assurances that medical error did not cause the injury).

In sum, the government would have the statute of limitations bar Ms. Arnold's claim before any of her numerous treating physicians correctly diagnosed her condition. The courts, however, have overwhelmingly rejected that unfair outcome. As the court summarized in *Harrison v. United States,* 708 F.2d 1023, 1028 (5th Cir. 1983), a plaintiff does not have the requisite knowledge "when doctors who knew immeasurably more than [the plaintiff] were stymied. . . ." Because the district court's holding conflicts with those decisions, it must be reversed.

2.   A Layperson's Mere Belief or Suspicion About an Illness or Its Cause Does Not Trigger the Accrual of a Claim Under the FTCA

Ms. Arnold received *no* medical corroboration of her correct condition until Dr. Wrede's diagnosis in 2016. Accordingly, the district court's ruling can stand only if Ms. Arnold's earlier speculation about her medical situation constituted sufficient "knowledge" of her condition and its cause. The case law, however, rejects the proposition that such suspicions — which amounted to nothing more than guesses about her illness — are sufficient for a cause of action to accrue under the FTCA.

Two decisions involving plaintiffs with similar suspicions about their illnesses support this conclusion. In the first decision, *Stoleson v. United States,* 629 F.2d 1265 (7th Cir. 1980), the plaintiff Stoleson worked in 1968 at an Army plant handling munitions and rocket propellants that contained nitroglycerin. She began to suffer severe chest pains and was diagnosed first with a coronary insufficiency and later with a myocardial infarction caused by a vascular spasm. *Id.* at 1266.

Stoleson suspected a connection between heart problems and her work conditions, but the treating physician informed her that exposure to nitroglycerin did not cause her problems. *Id.* at 1267. In 1969, she read a newspaper article suggesting that sudden withdrawal from exposure to nitroglycerin might cause anginal chest pains, and an occupational safety inspector told her that he believed exposure to nitroglycerin caused her heart problems. Stoleson then consulted another physician, but he rejected these suggestions. Finally, in 1971, the chief of cardiology at the Medical College of Wisconsin examined Stoleson and concluded that her cardiovascular problems were related to nitroglycerin exposure. *Id.*

The government contended that Ms. Stoleson's "suspicion that nitroglycerin was the culprit" constituted sufficient knowledge to trigger the statute of limitations, but the court of appeals rejected that argument. *Id.* at 1270. It emphasized that "[a] laymen's subjective belief, regardless of its sincerity or ultimate vindication, is patently inadequate to go to the trier of fact." *Id.* Thus, "[e]ven armed with the occupational safety expert's opinion and the newspaper article, the suggestion that Ms. Stoleson had a claim that she could judicially enforce is implausible." *Id.*

In the present case, Ms. Arnold had the same type of suspicion as the plaintiff in *Stoleson*. Both she and Ms. Stoleson had heard suggestions about causes of their conditions in the form of media articles and conversations with nonmedical individuals. In the end, however, both of them merely held suspicions, nothing more. Whether or not Ms. Arnold believed that suspicion, under *Stoleson* a suspicion like hers does not rise to the level of knowledge required for the claim to accrue.

A district court reached the same conclusion in a chemical exposure case factually similar to the present case. In *Frasure v. United States*, 256 F. Supp. 2d 1180 (D. Nev. 2003), a child who had previously undergone a kidney transplant played near his home on an abandoned industrial property called the "Monite site." *Id.* at 1182. In 1994, plaintiff's kidney transplant failed, and the child suffered bone marrow failure, aplastic anemia, and gastrointestinal bleeding, among other illnesses. *Id.* at 1183. A year later, his parents learned that explosives manufactured and dismantled on that site had contained high levels of trinitrotoluene, dinitrotoluene, and other hazardous substances. *Id.* at 1182, 1185. Only in 1998 did a specialist link the child's illnesses to chemical exposure from the Monite site where the child had played. *Id.* at 1187.

The government argued that the claim accrued in 1995 when plaintiff's parents were placed on notice that the Monite site contained hazardous wastes. The government cited media reports on the wastes located at the site as well as a fact sheet about the site distributed to the child's father at a public meeting. *Id.* at 1185. The court disagreed, citing *Stoleson*. The parents had stated that they thought the Monite site could be the cause of plaintiff's condition. *Id.* at 1188. Their statement, however, was insufficient to constitute the requisite knowledge. By themselves, these "layman's beliefs regarding the cause of his illness" were insufficient to start the claim accruing under the statute. *Id.*

In the present case, Ms. Arnold held the same type of "lay belief." While both she and the parents in *Frasure* "thought" that they knew the cause of the respective injuries, their beliefs stemmed from informal sources such as media reports rather than from expert analysis. Although a layperson may form a "belief" based on such reports, that belief does not amount to the qualitative knowledge needed for the claim to accrue. *See Thompson v. United States*, 642 F. Supp. 762, 766 (N.D. Ill. 1986) ("[Plaintiff's] 'wondering,' based on materials he had read, is not enough to start the statute running"); *Client Solutions Architects, LLC v. United States*, __ F. Supp. 3d __, 2020 WL 1169696 at *7 (S.D. Cal. 2020) (plaintiff's suspicions that mold at her work caused her symptoms were insufficient for a cause of action to accrue).

In sum, the government isolates one or two incidents from Ms. Arnold's years-long search for the cause of her condition and asserts that those incidents were sufficient for her claim to accrue. On numerous occasions during that period, Ms. Arnold speculated what the cause might be and then expressed her "belief" about that cause. In the end, however, those beliefs lacked medical or other solid confirmation. Thus, her "belief" at that time in the chemical exposure theory amounted to nothing more than the latest in a long line of theories. The conclusion here must be the same as in *Harrison v. United States*, 708 F.2d at 1028: "Harrison's suspicion or belief that her problems dated from Wilford Hall was merely one of a series of explanations that she seized upon in anguish and desperation to explain her illness."

C.   The Two Decisions Principally Relied Upon by the District Court Are Distinguishable, as the Plaintiffs in Both Decisions Were Aware of Their Injuries and Possessed Facts to Determine the Causes of Those Injuries

The district court's holding relied principally upon two Tenth Circuit decisions: *Plaza Speedway, Inc. v. United States*, 311 F.3d 1262 (10th Cir. 2002), and *Cannon v. United States*, 338 F.3d 1183 (10th Cir. 2003). Neither case, however, can reasonably be read to suggest that mere lay suspicion triggers the accrual of a claim, especially when the medical evidence discredits that suspicion.

In *Plaza Speedway*, the court held that a claim accrued when state environmental authorities called and notified a plaintiff landowner that testing had found contamination on its property. 311 F.3d at 1270-71. After that call, the plaintiff knew that (1) a well on its property had been tested for contaminants; and (2) an adjacent Army airfield — the plaintiff's only neighbor — had used jet fuels, solvents, and various chemicals. *Id.* At this point, declared the court, the plaintiff "had reason to suspect the source might have been the neighboring property." *Id.* at 1271. From this time, the court concluded, the plaintiff had two years to file a claim under the FTCA.

The *Cannon* plaintiffs knew even more about their injury and its cause than the landowner in *Speedway*. In *Cannon*, the plaintiffs were aware that the U.S. Army had previously tested explosive weapons on property that the plaintiffs later inherited. Indeed, the government had once compensated their grandfather for damages from this testing. 338 F.3d at 1185-86. The government also provided the plaintiffs with a "fact sheet" declaring it "highly probable" that additional contamination from hazardous ordnance and explosive waste remained on the property. *Id.* at 1187, 1191.

Given the plaintiffs' knowledge of this "highly probable" contamination, the court rejected plaintiffs' assertion that their claim did not accrue until a written report on the contamination formally issued two years later. The plaintiffs may not have known the full extent of long-term damage to their property before the release of that written report. However, they "undoubtedly had notice of the general nature of their injury and its cause" more than two years before they filed their administrative claim. *Id.* at 1192. That notice was sufficient to trigger the FTCA's statute of limitations. *Id.*

The circumstances of the present case differ from those in both *Plaza Speedway* and *Cannon* in decisive respects. The landowner in *Plaza Speedway* knew of its injury and that its only neighbor had used chemicals; connecting the injury with the neighbor's use of chemicals was obvious. In contrast, while Ms. Arnold knew that she had an injury of some sort, medical professionals diagnosed neither its precise nature nor its cause. Absent both sets of information, Ms. Arnold lacked the heightened knowledge possessed by the landowner in *Plaza Speedway*.

In the same way, although the plaintiffs in *Cannon* knew that toxic ordnance remained on their property and had damaged it, Ms. Arnold possessed no similar knowledge about the nature and source of her injuries. She acquired the same level of knowledge as the *Cannon* plaintiffs only after a doctor diagnosed her condition as caused by poisoning from sarin gas, whose source was very likely Fort Forester. Until that time, Ms. Arnold's cause of action could not have accrued under the FTCA.

In summary, the discovery rule protects plaintiffs who are "blamelessly unaware" of their claim because the facts establishing the link between the injury and its cause "are in the control of the tortfeasor or are otherwise not evident." *Robert L. Kroenlein Trust ex rel. Alden v. Kirchhefer*, 764 F.3d 1268, 1277 (10th Cir. 2014). Here, Ms. Arnold possessed that required knowledge only after she was diagnosed as suffering from poisoning caused by toxic nerve gas. Accordingly, she timely filed her claim, and this Court must reject the government's argument that the FTCA's statute of limitations bars her action.

III. The District Court Erred in Holding That the Doctrine of Equitable Tolling Did Not Prevent the Expiration of the Statute of Limitations Governing Ms. Arnold's Claims

The doctrine of equitable tolling can prevent a plaintiff's claim from being untimely where circumstances make it unfair to strictly apply the statute of limitations. Here, the district court held that the doctrine did not apply by limiting its reach to two narrow situations. It then held that, in any event, Ms. Arnold did not meet the doctrine's other requirements.

The court erred. The doctrine of equitable tolling applies broadly to situations under the FTCA. Here, the government does not contest that Ms. Arnold repeatedly sought a diagnosis for her serious ailments but did not receive one until 2016. Further, the Army classified as secret the key facts about the cause of Ms. Arnold's injury. Under these circumstances, the doctrine operates to toll the statute of limitations.

A. The Supreme Court Has Held That Equitable Tolling Is Available to Claimants Who Seek Recovery Under the Federal Tort Claims Act

The doctrine of equitable tolling applies "where the interests of justice require vindication of the plaintiff's rights." *Turgeau v. Administrative Review Bd.*, 446 F.3d 1052, 1058 (10th Cir. 2006) (quoting *Burnett v. New York Cent. R.R. Co.*, 380 U.S. 424, 428 (1965)). The doctrine allows a court to toll the running of a statute of limitations when plaintiffs have pursued their rights diligently, but some extraordinary circumstance prevents them from meeting a deadline. *Lozano v. Montoya Alvarez*, 572 U.S. 1, 10 (2014). Until relatively recently, the doctrine's applicability to deadlines under the FTCA remained an open question, although most of the courts of appeals had held that it did apply. *See, e.g., Santos ex rel. Beato v. United States*, 559 F.3d 189, 196-97 (3d Cir. 2009).

In 2015, the Supreme Court settled the issue. In *United States v. Kwai Fun Wong*, 575 U.S. 402 (2015), the government argued that, because the FTCA's statute of limitations and claim requirement were jurisdictional, courts possessed no authority to employ the doctrine of equitable tolling to ease those requirements. The Court, however, found that they were not jurisdictional. Accordingly, a court may apply the doctrine after the statutory time period has expired. *Id.* at 412.

In the present case, the district court construed the doctrine so narrowly as to render it inapplicable to Ms. Arnold's case. In doing so, it erred.

B. Equitable Tolling Is Not Limited to Situations Where a Plaintiff Has Timely Filed a Defective Pleading or the United States Has Fraudulently Concealed Information

In some decisions, courts have applied equitable tolling where plaintiffs filed timely but defective pleadings, or the United States fraudulently concealed critical facts that prevented the plaintiff from discovering a cause of action. *See Irwin v. Dep't of Veterans Affairs*, 498 U.S. 89, 96 (1990) (allowing equitable tolling where a complainant filed a defective pleading within the statutory deadline or "where the complainant has been induced or tricked by his adversary's misconduct into allowing the filing deadline to pass"), and *Valdez ex rel. Donely v. United States*, 518 F.3d 173, 182 (2d Cir. 2008). In the present case, however, the district court read these previous decisions as establishing rigid rules delineating the doctrine's scope. The court limited equitable tolling only to circumstances where a claimant has filed a timely but defective pleading, or has been induced or tricked by misconduct into missing a deadline. App. at 432. Thus, it found the doctrine inapplicable to Ms. Arnold's case.

The doctrine is not so narrowly constrained. While the *Irwin* Court identified these two scenarios as ones in which equitable tolling may apply, nothing in that opinion or subsequent Supreme Court opinions expressly limits the doctrine's scope to only those scenarios. Rather, the doctrine's equitable reach extends more broadly. The Supreme Court recognized as much in *Holland v. Florida*, 560 U.S. 631, 649 (2010), holding that a petitioner is entitled to equitable relief from a filing deadline upon a showing "'that some extraordinary circumstance stood in his way' and prevented timely filing." 130 S. Ct. at 2562 (quoting *Pace v. DiGuglielmo*, 544 U.S. 408, 418 (2005)).

14

The Court's later opinion in *Menominee Indian Tribe of Wisconsin v. United States*, __ U.S. __, 136 S. Ct. 750 (2016), is consistent with *Holland*'s broader statement of the doctrine. In *Menominee*, the Court held that the doctrine of equitable tolling was unavailable to the plaintiff in that case. The Court explained that presentment of the plaintiff's claim to the government "was blocked not by an obstacle outside its control, but by the Tribe's mistaken belief that presentment was unneeded." 136 S. Ct. at 756-57. If the restrictions imposed by the district court in Ms. Arnold's case had existed, the *Menominee* Court would not have applied the doctrine of equitable tolling as it did. Instead, it would have ruled that, because the facts of the case did not present either a timely filed but defective pleading, or fraudulent concealment of facts, the doctrine did not apply at all.

The Second Circuit likewise confirmed the doctrine's broader reach in *Valdez*. In that case, the district court found equitable tolling inapplicable because no acts of fraudulent concealment had occurred. The court of appeals, however, held that the district court's inquiry into the equitable grounds of the case was unduly narrow because "fraudulent concealment is not essential to equitable tolling." 518 F.3d at 182. The court cited *Cada v. Baxter Healthcare Corp.*, 920 F.2d 446 (7th Cir. 1990). Equitable tolling, said the *Cada* Court, "does not assume a wrongful — or any — effort by the defendant to prevent the plaintiff from suing." *Id.* at 451.

In short, the district court imposed limitations on the doctrine of equitable tolling that do not exist.

C. Ms. Arnold's Diligence in Pursuing Information About Her Symptoms and the Government's Secrecy About Its Sarin Testing Compel the Tolling of the Statute of Limitations in Her Case

The district court then went on to find that, had the doctrine of equitable tolling been available to Ms. Arnold, she could not have met its other requirements. In so concluding, the district court again erred.

The Supreme Court has established a two-part test to determine whether the doctrine of equitable tolling applies in a case. A plaintiff must demonstrate "(1) that he has been pursuing rights diligently, and (2) that some extraordinary circumstance stood in his way and prevented timely filing." *Menominee Indian Tribe of Wisconsin v. United States*, 136 S. Ct. at 755 (quoting *Holland v. Florida*, 560 U.S. at 649). The two parts of this test address separate factors: "the diligence prong . . . covers those affairs within the litigant's control; the extraordinary-circumstances prong, by contrast, is meant to cover matters outside its control." 136 S. Ct. at 756. Here, the stipulated facts show that Ms. Arnold easily meets both parts of the test.

1. Ms. Arnold Unquestionably Demonstrated Due Diligence in Searching for a Diagnosis of Her Medical Condition and Its Cause over an Eight-Year Period

The first requirement for equitable tolling is that the claimant act with due diligence. *See Irwin*, 498 U.S. at 96 ("We have generally been much less forgiving in receiving late filings where the claimant failed to exercise due diligence in preserving his legal rights"); *Bolarinwa v. Williams,* 593 F.3d 226, 231 (2d Cir. 2010) (litigants seeking equitable tolling must establish that they have been pursuing their rights diligently). This requirement need not long detain the Court, for Ms. Arnold's efforts far exceeded due diligence.

She consulted *11* doctors in trying to determine the source of her injury, and she persisted despite the false diagnoses of multiple sclerosis and a psychosomatic condition. After she read an article about chemical exposure at a different army base, she took a test in 2013 for exposure to chemical weapons. When that test came out negative, she did not cease her efforts. After she learned that a former government employee believed that he had been exposed to nerve agents while working at Fort Forester, she took another test for exposure to nerve agents, which again came up negative. Finally, she consulted a national expert on neurotoxicity, who diagnosed her condition.

This lengthy series of actions on her part — extending over eight years — unquestionably met the "due diligence" requirement for equitable tolling. Indeed, it is hard to imagine what other actions she could have taken to resolve her situation.

2. The Government's Withholding of Key Information Relating to the Cause of Ms. Arnold's Injuries Constitutes an Extraordinary Circumstance That Justifies Equitable Tolling

The second part of the test set forth in *Menominee Indian Tribe* asks whether "extraordinary circumstances" prevented a timely filing. Put another way, the litigant must show that the circumstances "were the cause of his untimeliness and . . . made it impossible to file the document on time." *Booth v. United States,* 914 F.3d 1199, 1207 (9th Cir. 2019) (quoting *Ramirez v. Yates,* 571 F.3d 993, 997 (9th Cir. 2009)). Here, the government's secrecy over its testing of sarin supplies the extraordinary circumstances that compel application of the doctrine.

Intentional concealment by the government of its connection with an injury provides a basis for applying the doctrine of equitable tolling. As the court of appeals explained in *Trinity Marine Products, Inc. v. United States,* 812 F.3d 481, 489 (5th Cir. 2016), one ground for equitable tolling is "where a plaintiff is unaware 'of the facts giving rise to the claim because of the defendant's intentional concealment of them'" (quoting *Granger v. Aaron's, Inc.,* 636 F.3d 708, 712 (5th Cir. 2011)). *See also Bradley v. Nat'l Collegiate Athletic Ass'n,* 249 F. Supp. 3d 149, 162 (D.D.C. 2017) (finding equitable tolling where the government concealed information that a doctor was a federal employee).

From the onset of her symptoms in 2007 until the correct diagnosis of her illness in 2016, Ms. Arnold faced an insurmountable barrier to her inquiries: the government had classified as secret the chemical source that caused her injuries. The highly unusual nature of her injury — exposure to neurotoxins secretly tested by the Army — rendered it impossible for her to connect the symptoms of that injury to their cause. For years, no facts obtained by Ms. Arnold indicated that a chemical exposure may have caused her condition. Not until 2013 did she receive even the first inkling of possible contamination by a federal source.

At this point, the key facts supporting the application of the doctrine of equitable tolling came fully into play. The government had classified as top secret the essential information necessary to put Ms. Arnold on notice of her claim — the testing of chemical weapons at Fort Forester. The only information available to the public took the form of unsubstantiated internet rumors. Accordingly, when Ms. Arnold learned in 2013 that a person formerly employed at Fort Forester suspected that he had been exposed to nerve agents there, she could not investigate that possibility. The government withheld, as top secret, all the information on Fort Forester that she needed.

Indeed, the government's resistance to revealing its activities at the fort continued through the present litigation, which Ms. Arnold brought after finally obtaining a correct medical diagnosis of her sarin exposure. The government's answer to her complaint denies that the government tested sarin gas at Fort Forester. App. at 12. Not surprisingly, then, the complete lack of public information about the sarin exposure rendered it impossible for Ms. Arnold to identify both her symptoms and their cause.

In other FTCA cases, the government's retention of similar vital information has supported the use of the doctrine of equitable tolling. For example, in *Glarner v. U.S. Dep't of Veterans Admin.*, 30 F.3d 697 (6th Cir. 1994), doctors in the Veterans Administration performed hip surgery on the plaintiff Glarner. After the surgery, he dislocated the hip, which was then placed in a cast. A later x-ray, however, showed that the hip had remained in a dislocated position when the doctors applied the cast. Thereafter, his hip dislocated again, and his condition greatly deteriorated. *Id.* at 699.

After these painful mishaps, Glarner went to a Veterans Administration Office and informed the personnel there that he wanted to file a negligence claim. The Administration officer filled out a form and had Glarner sign it. *Id.* Glarner believed that he had submitted the proper form, but it was not the official form required by the FTCA. Nor did the Veterans Administration ever inform Glarner that this form was incorrect. Later, when Glarner hired a lawyer who filed suit, the government claimed that Glarner had not timely filed a proper claim. *Id.*

Glarner argued that the doctrine of equitable tolling should apply, and the court of appeals agreed. Importantly, the pertinent regulations required the Veterans Administration to inform Glarner of the correct form, and it never did so. *Id.* at 701. In light of Glarner's "lack of actual or constructive knowledge" of the required form's contents, and his continued pursuit of remedies at each level, the court found that the doctrine of equitable tolling applied until he received the correct information. *Id.* at 702.

In the present case, the government likewise kept critical information from Ms. Arnold. Just as Glarner could not proceed with his claim until the government supplied the correct information about the form, Ms. Arnold could have discovered the circumstances behind her injury only if the government revealed its chemical testing. Ms. Arnold had no alternate source of information. Accordingly, just as in *Glarner*, the doctrine of equitable tolling should apply here until the date that a doctor actually diagnosed Ms. Arnold with sarin exposure and thus indirectly confirmed that the government's testing of nerve gas caused her exposure.

In short, Ms. Arnold's circumstances present a paradigmatic situation for the application of the doctrine of equitable tolling, one where the party invoking equitable tolling is unable to obtain vital information bearing on the existence of the claim. *Socop-Gonzalez v. I.N.S.*, 272 F.3d 1176, 1193 (9th Cir. 2001); *see also Cabello v. Fernandez-Larios*, 402 F.3d 1148, 1155 (11th Cir. 2005) ("extraordinary circumstances" may be met when the plaintiff "has no reasonable way of discovering the wrong perpetrated against her"). The government's secrecy made it impossible for Ms. Arnold to discover the wrongful exposure and caused her to miss the filing deadline.

CONCLUSION

For the reasons set forth above, Appellant Ann Arnold respectfully requests that this Court reverse the order of the district court granting the government's motion for summary judgment. Moreover, because the parties stipulated to the facts, Appellant must prevail as a matter of law. This Court should therefore order that the district court grant summary judgment to Ms. Arnold.

Dated: March 1, 2020

Respectfully submitted,

/s/ *Erin A. Rogers*

Erin A. Rogers, Esq.
ROGERS, SHOWELL, AND TAYLOR
Attorneys for Appellant Ann Arnold

CERTIFICATE OF COMPLIANCE

1. This brief complies with the type-volume limitation of Federal Rule of Appellate Procedure 32(a)(7)(B) because it contains 9,230 words, as determined by the word-count function of Microsoft Word, excluding the parts of the brief exempted by Federal Rule of Appellate Procedure 32(f).

2. This brief complies with the typeface requirements of Federal Rule of Appellate Procedure 32(a)(5) and the type style requirements of Federal Rule of Appellate Procedure 32(a)(6) because this brief has been prepared in a proportionally spaced typeface using Microsoft Word in 14-point Times New Roman font.

Dated: March 1, 2020

/s/ Erin A. Rogers
_____

Erin A. Rogers, Esq.
ROGERS, SHOWELL, AND TAYLOR
400 A Street, Suite 600
Springfield, Caledonia 01234
ERogers@RSTLaw.com
(980) 765-4321

CERTIFICATE OF SERVICE

I hereby certify that a copy of the foregoing **APPELLANT'S OPENING BRIEF** was served through (ECF) electronic service to the following on this the 1st day of March, 2020:

> James K. Loder, Esq.
> Appellate Division
> U.S. Department of Justice
> 200 Constitution Avenue
> Washington, DC 20012
>
> Attorneys for Appellee United States of America

> */s/ Erin A. Rogers*
> _____
> ROGERS, SHOWELL, AND TAYLOR
> 400 A Street, Suite 600
> Springfield, Caledonia 01234
> ERogers@RSTLaw.com
> (980) 765-4321

APPENDIX B

Each exercise relates to material in a particular chapter:

EXERCISE NO. 1

Which Standard(s) of Review will the appellate court apply to determine whether reversible error occurred in the following hypotheticals?

1. The appellant's only complaint about the trial is that the jury believed Witness A instead of Witness B. Appellant wants to challenge the jury's decision.
2. The appellant claims that the court should not have admitted Witness A's testimony because it was inadmissible under the rules of evidence.
3. The appellant complains the court erred in concluding that the appellant had the burden of proof on an issue at trial.
4. The appellant challenges the trial court's refusal to grant a continuance of the trial.
5. The appellant complains that the trial court erroneously rejected the appellant's jury instruction on its defense. The court's refusal to give the instruction was based on:
   a. a conclusion that the defense asserted did not apply as a matter of law;
   b. a finding that no reasonable juror would conclude that the appellant proved the defense.

EXERCISE NO. 2

What Standards of Review did the Court of Appeal apply here? (Excerpt from *People v. Esquibel*, 166 Cal. App. 4th 539 (2008))

The exclusion of spectators from the courtroom was a partial exclusion of two male spectators during the testimony of a single minor witness. There was no evidence of any special relationship between the spectators and the appellant, other than friendship. There seems to be no dispute that appellant's family members remained in the courtroom during this examination. These spectators were removed at the request of the prosecutor based on the concern and urging of the mother of the witness. Her principal concern in this gang-related case was that the spectators might be gang members and would recognize her child in the neighborhood, not that her child might recognize them. There was no evidence of intimidation or harassment. Over the objection of appellant, who argued that the trial court should comply with California Penal Code section 686.2, prior to excluding people from the courtroom, the court excluded these spectators during the child's examination.

We conclude that this exclusion was not a violation of appellant's constitutional right to an open trial. There was no order excluding the press or the public in general. Except for these two spectators, no one else connected with appellant was excluded from the courtroom and the exclusion was only during the testimony of the single witness. Members of appellant's family remained in the courtroom. There was no showing that the excluded individuals had any special relationship to appellant or were needed to provide him support during the trial.

We conclude the partial closure of a trial by the temporary exclusion of select supporters of the accused does not create an automatic violation of the constitutional right to a public trial. Furthermore, on the facts of this case, we conclude there was no constitutional violation of appellant's rights. To hold otherwise would not serve the purposes of the public trial right. Here, the exclusion of the spectators was for a minimal amount of time and appellant's family supporters remained in the courtroom.

In addition to state and federal constitutional requirements, in California there are statutes setting forth requirements for excluding certain spectators from a public criminal trial. "A trial court also retains broad discretion to control courtroom proceedings in a manner directed toward promoting the safety of witnesses. (See, e.g., §868.7, subd. (a)(2) [upon motion of the prosecutor, a magistrate may close the examination of a witness '[w]hose life would be subject to a substantial risk in appearing before the general public']; see also §686.2 [authorizing the trial court to remove any spectator who is intimidating a witness]; §867 [authorizing the magistrate to exclude potential and actual witnesses upon motion of either party]; §868 [authorizing the magistrate to exclude the public upon the request of the defendant and a finding by the magistrate 'that exclusion of the public is necessary in order to protect the defendant's right to a fair and impartial trial']; *People v. Woodward* (1992) 4 Cal.4th 376, 382-386 [14 Cal.Rptr.2d 434, 841 P.2d 954] [upholding the temporary closure of the courtroom to additional spectators during a murder trial, in view of the 'unusual security risks' posed by the trial]; *NBC Subsidiary (KNBC-TV), Inc. v. Superior Court* (1999) 20 Cal.4th 1178, 1222, fn. 46 [86 Cal.Rptr.2d 778, 980 P.2d 337] [noting that among the 'overriding interests' that may justify closure of a courtroom in an appropriate instance is the protection of witnesses from intimidation].)" (*Alvarado v. Superior Court*, supra, 23 Cal.4th at p. 1150, 99 Cal.Rptr.2d 149, 5 P.3d 203.)

Appellant, nonetheless, contends that the court erred in rejecting his request to comply with California Penal Code section 686.2, which provides that a court may order the removal of any spectator who is intimidating a witness, but only after holding a hearing and making the following findings by clear and convincing evidence:

"(1) The spectator to be removed is actually engaging in intimidation of the witness.

"(2) The witness will not be able to give full, free, and complete testimony unless the spectator is removed.

"(3) Removal of the spectator is the only reasonable means of ensuring that the witness may give full, free, and complete testimony."

We agree with appellant that the record shows the exclusion of the spectators in this case was not in compliance with section 686.2. However, we find that section 686.2 has no application to the facts of this case. By its own terms, it only applies when there is a proposed exclusion of a spectator who is engaged in the active intimidation of a witness. When the predicate facts are present, the statute directs the court how to handle the exclusion of the offending spectator. Here, there is no evidence of any intimidation by the spectators in this case. They were excluded based solely on the concerns of the witness's mother for the safety of her child. There is no evidence of any conduct, act or attitude by the spectators which would call for the application of section 686.2.

EXERCISE NO. 3

Set forth below are five sets of Statements of Issues. Evaluate each set for consistency with the principles discussed in Chapter Five.

Set No. 1

1. Whether the district court erred in denying Pendleton's motion for attorney's fees on grounds that Count 5 of Freedman's amended complaint (asserting a claim against Pendleton for breach of contract) did not constitute an "action arising out of contract" for purposes of S.T.S. §10-1234.01.

2. Whether the district court erred in denying Pendleton's motion to recover expert fees under Fed. R. Civ. P. 26(b)(4)(C) as non-taxable costs, on grounds that Pendleton failed to itemize and verify his claim for Rule 26 expert fees pursuant to Local Rule 4.60.

3. Whether the district court erred in denying Pendleton's motion for review of taxable costs awarded by the clerk, apparently on grounds that expert fees under Rule 26(b)(4)(C) are not taxable as costs.

Set No. 2

1. Whether, under Caledonia law, an indemnity agreement contains an implied covenant of good faith and fair dealing?

2. Whether a district court errs if, when faced with a motion for summary judgment on a claim for breach of an indemnity agreement that expressly requires good faith by the indemnitee (surety) when it pays on a claim against a performance bond covered by the agreement, the court weighs the evidence of good faith proffered by the indemnitee (surety) and the evidence of lack of good faith presented by the indemnitor, and decides to assign more weight to the evidence offered by the indemnitee (surety), and therefore grants summary judgment in its favor?

3. Whether a district court errs if, when confronted with an unconscionability defense to a claim for breach of an indemnity agreement, upon summary judgment, the court weighs the evidence submitted by the parties on the factual question of that agreement's unconscionability and finds in favor of the moving party?

Set No. 3

1. Was the evidence sufficient to support the verdict; was the verdict opposed by the great weight of the evidence?

2. Did the trial court err in refusing to grant an instruction of malicious mischief or vandalism?

3. Was the appellant's right to a speedy trial violated?

4. Was the sentence of life without parole as a habitual offender disproportionate?

Set No. 4

1. Did the trial court abuse its discretion and commit error of law when it failed to correct the illegal sentence on the S.I.C. charge, thereby violating the U.S. Constitution's Eighth Amendment ban on cruel and unusual punishment?

2. Did the trial court abuse its discretion and commit error of law when it failed to furnish Appellant with a copy of the missing portions of the trial transcripts, thereby violating the Fourteenth Amendment's Equal Protection and Due Process Clause?

3. Was trial counsel ineffective for failing to object to the prosecutor's impermissible reference to Petitioner's post-arrest silence, or failing to request a mistrial and/or curative instructions?

4. Was appellate counsel ineffective for failing to raise on direct appeal the claim that the evidence submitted at trial was insufficient as a matter of law to support a conviction for possession of an instrument of crime?

Set No. 5

1. Did the trial court err in failing to grant Mr. Trent's suppression motion because the search violated the Fourth Amendment?
2. Did the trial court err in admitting the chemical analyst's report?
3. Did the trial court err in admitting the prior testimony of Officer Morris and the chemical analyst Esmeralda Knight from the first trial?

EXERCISE NO. 4

Set forth below are two sets of Questions Presented from briefs filed in the United States Supreme Court. Each set contains the questions as framed by the opposing parties. Examine the questions in each set. For each set, how does the question framed by one party differ in emphasis from the question framed by the opposing party?

Set No. 1

Brief for Petitioner:

Whether a foreign corporation is subject to general personal jurisdiction, on causes of action not arising out of or related to any contacts between it and the forum state, merely because other entities distribute in the forum state products initially placed in the stream of commerce by the corporation.

Brief for Respondent:

Whether foreign-based subsidiaries of an American corporation that choose to become part of an ongoing and highly-integrated business enterprise operating within the forum may evade that state's general personal jurisdiction even though they regularly sell tens of thousands of their products through that enterprise in the forum state?

Set No. 2

Brief for Petitioner:

Whether imposing class arbitration on parties whose arbitration clauses are silent on that issue is consistent with the Federal Arbitration Act, 9 U.S.C. §§1 *et seq.*

Brief for Respondent:

Whether arbitrators "exceeded their powers" under the Federal Arbitration Act, 9 U.S.C. §10(a)(4), when they applied ordinary principles of contract interpretation to hold that a contract clause that broadly requires arbitration of "[a]ny dispute" arising from the contract permits class-wide arbitration.

EXERCISE NO. 5

This exercise is in two parts. Part I: Set forth below is a draft statement of Facts for an appellate brief. Evaluate it for consistency with the principles discussed in Chapter Six.

STATEMENT OF FACTS

On December 31, 2010, UPS, a postal service company, alerted the Indianapolis Metro Police Department about a parcel that contained three different vacuum sealed packages of marijuana (Tr. Vol. II, pp. 8, 11, 52). The parcel was addressed to "Matthew Davis" with a mailing address to the Wingate Hotel in Indianapolis (Tr. Vol. II, p. 20). Officers Robert Hicks ("Hicks") and Scott Wildauer ("Wildauer") retrieved the parcel from UPS and observed what they believed to be marijuana inside the parcel (Tr. Vol. II, pp. 11, 45). The officers then took the parcel to the police station and packaged it with a GPS tracking unit and an electronic parcel wire ("wire") that would alert the police once the parcel was opened (Tr. Vol. II, pp. 22, 24-25; State's Ex. 2).

After taping the original shipping label to the repackaged parcel, law enforcement went to the Wingate Hotel sometime around noon to conduct a controlled delivery of the parcel (Tr. Vol. II, p. 26). Wildauer spoke with the hotel clerk and learned that no one had checked into the hotel under the name of "Matthew Davis" (Tr. Vol. II, p. 55). According to the clerk, someone had called expecting a delivery and wanted the clerk to call once it was delivered (Tr. Vol. II, p. 55). Wildauer called the number the man provided and informed him that his delivery had arrived (Tr. Vol. II, p. 58). A man, later identified as Defendant, pulled up to the front entrance of the hotel and said the parcel was for him (Tr. Vol. II, p. 59). Around 12:15 p.m., Defendant picked up the parcel, placed it in his car, and left (Tr. Vol. II, pp. 37, 59, 67). At the time of delivery, the officers did not know of Defendant's identity or his address (Tr. Vol. II, pp. 28-29, 72).

Not knowing Defendant's final destination, the officers followed Defendant, who was driving at a very high rate of speed estimated at 90 to 100 miles per hour (Tr. Vol. II, pp. 40, 88). About ten minutes or so after receiving the parcel, Defendant arrived at his home and went inside with the parcel in tow (Tr. Vol. II, pp. 38, 68, 88). Within a "few minutes" the wire indicated that the parcel was open (Tr. Vol. II, p. 30). According to Officer Hicks, the presence of the wire and GPS unit alerts suspects to police involvement. Officer Wildauer described it would be "painfully obvious" that the police were involved (Tr. Vol. II, pp. 31, 62). The officers knocked on the front door numerous times and announced their presence (Tr. Vol. II, pp. 33, 44, 61). When no one answered the door, the officers forcibly entered the home to secure the residence and ensure that Defendant would not attempt to destroy the evidence (Tr. Vol. II, pp. 31, 33, 44, 61-62). The officers conducted a protective sweep of the home looking for other individuals or weapons in plain view (Tr. Vol. II, p. 95).

Officer Paul McDonald ("McDonald") secured Defendant in the upstairs hallway (Tr. Vol. II, pp. 63, 91). On the floor underneath Defendant was a pocket knife (Tr. Vol. II, p. 95). Three children were also in the home (Tr. Vol. II, pp. 76, 91). The police observed the re-packaged parcel open on top of the bed in the master bedroom with the wire outside of the box (Tr. Vol. II, pp. 62-64, 77-78).

When Defendant did not consent to a search by the police, the officers applied for a search warrant (Tr. Vol. II, pp. 34, 82). Defendant's wife arrived at the home a little after 2:00 p.m. and was informed that the police were in the process of obtaining a warrant (Tr. Vol. I, pp. 12-13). Law enforcement served the warrant at 3:36 p.m. and collected the marijuana that was in the parcel (Tr. Vol. II, pp. 47, 95; State's Ex. 1).

Part II: This exercise requires you to read the Statement of Facts in Appendix A, the sample appellate brief in the appeal entitled *Arnold v. United States*. After you have read the Statement of Facts, answer the following questions about it.

1. Do the subheadings lead the reader through the facts? If you would change the subheadings, how would you do so, and why?
2. The Statement of Facts is somewhat lengthy. What are the pros and cons of shortening the Statement of Facts within the context of what Ms. Arnold is claiming?
3. Does the Statement of Facts paint Ms. Arnold's situation favorably? What parts of the Statement of Facts do so?
4. What facts hurt Ms. Arnold's case? How were they portrayed in the Statement of Facts?
5. Is there a theme in the Statement of Facts? If so, what is it?

EXERCISE NO. 6

Read these fact statements (Versions 1 and 2) from the same case. (1) Which party (either the appellant or appellee) wrote each of the fact statements, and how did you make that decision? (2) Looking at the fact statements separately, evaluate the parts that were effective and ineffective in each in accord with the principles in Chapter Six.

Version 1:

On February 20, 2020, Jay Page was driving Jean Smith to work at the Angeles Crest Christian Camp in the Allegheny Mountains. On their way up to the mountains, the two stopped at a restaurant in Altoona where Page purchased take-out food. Page tried to eat as he was driving on Angeles Crest Highway, but it became too difficult. Smith offered to drive so that Page could eat, but he gave his food to Smith to hold until they reached the camp. It had been raining earlier in the day and the road, in addition to having many tight curves, was still wet. Both Page and Smith were wearing seat belts. They talked about how dangerous the road was as Page drove up the mountain.

As they came around a curve in the road, Smith saw a white truck coming toward Page's car. The truck, which was heading down the mountain, was partially in their uphill lane of traffic. Their conversation about Page's food and her brief sighting of the white truck were the last things Smith remembered before the accident. Then, Smith woke up in Page's mangled car. Page had been removed from the car, but Smith was still sitting in the front, passenger seat. A woman was talking to her from outside the car telling her that help was on its way. Smith had a cut above her left eye.

Jon Lee, an off-duty detective with the Blair County Sheriff's Department, and his wife were in their car following behind the white truck on Angeles Crest Highway. Lee was driving about 40 or 45 miles an hour and the white truck was going about the same. The speed limit on the road was 45. The rain had stopped but there was still a light mist and the road was wet. As Lee drove around the curve, he lost sight of the white truck for a few seconds. The last time Lee saw the white truck, it was properly inside the downhill traffic lane. Lee did not see or hear the accident. The next time he saw the white truck, it was stopped and off to the other side of the road. He identified appellant as the driver of the truck and noticed that appellant appeared dazed and confused from the accident but was otherwise all right.

Page's car, a Mitsubishi, was still in the uphill lane, but was up against the guard rail. The driver's side of the car was completely ripped off and Page was almost hanging out of the car and he was unconscious and appeared to have multiple fractures on his lower extremities. Page also had a large gash on the top of his head and his breathing was labored and shallow. Lee removed Page from the car and placed an item of clothing on Page's head to try to stop some of the bleeding. In ten to fifteen minutes, Page stopped breathing and had no pulse.

Emergency personnel responded to the scene of this accident. According to several of the first responders, there had previously been a lot of accidents at this particular curve on Angeles Crest Highway. The paramedics in an ambulance arrived at the scene of the accident and administered advanced life support to Page, but he was already in full cardiac arrest.

Page suffered significant blood loss, and the paramedics could not stop the bleeding. The coroner determined that Jay Page died from multiple traumatic injuries sustained in the car accident. His blood was tested for alcohol and drugs, but the test results were negative. Smith was airlifted to Huntington Memorial Hospital after she was extracted from the car. Smith recovered from her injuries, but she remained nervous while driving or riding in cars.

After the accident, appellant told a Highway Patrol officer that he was driving the white, Forest Service truck and was working for the Forest Service when the accident happened. Appellant also told the officer that he was not braking at the time of the impact because the road was slick and wet, and he feared sliding off the mountain.

Pennsylvania Highway Patrol officer Sean Price examined the highway where the two vehicles came to rest after this accident, the marks and debris he found in the road, and the damage to the two vehicles. In his opinion, it appeared that appellant drove across the double yellow lines and collided with Jay Page's car as it was going uphill. According to Price, crossing double yellow lines in a roadway was considered a violation of Vehicle Code.

Robert Stevenson, an investigator for the Pennsylvania Highway Patrol's Multi-Disciplinary Accident Investigation Team, also responded to the scene of this accident. Stevenson's team obtained a total survey of the accident scene, gathered evidence, and compared the roadway characteristics. According to the investigator, the debris from the accident indicated to him that the collision occurred in the uphill traffic lane. After the investigation, it was Stevenson's opinion that this accident occurred when appellant, the driver of the white Dodge truck, drove into the downhill lane, allowing his truck to cross the double yellow lines where it hit Page's Mitsubishi traveling in the uphill lane. In Stevenson's opinion, appellant, the driver of the truck, was in violation of Vehicle Code and was at fault for the accident.

According to appellant, on the day of this accident, he was working as a forest protection officer for the Forest Service. At about 2:00 p.m. on that day, he was driving down the mountain to go to the bank. As he came around a curve, he saw a vehicle coming uphill which appeared to be about two feet over the double yellow lines and coming into his traffic lane. Appellant believed he was driving at approximately 32 miles per hour and that the headlights on his truck were on. At that moment, appellant was afraid to step on the brakes because he thought his truck would slide off the slick, wet, mountain road. He tried to maneuver his truck closer to the mountain to give the Mitsubishi more room on the road but the collision happened anyway.

Appellant saw the car's air bags inflate and its windshield break. Next, his truck's air bags inflated and he began to choke on a yellow smoke that filled the truck's cabin. Then, a second, heavy impact occurred and the truck came to a stop. Appellant tried to get out of the truck but the driver's side door was stuck. Finally, he got out through the passenger door. A person came up to him and told him that help was on the way.

Appellant gave a statement about the accident to the law enforcement personnel who responded to the scene of the accident. Appellant believed the impact occurred in his downhill lane and that after the initial impact, the truck stayed on top of the car as the two vehicles slid together into the uphill traffic lane. At that time, the truck came off the car and ended up on the shoulder of the mountain side of the road.

Version 2:

A. Testimony of Surviving Victim

On February 20, 2020, Jean Smith lived in Allentown and was a student at Muhlenberg College. She also worked at the Angeles Crest Christian Camp and Jay Page was her co-worker. That day Page was driving them to the youth camp. They met at the university, picked up some food at a restaurant, and proceeded along State Road 2. Page stored the food, intending to eat it when he reached the youth camp. Smith had driven with Page on prior occasions, including two trips to the youth camp. She characterized Page as a "good driver" who was "cautious [and] careful."

It had been raining earlier in the day, but the rain had stopped sometime before they proceeded up the mountain. Smith and Page were both aware that there had been multiple accidents along the road to the youth camp. They had discussed the road's dangerousness. Both Smith and Page were wearing seat belts. As they proceeded around a curve, the last thing that Smith remembered was seeing a white truck coming down the hill.

The white truck had crossed over the double yellow lines and was partially in the wrong lane. When Smith regained consciousness, she was inside Page's mangled car. A woman told her help was on the way. Smith had a large cut above her eye. She was taken to the hospital by helicopter, where she received stitches for the cut, and was released the following day. After the accident, Smith found it difficult to be a passenger in another person's car and felt "a little jumpy" when she drove herself.

B. Testimony by Blair County Police Detective Lee

Blair County Police Detective Jon Lee had been a peace officer for 10 years at the time of trial. At about 2:00 p.m., Detective Lee was off-duty and he and his wife were driving on State Road 2 behind appellant's truck. The posted speed limit was 45 miles per hour. Both Detective Lee and appellant were proceeding at about 40 to 45 miles per hour. The road was wet due to some mist and sporadic rain. Detective Lee lost sight of appellant's truck for three to five seconds as appellant proceeded around a curve.

When Detective Lee rounded the curve, he saw that appellant's truck had collided with another car. Both vehicles had come to a rest in the road. The driver's side of Page's vehicle had been ripped apart. Page appeared to have suffered several extreme injuries to his head and body. Appellant was walking around and appeared confused or dazed from the accident. Detective Lee's wife summoned help. Page was alive when Detective Lee removed him from the vehicle, placed him on the ground, and administered aid. Page stopped breathing before emergency personnel arrived about 10 to 15 minutes after the accident. Emergency personnel were unable to revive Page and he died as a result of multiple traumatic injuries to his brain, heart, lungs, and legs.

C. Post-Collision Investigation

Pennsylvania Highway Patrol Sergeant Sean Price had been a peace officer for 10 years at the time of trial. Sergeant Price had over 120 hours of accident collision investigation training during this period. He personally investigated hundreds of traffic accidents and had been involved in thousands of traffic accident investigations. These accidents involved 15 to 20 fatalities. Over seven years, Sergeant Price had investigated 50 to 100 accidents in the area where the collision took place. Sergeant Price investigated the collision between appellant's vehicle and Page's vehicle.

Page's vehicle had been struck on the front of the car on the driver's side. The damage extended to the back of Page's car. The collision appeared to be an off-set head-on collision rather than a full head-on collision. Sergeant Price took measurements at the scene, reviewed the collision debris, and studied the damage to both vehicles. Sergeant Price explained that a vehicle heading up the road and into the curve where the accident occurred would naturally tend to go to the outside edge of the road. In other words, if the driver did not turn the wheel to the left as he entered the curve, the vehicle would hit the guard rail on the outside of the road (to the driver's right-hand side).

Sergeant Price also explained that a vehicle headed down the road and into the curve would also naturally tend to go to the outside edge of the road. In other words, if the driver did not turn his wheel to the right as he entered the curve, the vehicle would cross the center line into the oncoming lane of traffic and eventually hit the outside guard rail. Sergeant Price had never investigated an accident where an uphill driver crossed over the center lines into the oncoming lane of traffic, with the exception of motorcycle riders proceeding uphill at high rates of speed.

Sergeant Price opined that appellant's truck came across the double yellow lines and collided with Page's car. His opinion was based on several factors. First, the debris was all in Page's lane. If the collision had occurred in the other lane, there would have been debris in that lane. Second, the damage to the vehicles informed Sergeant Price's conclusion. If Page's car had crossed the double yellow lines, then the angle of the collisions would have been different, and the damage to the vehicles would have been different. Third, there was a gouge in the road in Page's lane caused by one of the vehicles after the collision. Sergeant Price also opined that when appellant crossed the double yellow lines, he committed an infraction under Vehicle Code section 21460, subdivision (a). Finally, Sergeant Price opined that Page was driving lawfully.

Pennsylvania Highway Patrol Officer Robert Stevenson was assigned to the Multi-Disciplinary Accident Investigation Team ("MATT") located in Blair County. Each MATT team consisted of investigators with specialized skills in training and accident reconstruction, automotive engineering, and mechanical engineering. Each team consisted of at least three members.

Officer Stevenson had extensive training and experience in accident investigation. The MATT team arrived at about 5:00 p.m. The team conducted an investigation, which included using a laser device to calculate the various distances involved. The information was loaded onto a flash card and brought back to the station for computer analysis. Officer Stevenson opined that appellant's truck came across the double yellow lines and collided with the front of Page's car on the driver's side. This opinion was based on several factors, including the damage pattern to the vehicles, the position of the vehicles in the roadway, and gouges to the roadway caused by the collision.

Rowan Brown was a law enforcement officer for the United States Forest Service. He spoke to appellant at the scene of the collision. Appellant was drinking from a thermos cup. Appellant did not appear injured. Appellant did not seem upset or tense.

D. The Defense

On February 20, 2020, appellant was employed as a forest protection officer for the United States Forest Service. At about 2:00 p.m., appellant was driving to the bank to make a deposit. Appellant was traveling at 32 miles per hour. As he entered the curve, appellant saw a car in the oncoming traffic lane. The car had crossed over the double yellow line into appellant's lane by two or three feet. Appellant did not apply his brakes because he was concerned about additional oncoming traffic. He was unable to steer his car to the inside of his lane before the vehicles collided. The air-bag deployed in appellant's vehicle, and he became disoriented. Appellant's legs were pinned down by his vehicle. Appellant felt a strong secondary impact, which sounded like scraping metal. At trial, appellant admitted that he could simply be mistaken about the details of the collision.

EXERCISE NO. 7

The subheadings for a Statement of Facts should lead the reader through the story in the Statement. Set forth below are five sets of subheadings used in Statements of Facts. Analyze them and determine how well they help the reader.

Set No. 1

STATEMENT OF FACTS

    A. The Background of the TASER Model K26
    B. The Operation and Effects of the Model K26
    C. The Model K26's Electrical Current and the Dataport
    D. Deaths Caused by TASER Products
    E. The Death of John Allen
    F. The Autopsy and the Cause of Death

Set No. 2

    A. Factual Background
        1. The Parties
        2. Criminal Activity in the Apartment Building and the Neighorhood
        3. The Broken Front Door
        4. The Murder

Set No. 3

STATEMENT OF FACTS

    A. The Development of the North Coast Business Center

B. The Construction Defect Action
C. The Mary Carter Settlement Agreement Entered into by American Life Insurance Company and Ford Construction Company
D. The Notice of Motion and Motion for Good Faith Settlement, the Oppositions, and the Replies
E. The Trial Court's Hearing on the Good Faith Issue and Its Finding That the Settlement Was in Good Faith

Set No. 4

A. Generally, the Issues Presented at Trial
  1. Pre-Operative Findings and Beliefs
     a. Bleeding and pain
     b. The diagnosis of a complex ovarian cyst
     c. The risk of cancer from a complex ovarian cyst
     d. Dr. Jorgensen's reasonable assumption about Mrs. Rowen's condition
  2. The Surgery
  3. The Post-Surgery Condition
B. Testimony Regarding the Consent Issue

Set No. 5

A. Plaintiff-Appellant Kelly Brown Is Employed by Defendants-Appellees Northern Supply Co. and Moveit Corporation and Dedicates 30 Years of Her Life to Her Male-Managed Employer Becoming a Jack of All Trades
B. Female Brown Was the Victim of Gender Segregation in Job Assignments That Prevented Her from Being Promoted to and Learning the Higher Paying Crane Operator Position While Forced to Contend with an Undercurrent of Sexism by Her Primary Supervisor Defendant Fred Heller
C. Defendants-Appellees' Outdated, Antiquated Discrimination Policies and Lack of Discrimination Policy Training
D. Brown Complained to Her Supervisors
E. Brown Is Laid Off; Defendants-Appellees' RIF Targets Women
  1. Reduction in Force Occurs, Women Workers Disparately Affected as a Result
  2. Aftermath of RIF and the Men Who Remained Employed

EXERCISE NO. 8

Set forth below are six sets of Point Headings. Evaluate them for consistency with the principles discussed in Chapter Seven.

Set No. 1

ARGUMENT

    A. The Trial Court Erred in Ruling that Respondents Owed No Duty to Appellants to Repair the Door as a Matter of Law

        1. Respondents Owed Appellants a Statutory Duty to Repair the Door

        2. Respondents Owed Appellants a Contractual Duty to Repair the Door

           a. The implied warranty of habitability

           b. Respondents assumed a duty to repair the door

    B. The Trial Court Erred in Holding that the Criminal Intrusion into the Bakers' Apartment Was Not a Foreseeable Consequence of Respondents' Failure to Repair the Door

        1. The Trial Court Misapplied *Alouette v. Hanson* and State of Caledonia Law in General Regarding Foreseeability

        2. *Alouette*'s Analysis Is Inapposite

        3. The Risk of Harm to Appellants Would Be Reasonably Foreseeable Under the *Alouette* Analysis

    C. The Record Raises Triable Questions of Fact as to the Other Elements of the Tort

Set No. 2

ARGUMENT

    A. Deputy Nielson Is Entitled to Qualified Immunity from Claims That Plaintiff Was Arrested Without Probable Cause in Violation of Plaintiff's Fourth Amendment Rights.

        1. No Fourth Amendment Violation Occurred Because Deputy Nielson Had Probable Cause to Arrest Plaintiff for Public Intoxication

        2. Even If Deputy Nielson Did Not Have Probable Cause to Arrest Plaintiff, He Was Nonetheless Entitled to Qualified Immunity Because a Reasonable Officer in His Shoes Could Believe Probable Cause Existed

    B. Deputy Nielson Is Entitled to Qualified Immunity on Plaintiff's First Amendment Claims

1. Because Probable Cause Existed to Arrest Plaintiff, Deputy Nielson Is Entitled to Qualified Immunity on Plaintiff's First Amendment Retaliation Claims
2. The Record Does Not Contain Requisite Specific Evidence That Plaintiff's Arrest Was Born of an Intent to Retaliate Against Him for Exercising Free Speech Rights
3. Plaintiff Has No Constitutionally Protected Right to Stay on the Phone with a 911 Operator on Saturday Night to Demand to Speak to the Sheriff
4. Sheriff Joyce Violated No Clearly Established Constitutional Rights and Is Thus Entitled To Qualified Immunity on Claims Against Him in His Individual Capacity

Set No. 3

ARGUMENT

I. STANDARDS OF APPELLATE REVIEW
II. THE COURT SHOULD DISMISS THE SUBJECT MATTER JURISDICTION APPEALS FOR LACK OF APPELLATE JURISDICTION
   A. Interwire and STS Have No Jurisdictional Basis for Their Interlocutory Appeal of the Subject Matter Jurisdiction Issues and Those Claims Must Be Dismissed from Proceedings at the Twelfth Circuit
   B. STS Has No Basis for Its Interlocutory Appeal Based on Pendent Appellate Jurisdiction
   C. Interwire Has No Basis for Its Interlocutory Appeal Based on Pendent Appellate Jurisdiction Because It Cannot Appeal the Sovereign Immunity Issue
III. THE TRIAL COURT CORRECTLY UPHELD THE BANKRUPTCY COURT'S DECISION AND STS WAIVED ITS SOVEREIGN IMMUNITY WITH RESPECT TO PLAINTIFFS' CLAIMS
   A. STS Waived Its Sovereign Immunity Through Active and Lengthy Participation in the Bankruptcy Cases
   B. The Trial Court Properly Held That STS Waived Sovereign Immunity By Filing Proofs of Claim in the Debtors' Bankruptcy Cases
      1. STS's and Plaintiffs' Claims Are Logically Related
      2. STS's Waiver of Immunity Is Not Limited to Recoupment Claims, but Extends to Plaintiffs' Claims for Damages in Excess of STS's Original Claims
   C. *Broderick* is Inapplicable to Plaintiffs' Claims Because the Appellant in That Case Deliberately Waived Its Immunity

Set No. 4

ARGUMENT

I. FIRING A GUN HELD INSIDE THE THRESHOLD OF A CAR IS NOT DISCHARGING A FIREARM "AT" AN OCCUPIED VEHICLE WITHIN THE MEANING OF PENAL CODE SECTION 123

    A. The Courts Have a Well-Established Process to Determine the Meaning of a Law

    B. Statutory Construction of Penal Code Section 123 Shows It Does Not Apply to the Discharge of a Weapon That Is Inside an Occupied Vehicle

        1. The Language of Section 123

        2. The Legislative History and Object to Be Achieved by the 1990 Addition to Section 123

            a. "At" and "into" are not synonyms; respondent's analysis of Section 123 is undermined by its replacement of the word "at," which is in the statute, with word "into," which is not

            b. The legislative history of the 1990 addition of "occupied vehicle" to the proscribed targets in Section 123 shows the concern was to avoid having to prove someone who shot at a car intended great bodily harm to people in the car

        3. Policy Considerations in the Interpretation of Section

    C. The Evidence in this Case—That the Shooter Was Standing Outside the Truck and Held the Gun Inside the Truck as He Discharged It—Does Not Support a Conviction Under Section 123

Set No. 5

ARGUMENT

I. APPELLANT WAS PUNISHED SEPARATELY AND CONSECUTIVELY FOR THE GANG PARTICIPATION CHARGE (§678(a)) AND FOR THE VIOLATIONS OF SECTIONS 789, SUBDIVISION (a)(2) AND 2021, WHICH SUPPLIED THE PROOF OF ONE OF THE ELEMENTS OF THE GANG CHARGE; HIS CONVICTION OF THE GANG PARTICIPATION CHARGE, THEREFORE, RESULTED FROM THE COMMISSION OF A SINGLE "ACT OR OMISSION" AND SEPARATE SENTENCING FOR THAT CHARGE WAS BARRED BY SECTION 123.

    A. The Terrorism Enforcement and Prevention Act

    B. Section 123 Bars Multiple Punishment Where a "Single Act or Omission" Violates More Than One Penal Statute, or Where More Than One Statute Is Violated by the Commission of More Than One Act in an "Indivisible Course of Conduct" Committed with but One Intent or Objective

C. Appellant's Conviction for Being an Active Participant in a Criminal Street Gang Was Supported Solely by His Commission of the Crimes of Assault with a Firearm and Being an Ex-Felon in Possession of a Firearm; His Commission of the Gang Participation Offense Was, Therefore, Based Upon the Same Act or Omission as His Commission of the Other Offenses, and Separate Sentencing for the Gang Participation Charge Was Precluded by Section 123

D. Section 123 Bars Multiple Punishment in This Case Even Under the "Intent and Objective" Test Because the Underlying Felonies Were the Means by Which Appellant Committed the Gang Participation Charge; Appellant, Therefore, Had but One Criminal Intent in Committing the Crimes Charged Against Him

Set No. 6

ARGUMENT

I. THE DISTRICT COURT ERRED IN IMPOSING LIABILITY ON THE UNITED STATES BASED ON AN IMPLICIT WAIVER OF SOVEREIGN IMMUNITY.

A. FISA Section 1810 Contains No Express Waiver of the Government's Sovereign Immunity

B. The Explicit Sovereign Immunity Waiver in 18 U.S.C. §2712 Refutes the District Court's Interpretation of 50 U.S.C. §1810

C. The District Court's Reasoning Regarding Punitive Damages and Attorney Fees Confirms the Error in its Sovereign Immunity Analysis

II. THE DISTRICT COURT ERRED IN HOLDING THAT THE FISA IMPLICITLY DISPLACES THE STATE SECRETS PRIVILEGE

A. Had Congress Intended to Displace the State Secrets Privilege, It Would Have Done So Expressly

B. Congress' Regulation of Foreign Intelligence Surveillance Does Not Imply Displacement of the State Secrets Privilege

C. FISA Section 1806(f) Does Not Codify the State Secrets Privilege

III. THE DISTRICT COURT ERRED IN BASING GOVERNMENT LIABILITY ON INFERENCES FROM PUBLIC INFORMATION

A. The District Court's Liability Ruling Rests on Improper Speculation and Is Inconsistent with This Court's 2007 Decision

B. The District Court Erred in Effectively Penalizing the Government for Refusing to Waive the State Secrets Privilege

C. The District Court Erred in Suggesting That Due Process Would Bar in Camera, *Ex Parte* Review of Classified Information

EXERCISE NO. 9

Set forth below is a set of Point Headings filed in the United States Supreme Court. First, examine each overall heading (i.e., I, II, and III). Can you determine the logic of the order in which the argument is laid out? Second, look at the subheadings under each overall heading. Can you determine how the subheadings logically break down the overall argument?

ARGUMENT

I. THE FAA DOES NOT AUTHORIZE THE IMPOSITION OF CLASS ARBITRATION WHERE, AS HERE, THE PARTIES NEVER AGREED TO CLASS PROCEEDINGS
   A. The FAA Authorizes Courts to Enforce Arbitration Agreements Only in Accordance with Their Terms
   B. The Arbitration Proceedings Here Confirm That the Parties Never Agreed to Class Arbitration
II. IMPOSING CLASS ARBITRATION ON UNCONSENTING PARTIES WOULD FUNDAMENTALLY ALTER, NOT ENFORCE, ARBITRATION AGREEMENTS
   A. Requiring Arbitration with a Class, Rather Than an Individual Counterparty, Fundamentally Alters the Risk Involved in the Arbitration Bargain
   B. The Procedural Complexity and Uncertainty of Class Arbitration Fundamentally Alter the Benefits of the Parties' Arbitration Bargain
III. THIS CASE OFFERS NO BASIS FOR DEPARTING FROM THE FAA'S MANDATE THAT ARBITRATION AGREEMENTS BE ENFORCED ACCORDING TO THEIR TERMS

EXERCISE NO. 10

This exercise requires you to read Appendix A, the sample appellate brief in the appeal entitled *Arnold v. United States*. After you have carefully read the brief, answer the following questions about the Argument part of the brief. To answer the questions, you will have to refer back to specific parts of the brief.

The Table of Contents

1. Look at the point headings in the Table of Contents. How did the brief organize the issues presented to the Court?
2. What are the arguments made under Point Heading II, subheadings A, B, and C? Why was this order chosen?
3. Under Point Heading II, subheading B, how do the two subarguments differ? Why would the brief writer have chosen to use these two particular subarguments?
4. Under Point Heading III, how is the argument broken down in subheadings A, B, and C?

Part IIA of the Argument

5. What was the goal of Part IIA of the brief?
6. What preliminary legal information did this part of the brief give to the court?
7. Why didn't this part of the brief use precedents and compare the facts of the precedents with those of Ms. Arnold's case to show that she met the discovery rule?

Part IIB of the Argument

8. Do the two paragraphs immediately below Heading B and before subheading 1 adequately preview the argument for the Court? If you think they do not, what would you have said?
9. Beginning on page 180, this section of the brief applies the *Winter* case to the facts of Ms. Arnold's case. Why do you think the *Winter* case was chosen to play such a principal role in the brief? Where does the brief identify the issue to be decided? Did the brief use all six steps in applying *Winter*? Where is the comparison of facts? Is that comparison convincing?
10. The application of the *Winter* case quotes three sentences from *Winter* in a blocked, indented quote. Why were those sentences chosen to be quoted?
11. Is there a transition when the brief finishes its discussion of *Winter* and begins using *Nicolazzo v. United States*?
12. On page 182, the decision in *Schnurman v. United States* is discussed in a "see also" parenthetical. How did the quotation used relate to the discussion of *Nicolazzo*? Why do you think that particular quotation was used?
13. On page 182, the first full paragraph cites three cases and summarizes them in parentheticals. Why were the cases cited in this fashion? Were too many cases used?
14. What purpose does the last paragraph of Argument IIB1 on page 182 serve? Does the paragraph adequately fulfill this purpose? Was the short quotation effective?

Part IIC of the Argument

15. Locate and circle all the transitions (whether words, phrases, or sentences) used in the seven paragraphs of Argument IIC.
16. Do the comparisons in Argument IIC work? Were you convinced?
17. If the appellant believes that two principal cases discussed in this part (*Plaza Speedway* and *Cannon*) are inapposite, why did it devote an entire subsection of the brief to distinguishing them? Should the brief have dealt with those cases in some other way? Could the discussion of them have been placed in a footnote?
18. Looking back at Part II of the Argument as a whole: why did it use so few district court cases?

Part III of the Argument

19. What is the argument previewed in the paragraph immediately under Heading III? Is the preview adequately carried out?
20. Why was the argument under Section IIIA so short?
21. Should the argument under Section IIIA have been combined under one subheading with the argument in Section IIIB? What are the pros and cons of combining the two?
22. Was the use of the *Menominee* case in Section IIIB convincing? Do you see a problem using the case to support Ms. Arnold's position?
23. Should the argument in Section IIIB have included a policy subargument about why the doctrine's reach should be broad?
24. Under the heading for Section IIIC, the brief sets forth a two-part test. Should that test have been set forth earlier under Section IIIA? Why was it left for this point?
25. In Argument IIIC, the brief uses the *Glarner* case to emphasize how the government has kept the testing information secret. The brief writer had to choose how to characterize the secrecy—by treating it as an important fact that is addressed neutrally, or by inferring or directly charging that the government was acting improperly by "hiding" the information. Which approach did the brief use on these pages? Do you agree with this approach?

The Brief Overall

26. Which part of Ms. Arnold's argument did you find most persuasive? Why?
27. Which part of the argument did you find least persuasive? Why?
28. How would you have changed the brief in light of your conclusions?

EXERCISE NO. 11

Set forth below is a short argument that a landlord did not owe a duty of care to prevent his tenant's dog from injuring the plaintiff. Read the argument and then answer the questions posed at the end.

II. THE TRIAL COURT CORRECTLY DISMISSED THE CASE BECAUSE SMITH DID NOT PROVE THAT THE LANDLORD THOMAS OWED A DUTY TO RESTRAIN THE DOG OWNED BY HIS TENANT

A. A Landlord Owes a Duty of Care to His Tenant's Invitee Only if the Landlord (1) Has Actual knowledge of a Tenant's Dog and Its Vicious Nature, and (2) Could Have Prevented an Attack on the Invitee

In this appeal Appellant Smith alleges that Thomas, the defendant landlord, owed a duty of care to prevent Smith's injury inflicted by a dog owned by Thomas's Tenant, Fred Gray. At trial, however, Smith did not prove facts sufficient to establish this legal duty.

The Caledonia Supreme Court has held that a landlord generally is not liable for injuries to his tenant's invitees from a dangerous condition on the premises that comes into existence after the tenant takes possession. *Costello v. Enright*, 586 No. 876, 885 (1988). An exception to this general rule involves dogs but arises only when two conditions are met. First, the landlord must have actual knowledge of a tenant's dog and that dog's vicious nature. *Id.* at 888. Second, the landlord must have the ability to control the property and thus have been able to prevent the attack. *Id.*

Under this test, Smith did not prove facts at trial sufficient to establish a duty on the part of Thomas as a landlord.

B. Smith Did Not Prove That Thomas Had Actual Knowledge of His Tenant's Dog, Much Less That Thomas Knew of the Dog's Vicious Propensities

The first issue is whether Thomas had actual knowledge of a vicious dog on his tenant's premises. In *Luna v. New Caledonia Realty*, 125 No. 2d 456 (2002), which addressed this issue, a rental agreement allowed a tenant to keep a German Shepherd dog named Thunder. The landlord, however, had neither seen nor received any complaints about the dog before it attacked and injured the plaintiff. *Id.* at 458. The court held that under these circumstances the landlord did not have the requisite knowledge that would give rise to a duty of care in tort. *Id.* at 460.

At trial in the present case, Smith proved that a neighbor had told Thomas about a dog in the yard of the house which Thomas owned. Smith also showed that physical objects associated with dogs, such as stuffed toys and bones, were scattered about that yard. Tr. 93: l. 6-12. However, just as the plaintiff in *Lundy* never proved that the landlord ever saw or received any complaints about the dog, here no proof showed that Thomas had ever seen the dog or heard complaints about the dog. Accordingly, Thomas had no knowledge of the dog's viciousness before the attack on Smith, and under *Luna* no duty of care arose.

Two other cases illustrate circumstances concerning dogs that will impose a duty of care upon a landlord. The facts in both cases, however, are quite different from the case now before the court.

In the first case, *Pregerson v. Hillstrom*, 443 No. App. 2d 666, 672 (2008), the court found that a landlord had the requisite actual knowledge where he had a close relationship with the tenant, who was her nephew, and often saw the dog on the property. The police had also warned the landlord of a previous attack by the dog on a neighbor. *Id.* at 673. The second case, *Adams v. Noriega*, 601 No. App. 33 (1992), involved a similar level of knowledge by the landlord. In that case the landlord lived near his rental unit during portions of the tenancy period, permitted the tenant to keep a dog in the rental agreement, and frequently saw the dog. Unsurprisingly, in both cases the courts found that the landlord had the requisite actual knowledge for a duty to arise. *Pregerson*, 443 No. App. 2d at 676; *Adams*, 601 No. App. at 38.

Unlike the landlords in *Pregerson* and *Adams*, who actually saw their tenants' dogs, here Thomas never saw Smith's dog. While Thomas had heard stories about a dog in the neighborhood that barked excessively and chewed up furniture, such behavior is common in dogs that are not vicious. Accordingly, Thomas did not possess the requisite knowledge of the dog's vicious nature for a duty of care to arise.

C. No Proof at Trial Showed That Thomas Had the Ability to Control His Tenant's Dog

The supreme court's decision in *Costello* also requires that, for a duty to arise, a landlord must have the ability to control the tenant's dog. 586 No. at 885. In *Costello*, the court held that a landlord had sufficient control when he could have terminated a month-to-month tenancy and thereby regained possession of the premises. *Id.* at 887. Likewise, the landlord in *Pregerson* had sufficient control because his tenant's lease was an at-will arrangement. Under that lease, the landlord could have demanded immediate possession of the premises. 443 No. App. 2d at 675.

In the present case, an important feature of the tenant's lease distinguishes both *Costello* and *Pregerson*. Unlike the short-term leases held by the tenants in those cases, Gray and Thomas had signed a two-year lease. While the landlords in *Costello* and *Pregerson* could have quickly regained possession of their premises, Thomas did not have this legal right. Consequently, Thomas did not have the control over the property required for a duty to arise, and the trial court correctly dismissed Smith's case at trial.

To summarize, Smith did not prove facts sufficient to show either the required knowledge by Thomas of the dog's viciousness or his ability to control the dog. As a result, Thomas had no legal duty to protect Smith from injury.

Answer the following questions about the argument that you just read:

1. Where did the argument set up the necessary legal background for deciding the issues?
2. What were the issues that the argument raises?
3. Did the argument specifically compare the facts of the precedents with the facts of the present case? Were any of the comparisons more convincing than others?
4. Go back and identify all of the transitions used in the argument: words, phrases, and sentences. Did the transitions perform their function of helping the reader follow the argument?

EXERCISE NO. 12

This exercise has two parts. Part I: Set forth below are five Introductions. Analyze them for consistency with the principles set forth in Chapter Nine.

Introduction No. 1

The trial court erred when it granted defendant's motion to suppress evidence obtained as a result of a warrantless entry into defendant's apartment. City of Oxford Police Officer Gabriela Rodriguez responded to a dispatch report of an intoxicated driver involved in a hit-and-run collision that occurred in an apartment complex parking lot. At the apartment complex, Rodriguez learned from witnesses that defendant had struck another vehicle, that she appeared visibly intoxicated and smelled of alcohol, and that she "stumbled" into her apartment. Based on those witness reports, Rodriguez had probable cause that defendant committed DUI. In addition, defendant's dissipating blood-alcohol presented exigent circumstances that justified Rodriguez' warrantless entry into defendant's apartment for the purpose of making contact with her regarding the DUI. In light of *State v. Grant*, 147 N.P. 644 (2010), the trial court erred when it concluded that exigent circumstances were not present in light of the possibility that Rodriguez could have obtained a telephonic search warrant to enter the apartment. Moreover, this is not a "rare case" in which *Grant* might not apply as the only evidence shows that a warrant was available within 30-60 minutes, and that even based on the trial court's unsupported finding that it might take 10 minutes, that time still was not "significantly faster" than the time it took Rodriguez to enter defendant's apartment.

Introduction No. 2

In the early morning hours of October 3, 2009, a group of teenagers and young adults were walking southbound on the eastside of Adams Avenue and Second Street when a white vehicle drove by them and the driver shot at them.

The group scattered and some of the teenagers and young adults ran southbound to the northeast corner of Adams Avenue and Second Street where they stopped and called the police.

Officer Sampson responded to the radio call. As he was interviewing the teenagers and young adults, he heard a car stop north of his location at Second Street facing east. Officer Sampson heard a female exclaim, "That's the car." Officer Sampson observed the driver walk to the front of the vehicle near the headlights and start firing a handgun in the direction of the homes on the eastside of Adams Avenue.

Officer Sampson put out a radio broadcast of "shots fired" and ran north to the location of the suspect shooting into the homes. The suspect returned to his vehicle as Officer Sampson ran northbound. When Officer Sampson observed the vehicle to start moving, he stopped. The vehicle suddenly turned southbound toward Officer Sampson and the prior victims. As the vehicle approached, he observed the silhouette of a second suspect in the dark interior of the vehicle and observed an arm rise, extend and point in his direction as the vehicle approached him and the prior victims.

Officer Sampson fired one round at the arm in the vehicle as it accelerated toward him and the prior victims/witnesses. The single round fired by Officer Sampson struck the second suspect in the vehicle who was later identified as Emily Hindman (hereinafter "Decedent" or collectively with the driver, Walter Williams, "suspects").

Decedent, the girlfriend of the driver, suspect Walter Williams (hereinafter "suspect" or "Williams"), was killed by the bullet fired by Officer Sampson.

Decedent's daughter, Alice Hayes, and decedent's mother, Mary Morton (hereinafter collectively "Plaintiffs") filed a complaint alleging, among other causes of action, negligence and violation of civil rights (42 USC 1883).

A jury trial was held and the jury reached a verdict in favor of the Defendants. The jury found that Defendant Officer Sampson was not negligent and that he had not used excessive force against Emily Hindman.

In their appeal, Plaintiffs allege that the trial court committed five errors which require reversal. Plaintiffs' allegations are without merit and each will be addressed below.

Introduction No. 3

Appellant Christopher Walsh ("Walsh") was terminated at age 54 by Opticon, Inc. ("Opticon"), after enduring 21 months of age discrimination by the youth-obsessed start-up company. The under-thirty co-founders made clear they did not want the average age at Opticon to be higher than their own; as Simpson remarked in front of Walsh, hiring younger workers "just worked better." Opticon's Board members wanted to hire 25-year-olds, who could work without "distractions like families and children and other things that get in the way of business." The discriminatory preferences were instilled in Opticon's CEO, who commented that "there are actually laws here that you want to avoid breaking" and then explained the way to "solve [the] problem" is to "pay really low salaries and all the right things occur. "

Walsh was the recipient of repeated ageist comments by decisionmakers and co-workers at Opticon, who called him "old man" and "ancient," told him his ideas were "too old" and "obsolete," that he was "slow" and "fuzzy," and that he was not a "cultural fit," which was Opticon-speak for "too old." A Ph.D. computer scientist with 25 years accomplishment in his field, Walsh was demoted from Director of Operations to run a college program, only to be terminated four months later on the pretext of "job elimination," just months before Opticon's lucrative initial public offering. Walsh lost 90,000 shares in stock options.

Walsh sued Opticon for unfair business practices under Caledonia's Unfair Competition Law ("UCL"), Civil Code section 400 *et seq.,* based on Opticon's discriminatory practices of refusing to hire workers age 40 and over and, for the limited number of older workers who are hired, including Walsh, subjecting them to discriminatory treatment. In addition, he filed claims for disparate treatment and disparate impact age discrimination under Caledonia's Fair Employment Act, wrongful termination, failure to prevent discrimination, and emotional distress.

Although Walsh presented significant evidence of Opticon's age discrimination, including "highly statistically significant" expert findings of discriminatory practices at Opticon, the trial court dismissed his entire suit by granting Opticon summary judgment as to the remaining causes of action.

The trial court's rulings constitute reversible error. The court's summary judgment ruling ignored triable issues of fact on multiple material points, including: the weight to be attributed to Walsh's expert statistician's findings of discriminatory practices; the weight to be attributed to age discriminatory statements made by

Walsh's superiors and peers; whether Walsh was demoted into a non-viable position as a precursor to a discriminatory termination; whether job elimination was a pretext to Walsh's discriminatory termination; whether performance played a role in Walsh's termination; and who at Opticon was responsible for the discriminatory decisions impacting Walsh.

The judgment should be reversed.

Introduction No. 4

James Hull was convicted of possession of a controlled substance based on illegally obtained evidence. Sheriff's deputies pulled him over for failing to transfer the title in his new car, and then arguably developed a reasonable suspicion that he was driving under the influence of an intoxicant. But they did not cite him for either of those offenses; instead, they detained him in order to wait for a K-9 unit to indulge their suspicion that he currently possessed a controlled substance. But because that suspicion was not reasonable, the detention was illegal, and all evidence that resulted from it must be suppressed.

Furthermore, the search warrant later obtained for Mr. Hull's car was invalid. The warrant was based on an illegal warrantless search, and the warrant affidavits failed to establish either that the dog-handler team was properly certified or that the dog was reliable. Because the warrant relied on illegally obtained and unreliable information, it was defective. This Court should therefore reverse the trial court, suppress the illegally obtained evidence, and vacate Mr. Hull's conviction.

Introduction No. 5

John Cannon died after two Oceanview Police Department officers subjected him to more than 50 seconds of electrical current from Model T26 electrical control devices ("ECDs") manufactured by defendant TASER International, Inc. ("TASER"). Plaintiffs are his adult daughter and successor in interest, Helen Cannon, and his parents Robert and Marie Cannon. According to plaintiffs' experts, the multiple ECD discharges caused severe muscle contractions, which elevated Mr. Cannon's blood acid, causing metabolic acidosis, while overly stimulating his heart, resulting in ventricular fibrillation, cardiac arrest, and death.

Plaintiffs alleged federal civil rights claims against the involved police agency and officers, and state-law product-liability claims against TASER. After discovery, plaintiffs settled their claims against the governmental defendants. At the eve of trial on the remaining state-law claims, however, the district court reversed its oral tentative ruling (1 ER 1, 4-5), granting TASER's Rule 56 motion for summary judgment. The district court found no triable issues as to whether the risk of prolonged or multiple ECD applications causing metabolic acidosis and cardiac arrest was "known or knowable," as required for plaintiffs' strict liability claim, and whether TASER "knew or should have known" of that risk, as required for their negligent failure-to-warn claim. *Cannon v. City of Oceanview*, 657 F. Supp. 2d 100, 101-2 (N.D. Cal. 2010).

Plaintiffs contend that they produced adequate evidence to meet their Rule 56 burden to establish triable issues on whether the risk of cardiac arrest due to metabolic acidosis from repeated ECD exposures was knowable prior to this 2004 death. Here, this basic property of human physiology was demonstrated by, among other things, a 1999 hazard analysis for another ECD under development, and a 2001 commentary in the prestigious British medical journal, *The Lancet*.

Because there are triable issues of fact, the case should be remanded for trial on the merits.

Part II: Read the Summary of the Argument on pages 176-178 in the sample appellate brief found in Appendix A. Then answer the following questions:

1. Does the Summary tell a story? If so, what is that story?
2. In the first couple of paragraphs, does the Summary state the basic premise of the appeal and the outcome sought?
3. Does the Summary quickly capture the reader's attention?

EXERCISE NO. 13

Part I: Review the writing principles in Chapter Ten. Then take the following test to measure your knowledge of them.

In the space below each of the following sentences, (1) list the writing problem or problems (e.g., passive voice, improper punctuation, etc.) that you identify in that sentence, and (2) rewrite the sentence above the existing lines to fix the problem(s).

1. The plaintiff's allegations were that a jet engine parts list was exchanged

   by the defendant manufacturers, and that the manufacturers had made an

   agreement to set a fixed price.

   Problem(s):

2. There were three grounds stated by the court as the reasons for the approval

   of the partition in order to end the matter.

   Problem(s):

3. The defendant is in agreement with your position, however if you intend to

   delay, he will raise opposition, and make objections.

   Problem(s):

4.   The plaintiffs' allegations were that the government didn't warn him of the aforementioned dangers of handling radioactive waste, and that he suffered damage therefrom.

Problem(s):

5.   The question in *Jones v. United States*, 432 F.3d 1131 (1985), was whether Smith informed the plaintiff of the defect in the chemical tank design projection and if this led to the plaintiff's response.

Problem(s):

6.   The defendant, in addition to having to pay punitive damages, may be liable for plaintiff's costs and the attorney's fees.

Problem(s):

7.   On September 7, 2008 the defendant filed a motion to dismiss the complaint, and started discovery.

Problem(s):

8.   In many cases the fact that the testator had died means that, until a personal representative is appointed by the court, no action is taken by the parties.

Problem(s):

Part II: Recognizing the passive voice is important to improving your legal writing. In the 12 examples below, circle all the passive voice constructions that you find. Be prepared to explain how you identified each one.

1.   The filing is longer than the norm, which is about 20 pages in length.
2.   The filing was made in the morning.
3.   The admissibility of that evidence is an issue that was questioned in the *Smith* case.
4.   The *Smith* case was the cause of a split among the circuits, which has continued to exist.
5.   It is evident that the defendant was the cause of the damage.
6.   If a writing was used to refresh the witness's recollection, the plaintiff was entitled to see it.

7. At issue is the perception by the witness of the key events.
8. The due process clause is constitutional in origin and was violated under the circumstances.
9. The argument was a long one and was based on 120 years of precedent.
10. Good faith efforts, which the lawyer was making, shall be taken into consideration at the contempt hearing.
11. The jurors should be respected by the attorneys, but undue solicitude should be avoided.
12. If no request for legal services has been made, then Friday is the day on which the hearing will be held.

EXERCISE NO. 14

Set forth below is a draft of an Introduction. Edit the draft using the writing principles set forth in Chapter Eleven.

<u>INTRODUCTION</u>

Plaintiff and Appellant John Parker (hereinafter "Parker"), a police officer, seeks bodily damages from Defendant and Respondent George Donkin (hereinafter "Donkin") for striking Parker while Parker arrested a suspect during an altercation that occurred in a parking lot outside of a motel. Parker alleged that on February 20, 2012 an automobile was driven at him by Donkin at a point in time where Parker was putting a prostitute inside a squad car. As a result of this, Parker, according to the complaint, suffered a broken nose and injuries to his neck, legs, and foot.

Donkin's answer included a denial of these allegations.

Donkin brought a motion for summary judgment on two grounds unrelated to whether Donkin was driving the vehicle. First, Donkin argued that Parker's testimony demonstrates that he can't bring this suit because of the so-called "Firemen's Rule." A police officer under that can't recover for risks of injury arising during the normal and usual course of employment.

Second, Donkin argued that the statute of limitations is a bar to Parker's claim. Under that statute any personal injury action lawsuit must be brought within one year after accrual of the cause of action. Parker was injured on or about February 20, 2012, but he did not file his complaint until February 22, 2013. Accordingly, summary judgment was granted by the trial court for Donkin, however, Parker contends this was incorrect and should be reversed.

EXERCISE NO. 15

Read the following paragraph, which is intended to provide contextual background information about the defendants, who were accused of engaging in terrorist activities. Focusing on the order in which the information is presented in this section of the brief, revise and edit the paragraph while keeping in mind the principles set forth in Chapter Eleven.

Terrorist organizations want global attention and support from other states. Attacks perpetrated by terrorists gain international attention. Secular terrorist organizations have used female suicide bombers without hesitation because incursions conducted by females are substantially more pernicious than those completed by a man. On average, a woman kills four times more people than a male counterpart. According to O'Rourke (2008), secular terrorist organizations are culpable for about 85 percent of attacks perpetrated by women. Secular terrorist organizations recruit women for terrorist attacks by reinforcing the idea that women are equal with men in fighting for that terrorist organization's particular cause. The first known woman suicide bomber was Sana'a Mehaydali from the Syrian Socialist Party. Mehaydali, in 1985, killed five Israeli soldiers near an Israeli convoy in Lebanon. Whereas religious terrorist organizations use sacred texts to justify their attacks and view women as innocuous. It was not until recently that religious radical groups began to use women as part of their attacks. Religious divergent organizations acknowledged that women attacked with greater precision than men. Secular terrorist organizations do not use sacred texts to justify their actions.

EXERCISE NO. 16

Set forth below is a draft of an Introduction to an appellant's brief. The draft needs considerable editing. Read and edit it to be consistent with the principles set forth in Chapter Eleven.

INTRODUCTION

It should not be the policy of the state of Caledonia to promote the litigation of claims just because claimants cannot rely on the representations regarding the existence of insurance coverage or of a dispute regarding coverage by the exclusive agent of a responsible driver.

In this case, during pre-filing negotiations, a claimant was told that the only insurance available to pay his claim was the $20,000.00 afforded under the bodily injury coverage of the responsible driver's "personal" policy of automobile liability insurance. The agents of the responsible driver had a duty to accurately state the "pertinent facts or insurance policy provisions relating to any coverages at issue." Insurance Code section 123.456(a). Despite that duty, they misrepresented the factual basis for the denial of coverage by the employer's automobile liability insurance. As a result of that misrepresentation, the claimant (who has damages well in excess of $100,000.00) settled his claims against the responsible driver for $20,000.00 and was denied the opportunity to pursue the $5,000,000.00 in insurance coverage which might be available to indemnify the responsible driver.

The claimant asked the trial court to exercise its equitable powers to relieve him of the onerous result of the release. The trial court held that it could not grant that relief.

The ruling in this case is not good policy for the Court and the administration of justice in the state of Caledonia. The ruling increases the need for litigation, because a claimant's attorney has little opportunity to speak directly to a responsible party while negotiating through a claims adjuster. He has no right of discovery. In practice, the policy reflected in this ruling forces the claimant's attorney to unreasonably take the risk of relying on the statements made by the claims adjuster on behalf of the responsible driver—without the legal ability to compel the verification of the coverage information—or to incur greater costs for the claimant just because the responsible driver and his insurance coverage have no responsibility for their representations. Worse than that: the responsible driver and/or his insurance coverage can actually profit from their misrepresentations.

There are triable issues of fact upon which a trial court might exercise its equitable powers to set aside the Release in this matter. Plaintiff asks this Court to return this matter to the trial court for that trial.

Made in the USA
Coppell, TX
03 August 2022

80797556R00136